Study Guide for Principles of Microeconomics

Seventh Edition

Companion volumes by Edwin Mansfield

PRINCIPLES OF MICROECONOMICS *Seventh Edition*

PRINCIPLES OF MICROECONOMICS:
 READINGS, ISSUES, AND CASES *Fourth Edition*

Study Guide for Principles of Microeconomics

Seventh Edition

EDWIN MANSFIELD

DIRECTOR, CENTER FOR ECONOMICS AND TECHNOLOGY
UNIVERSITY OF PENNSYLVANIA

W•W•NORTON & COMPANY NEW YORK • LONDON

To Ruth Brennan, with the
hope that she will be amused

ISBN 0-393-96176-1

W.W. Norton & Company, Inc. 500 Fifth Avenue,
New York, N.Y. 10110

1 2 3 4 5 6 7 8 9 0

Contents

Preface

The *Study Guide for Principles of Microeconomics*, seventh edition, is a substantially revised version of the *Study Guide* which accompanied the sixth edition of my text *Principles of Microeconomics*. It contains a number of new questions, many of which should whet the interest of students and extend their capabilities, without making the analysis too difficult.

This program of review and exercise material has been prepared with one overriding objective—to facilitate self-paced study of introductory economics. Each chapter parallels closely the content of the corresponding chapter in my text *Principles of Microeconomics*, seventh edition. In order to give comprehensive and varied coverage, a six-pronged approach has been developed:

1. *Chapter Profiles* that highlight principal points and that are followed by a set of *Behavioral Objectives* that indicate the main things students should be able to do once they have completed the chapter.

2. *A Case Study* (in practically every chapter) which shows how the chapter's principles and concepts can be useful in shedding light on major issues of public and private policy.

3. Limbering-up exercises in the form of *Matching Questions* and *Completion Questions* that open the way to systematic review of each chapter.

4. Self-tests in the form of numerous *True-False* and *Multiple-Choice* questions.

5. A number of *Discussion and Extension Questions*, many rather open-ended, to stimulate classroom discussion (or for further homework assignment).

6. Short cases in the form of *Problems* that simulate real-world situations and require the student to work with actual data in tabular and diagrammatic form.

Answers to all the objective questions and problems are contained at the end of each chapter. No answers are given for the Discussion and Extension Questions, since they are essay questions that can be answered in a variety of ways. Answers to the cases are found in the text's *Instructor's Manual*, prepared by Michael P. Claudon of Middlebury College. (Answers to the odd-numbered Test Yourself questions are given at the end of the text *Principles of Microeconomics*.)

Since a study guide should be a flexible learning tool, I have sought to provide not only a large number of questions but also a wide range in terms of difficulty. Each chapter begins at a relatively easy level, increasing gradually in rigor as students build confidence along with competence. The more demanding an economic concept, the more extensive the amount of review material given to it. Some of the problems at the ends of chapters are hard enough so that the typical student should not expect to answer them all. Even the best students should be challenged by some of them.

The seventh edition of the *Study Guide* contains many improvements prompted by suggestions from instructors throughout the country. I appreciate their contributions. Also, a debt is owed to my wife, Lucile, for helping me with the preparation of many objective questions.

E.M.

Philadelphia
September 1991

Study Guide for Principles of Microeconomics

Seventh Edition

CHAPTER 1

Economic Problems and Analysis

Chapter Profile

Economics promotes a better understanding of the nature and organization of our society (and other societies), the arguments underlying many of the great public issues of the day, and the operation and behavior of business firms and other decision-making units.

According to one standard definition, economics is concerned with the way resources are allocated among alternative uses to satisfy human wants.

Economics relates to many problems in the real world. Here is a representative sample: (1) What determines the extent of unemployment, and what can be done to reduce it? (2) Why should we expect competition among firms to produce socially desirable effects? (3) Why does poverty exist, and what can be done to abolish it?

A resource is a material or service that is used to make goods (or services). Not all resources are scarce. Free resources, such as air, are so abundant they can be obtained without charge. Scarce resources are called economic resources.

Resources are often classified into three categories: land, labor, and capital. Because resources are scarce, only a limited amount of goods and services can be produced from them, and there arises the necessity for choice. If society increases the output of one good, it must decrease the output of some other good (if resources are fully employed). The opportunity cost of using resources to increase the production of the one good is the reduction in the output of the other good.

Economists are particularly interested in four basic questions: (1) What determines what society produces? (2) What determines how it is produced? (3) What determines how society's output is distributed among the people? (4) What determines the rate at which the society's productive capacity will grow?

Economists often distinguish between positive economics and normative economics. *Positive economics* contains descriptive statements, propositions, and predictions about the world; the results you get are testable, at least in principle, by an appeal to the facts. *Normative economics* contains statements about what ought to be, or about what a person, organization, or nation ought to do; the results you get depend on your basic values and preferences.

Behavioral Objectives

A. You should be able to define and explain the following key concepts in this chapter:

Economics	Economic resources	Human wants
Unemployment	Free resources	Choice
Inflation	Land	Opportunity cost
Government regulation	Labor	Alternative cost
Labor productivity	Capital	Positive economics
Poverty	Technology	Normative economics
Resources		

B. Make sure that you can do each of the following:

1. Define economics, and be sure to include in your definition the concepts of resources, scarcity, and choice.

2. List the four basic questions that must be answered by any economic system.

3. Describe the doctrines of Adam Smith.

4. Indicate the general approach that economists take to any problem of choice.

5. Indicate the role of economics in public policy and private decision making.

Matching Questions

_____ 1. Antitrust laws

_____ 2. Less developed countries

_____ 3. Opportunity cost

_____ 4. Inflation

_____ 5. Resources

A. Increasing price level

B. Things or services used to produce goods that can satisfy human wants

C. Measures designed to promote competition

D. Areas of poverty

E. The value of what could have been produced if resources had been used in the best alternative way

Completion Questions

1. The growth of output has not been steady or uninterrupted; instead, output has tended to fluctuate—and so has _____.

2. The level of _____ may tend to rise when we reduce the level of unemployment. In other words, _____ may occur.

3. The American economic system is built on the idea that firms should (compete, cooperate) _____ with one another. In particular, the producers of steel, automobiles, oil, toothpicks, and other goods are expected to set their prices

_____.

4. Although relatively few people in the United States lack food desperately, about _____ American people, about _____ of the population of the United States, live in what is officially designated as poverty.

5. The industrialized countries of the world, like the United States, Western Europe, and Japan, are really just rich islands surrounded by seas of poverty. Over _____ of the world's people live in countries where the income per capita is less than $5,000 per year.

6. Economic problems generally involve _____. There are often a number of alternative ways to handle a problem, and the question is which is

_____.

7. A characteristic of many economic problems is that, to choose among a number of feasible solutions, one must _____ what will occur if each solution is adopted. This emphasis on the future necessarily entails some

_____.

8. Economic resources are sometimes classified into the three categories of _____, _____, and _____.

9. _____ is society's pool of knowledge regarding the industrial arts.

10. An economic system must determine the level and composition of society's

_____.

11. Adam Smith was among the first to describe how a free, competitive economy can function—without central planning or government interference—to allocate _____ efficiently. He emphasized the virtues of the _____ that leads the private interests of firms and individuals toward socially desirable ends, and he was suspicious of firms that are sheltered from _____, since he believed there would be _____ effects on resource allocation.

12. Smith's optimism was in keeping with the intellectual climate of his time—the Age of Enlightenment, when people believed in rationality. Leave markets _____, said Smith, and beware of firms with too much _____ and of unnecessary government _____.

13. Value judgments are in the realm of _____ economics. They (can, cannot) _____ be tested by an appeal to facts. They (can, cannot) _____ be proved in the way that the laws of physics can be.

14. The forests of the United States are an important national resource. If these forests are used for lumber, they (can, cannot) _____ be used for recreation. There (are, are not) _____ enough forest lands for both recreation and lumber. If we use a certain portion of the nation's forests for recreation, the _____ is the forgone lumber that could have been derived.

True-False

_____ 1. When economists refer to goods as being scarce, they mean that these items are monopolized by a few people. If goods were distributed equitably, there would be no problem of scarcity.

_____ 2. When economists refer to goods as being scarce, they mean that goods are scarce for a particular consumer or family. Viewed in the aggregate, there can be no scarcity of goods for a society as a whole.

_____ 3. If every resource is so specialized that it can produce only one good or service, and if all resources are fully employed, society has no choice concerning how much of each good or service will be produced.

_____ 4. The problem of choosing what goods to produce is not likely to confront a firm, once it is established, but it does confront society.

_____ 5. Since it passes the tax laws, Congress is the only branch of the government concerned with economics.

_____ 6. Economics now plays a considerable role in the decision making of the Department of Defense.

_____ 7. Measures designed to reduce the rate of inflation may increase unemployment, unless the government is very careful.

_____ 8. Avoiding excessive unemployment is not a task that can be assigned to a particular individual, family, or firm.

Multiple Choice

1. Adam Smith emphasized how the fundamental economic problems could be solved efficiently by:

   a. command.
   b. tradition.
   c. the price system.

   d. monopoly.
   e. government agencies.

2. When we reduce the level of unemployment, the effect may be:

   a depression.
   b. inflation.
   c. decreased output.
   d. deflation.
   e. increased purchasing power of the dollar.

3. In 1989, the percentage of U.S. households with incomes less than $25,000 equaled:

   a. less than 10 percent
   b. 10-29 percent
   c. 30-49 percent
   d. 50-59 percent
   e. 60 percent or more

4. The problem of distributing society's output among its members must be resolved by:

   a. planned economies.
   b. any society that survives.
   c. any society based largely on the price system.
   d. any society based largely on tradition.
   e. any society.

5. Which of the following is *not* included as capital?

   a. a new taxicab
   b. an old taxicab
   c. a school building
   d. a pencil used by an author
   e. a hot dog eaten by an author while writing a book

6. Susan Smith's father asks her to help her younger brother with his homework. She refuses until her father promises to pay her $5. She could obtain $6 by babysitting for the equivalent length of time. The opportunity cost of having Ms. Smith help her brother in this way is:

   a. $5.
   b. $6.
   c. less than $5.
   d. more than $6.
   e. zero.

7. Holding constant the amount of capital and natural resources, the greater a country's labor force:

   a. the greater the amount of equipment that each worker will have to use.
   b. the greater its rate of investment.
   c. the greater its inefficiency.
   d. the greater its output of capital goods.
   e. none of the above.

Discussion and Extension Questions

1. "The best things in life *are* free, and hence outside the realm of economics: the air we breathe, a view of a sunset, libraries, and free speech. Many other things ought to be free as well, like medical care." Discuss.

2. Robinson Crusoe apparently spent a lot of his waking hours in what we would usually deem "leisure activities." Does this not imply that he had a severe unemployment problem? Why would you not be worried about his unemployment but yet you would be concerned about the unemployed in the United States?

3. How do families, as opposed to an entire economy like the United States or Japan, solve the four basic economic problems?

4. Someone has said that economists study how people make choices and that sociologists study why people don't have any choices to make. What does that statement mean?

5. A lawyer charges what some would regard as an exorbitant sum for a simple matter like drawing up a will. How do economic principles in this chapter help you understand this?

6. What is the opportunity cost of (a) spending an evening at a movie; (b) a college education?

7. What characteristics do economic problems tend to have in common?

8. Is economics concerned solely with solving practical problems?

9. If resources are not fully employed, is it true that an economy must give up some of one good in order to get more of another good?

10. Adam Smith was suspicious of firms that are sheltered from competition. Can you think of some reasons for this suspicion? Is the Philadelphia Electric Company sheltered from competition? If so, how? Is the typical American wheat farmer sheltered from competition? If so, how?

Problems

1. Suppose that the costs due to crime and the opportunity costs of resources used in law enforcement are as follows:

Proportion of criminals that are caught and convicted	Costs due to crime	Opportunity costs of resources used in law enforcement (billions of dollars)	Total costs
0.4	60	10	70
0.5	50	—	68
0.6	40	30	—
0.7	30	50	80
0.8	—	80	100

a. Fill in the three blanks above.
b. What proportion of criminals should society try to catch and convict? Why?
c. Suppose the costs due to crime were to increase by $5 billion at each possible level of law enforcement. In other words, suppose that each of the figures in the second column of the table (headed *Costs due to crime*) were to increase by $5

billion. Would this affect the optimal proportion of criminals that society should try to catch and convict? Why or why not?

2. Suppose that the average cost per mile of operating your car (including insurance and taxes) is 18 cents. If you are contemplating taking a 200-mile trip, are you correct in assuming that your out-of-pocket costs for the trip will be 18 cents per mile? Why or why not?

3. If the opportunity cost of producing an extra million tons of steel exceeds the value of the extra million tons of steel, should society produce the extra million tons of steel? Why or why not?

4. Indicate whether each of the following resources is land, capital, or labor: oil deposits in Saudi Arabia _____; Thomas Edison's work on the lightbulb _____; the Empire State Building in New York City _____; the copies of this textbook on the shelves of your college bookstore _____; Big Sur _____.

5. Peter Jones stumbles accidentally onto a large cache of rifles buried in his backyard. He donates them to the local police department. The police commissioner, in a speech lauding Jones for his altruism, says that Jones has given an important resource (namely, the guns) to the city government, thus making them a free resource. From the point of view of economics, is this use of terms correct? Why or why not?

6. During the past fifty years, the U.S. economy has increased its automobile production by an enormous amount. At the same time it has increased its production of most other types of goods and services. Does this mean that the opportunity cost of the increased automobile production was negative? Why or why not?

7. In 1991, over 6 percent of the labor force was unemployed; how can anyone say that labor is scarce?

8. Mary Mineo, a graduate student, has one 8-hour day per week that she can devote to earning extra money. She can write stories for the local newspaper, or she can babysit, or she can divide her time between the two jobs. (For example, she can spend 3 hours writing stories and 5 hours babysitting.) If she babysits, she gets $4 per hour. If she spends her day writing stories, it takes her 1 hour to write the first story, 2 hours to write the second story, and 5 hours to write the third story because she runs out of ideas and becomes less productive as time goes on. Assume that she must write an integer number of stories in a day.

   a. If she receives $15 per story, should she do any babysitting if she wants to maximize her income during the day?
   b. If she receives $25 per story, should she do any babysitting if she wants to maximize her income during the day?
   c. What is the lowest price per story that will result in her doing no babysitting, if she maximizes her income?
   d. If she spends the first 5 hours of the day babysitting, what is the opportunity cost to her of spending the remaining 3 hours babysitting?
   e. If she spends the first 7 hours of the day babysitting, what is the opportunity cost to her of spending the remaining hour babysitting?

Answers

Matching Questions
1. C   2. D   3. E   4. A   5. B

Completion Questions
1. unemployment   2. prices, inflation   3. compete, independently   4. 32 million,
13 percent   5. half   6. choice, best   7. forecast, uncertainty   8. land, labor, capital
9. Technology   10. output   11. resources, invisible hand, competition, undesirable
12. alone, economic power, intervention   13. normative, cannot, cannot   14. cannot,
are not, opportunity cost

True-False
1. False   2. False   3. True   4. False   5. False   6. True   7. True   8. True

Multiple Choice
1. c   2. b   3. c   4. e   5. e   6. b   7. e

Problems
1. a. The blank in the second row is 18, the blank in the third row is 70, the blank in
    the fifth row is 20.
   b. 50 percent, because this minimizes the total costs to society.
   c. No, because the minimum total costs to society would still be achieved when 50
    percent are caught and convicted.
2. No, because some of the costs are not out-of-pocket costs. You pay a fixed amount
   for insurance and (some) taxes, regardless of how many miles you drive. Thus, you
   won't increase these costs by making the trip.
3. No, because the forgone output of other goods is more valuable than the extra steel.
4. land, labor, capital, capital, land
5. No, because rifles are not free. They have a positive price in the market place, even
   though Jones happened to donate them.
6. No. During the past fifty years, the amount of resources and the available technology
   in the American economy have changed greatly, thus allowing increased production
   of automobiles and other goods. But if we had chosen to produce fewer automobiles,
   we surely could have produced more of other things. Thus, the opportunity cost was
   positive.
7. It is not possible to get all of the labor one wants for the asking. The price of labor
   is positive.
8. a. She has three alternatives. (1) She can devote 1 hour to writing and 7 hours to
    babysitting, which will bring in $43. (2) She can devote 3 hours to writing and
    5 hours to babysitting, which will bring in $50. (3) She can devote 8 hours to
    writing which will bring in $45. Thus, she should do some babysitting.
   b. The opportunity cost of writing the third story is $20, since this is what she
    could earn in 5 hours of babysitting. Since she gets $25 for this story, she is
    better off writing the story than devoting the 5 hours to babysitting.
   c. $20.
   d. The amount that she could earn by writing two stories.
   e. The amount that she could earn by writing one story.

Economic Models and Capitalism, American Style

Chapter Profile

The methodology used by economists is much the same as that used in any other kind of scientific analysis. The basic procedure is the formulation and testing of models.

A model must in general simplify and abstract from the real world. Its purpose is to make predictions concerning phenomena in the real world, and in many respects the most important test of a model is how well it predicts these phenomena.

To test and quantify their models, economists gather data and utilize various statistical techniques.

The American economy, like any economic system, must perform four basic tasks: (1) It must determine the level and composition of society's output. (2) It must determine how each good and service is to be produced. (3) It must determine how the goods and services that are produced are to be distributed among the members of society. (4) It must maintain and provide for an adequate rate of growth of per capita income.

The production possibilities curve shows the various production possibilities a society can attain.

The task of determining the level and composition of society's output is really a problem of determining at what point along the curve society should be.

A society has to recognize that it cannot get more of one good without giving up some of another good, if resources are fully and efficiently used. However, if resources are not fully and efficiently used, it will be possible to obtain more of one good without giving up some of another good.

The production possibilities curve does not tell us anything about the distribution of income, but it does indicate various ways that a society can promote growth in per capita income. By doing lots of research and development, or by producing lots of capital goods (rather than consumers' goods), society can push its production possibilities curve outward, thus increasing per capita income.

To a considerable extent, ours is a capitalistic economy, an economic system in which there is private ownership of capital, freedom of choice, freedom of enterprise, competition, and reliance upon markets.

Under pure capitalism, the price system is used to perform the four basic economic tasks. Although it is not controlled by any person or small group, the price system results in order, not chaos.

A purely capitalistic system is a useful model of reality, not a description of our economy as it exists now or in the past.

The American economy is a mixed capitalistic economy, in which both government and private decisions are important. Many vital public services, like fire protection and schools, cannot be left to private enterprise. In addition, society has said that certain possible consequences of the price system—like the existence of abject poverty—are unacceptable.

Behavioral Objectives

A. You should be able to define and explain the following key concepts in this chapter:

Consumer	Production possibilities curve	Freedom of enterprise
Firm	Capital goods	Competition
Market	Consumers' goods	Price system
Perfect competition	Capitalism	Consumer sovereignty
Model	Freedom of choice	

B. Make sure that you can do each of the following:

1. Explain the role of models in economics, as well as the criteria used to determine whether a particular model is adequate or not.

2. Describe how a relationship between two variables (for example, a commodity's price and the quantity demanded) can be plotted in a graph, and the difference between a direct and an inverse relationship.

3. Explain how the production possibilities curve sheds light on the basic economic problems of determining what is produced, and of determining how goods are produced.

4. Explain how the production possibilities curve sheds light on the basic economic problem of achieving economic growth.

5. Define opportunity cost, and explain why, as more and more of a good is produced, the production of yet another unit of this good is likely to entail a larger and larger opportunity cost.

6. Describe how capitalism differs from a planned economy like China.

7. Explain how the price system, which lies at the heart of capitalism, can be used to carry out the four basic functions of any economic system.

8. Describe the role of government in our mixed capitalist system.

Getting Down to Cases: The Military Buildup and the Production Possibilities Curve

In the early 1990s, there was considerable talk about the reduction of America's defense expenditures. This was quite different from the early 1980s, when the United States began to increase its military expenditures considerably. Whereas defense spending equaled less than 5 percent of the nation's total output in 1976–80, it rose to almost 7 percent in 1982, according to the *New York Times*. Some economists were concerned that large outlays for defense would cause bottlenecks in the supply of civilian goods. Others felt that the military services could be more efficient in their operations.

    a. Suppose that the production possibilities curve at that time was curve *A* at the top of the next page. What effect would lower efficiency by the military services have had on the shape and position of this curve?

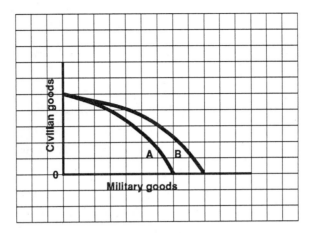

b. Suppose that the production possibilities curve shifted from *A* to *B* above. A newspaper reporter attributed this to an increase in the labor force. Was this reasonable? Why or why not?

c. A television commentator said that this shift was due to the nation's agricultural research and development program. Does this seem reasonable? Why or why not?

d. An economist at a midwestern university said that this shift was due to the nation's military research and development program. Does this seem reasonable? Why or why not?

e. An official of the Department of Defense said that this shift meant that the nation would produce more military goods. Can we be sure of this?

f. An official of the Department of Commerce said that if the nation produces the same amount of civilian goods as before, this shift meant that the nation would produce more military goods. Can we be sure of this?

Matching Questions

_____	1. Law of increasing cost	A.	Theory
_____	2. Technological change	B.	Nylon in the 1930s
_____	3. Economic growth	C.	Results in production possibilities curve having "bowed-out" shape
_____	4. Consumers' goods	D.	Increase in per capita income
_____	5. Consumer sovereignty	E.	Producers catering to consumer tastes
_____	6. Model	F.	Clothing, food, and drink

Completion Questions

1. A firm is an organization that produces a good or service for _____.

   In contrast to _____ institutions such as universities and hospitals, firms attempt to make a _____. There are over _____ firms in the United States. About _____ of the goods and services produced in this country are produced by firms.

2. A market can be defined as a group of _____ and _____ that are in touch with each other in order to _____ or _____ some good. A person or firm is part of a market even if it is in contact with only a _____ of the other persons or firms in the market.

3. Economics is concerned with the _____ and _____ of observed phenomena, regardless of their immediate application to practical problems.

4. A _____ is composed of a number of assumptions from which conclusions or predictions are deduced.

5. The most important test of a model is how well it _____.

6. _____ economics contains descriptive statements, propositions, and predictions about the world.

7. In _____ economics, the propositions depend on one's values.

8. The _____ shows the various combinations of output of different goods that society can produce.

9. The relationship between the price and quantity sold of a good generally is (direct, inverse) _____.

10. A model may be so _____ and distorted that it is utterly useless. A model should be constructed so that _____ and unimportant considerations and _____ are neglected, but the major factors—those that seriously affect the phenomena the model is designed to predict—are included.

11. Measurements enable economists to _____ their models. In other words, they enable them to construct models that predict _____ effect one variable has on another.

12. If two points on a straight line are $(x, y) = (10, 10)$ and $(x, y) = (12, 14)$, the slope of the line is _____.

13. Capital is owned by the government under _____.

14. The _____ is a way of organizing and coordinating an economy. A purely capitalistic economy relies entirely on this mechanism.

15. In the industrialized nations, the goal of _____ has become controversial. But in the _____ countries, economic growth is desired because these nations want to raise _____ income.

16. The first function of any economic system—to determine the _____ and _____ of society's output—is really a problem of determining at

what point along the _____ curve society should be. In making this choice, one thing is obvious: you cannot get more of one _____ without giving up some of another _____, so long as resources are fully and efficiently utilized.

17. It is desirable to produce each good and service in such a way that you wind up on the _____ curve, not on a point _____ it. Of course it is not that simple, but at least our model indicates what to watch out for: _____ of resources and _____.

18. One way for an economy to increase its output—and its per capita income—is to invest in _____. Another way is by devoting more of its resources to the production of _____ goods rather than _____ goods.

19. The United States is basically a _____ system, but there are certain areas where the government, not individuals, owns _____ , and where individual property rights are limited in various ways.

20. Within a capitalistic system firms compete with one another for _____. Under _____ , there are a large number of firms producing each product; indeed, there are so many that no firm controls the product's _____.

21. Suppose that a nation's production possibilities curve is as shown below: The only two goods produced by this nation are _____ and _____. The maximum output of _____ is 5 million bushels; the maximum output of _____ is 10,000.

22. In the previous question, the opportunity cost of a machine tool is _____ bushels of corn. The opportunity cost of a bushel of corn is _____

machine tools. If the diagram in the previous question is correct, the law of

_____ is violated.

23. Suppose that a nation's production possibilities curve is as follows:

The opportunity cost of a bushel of corn is _____; the opportunity

cost of a machine tool is _____.

Machine tools (thousands)

24. The production possibilities curves shown in questions 21 and 23 (do, do not)

_____ have the shapes typically encountered in the real world.

True-False

_____ 1. Theories generally do not work out in practice; if they did work out, they would not be called theories.

_____ 2. If some of a theory's predictions are wrong, the theory should be discarded since it can be quite misleading.

_____ 3. The most important test of a model is how well its assumptions replicate reality.

_____ 4. There is a substantial amount of agreement with regard to most of the propositions of positive economics.

_____ 5. Propositions in normative economics can be tested entirely by an appeal to the facts.

_____ 6. Economists are still uncertain about many effects of the government's monetary and fiscal policies.

_____ 7. To be useful, a model must not simplify and abstract from the real situation.

_____ 8. The basic reason for using a model is that the real world is so complex that masses of detail often obscure underlying patterns.

_____ 9. If one wants to predict the outcome of a particular event, he or she will be forced to use the model that predicts best, even if this model does not predict very well.

_____ 10. Liberal economists often differ from conservative economists in their conclusions on public policy, and the disagreements can be over means as well as ends. However, there is very substantial agreement on most of the propositions of positive economics.

_____ 11. The following statement is positive, not normative, economics: One way to increase total output in the United States is to reduce unemployment.

_____ 12. The following statement is positive, not normative, economics: The United States should reduce inflation to not more than 3 percent per year.

_____ 13. Whenever a model's predictions have been at variance with prevailing common sense, it always has been the model, not common sense, that was wrong.

_____ 14. The economy of Zanadu produces only two goods. If its production possibilities curve is of the ordinary shape, it is never possible for Zanadu to increase its output of both goods.

_____ 15. If Zanadu reduces the percentage of its output going for capital goods, its production possibilities curve will have to shift to the left.

_____ 16. If Zanadu's production possibilities curve is a straight line, the law of increasing cost does not apply in this country.

_____ 17. Points on the production possibilities curve can be attained whether there is full or partial employment of resources.

_____ 18. The production possibilities curve indicates how output is divided among the members of the society.

_____ 19. Increases in a commodity's price generally tend to increase the amount of it that is produced.

_____ 20. Few people favor a thoroughly egalitarian society, if for no other reason than that some differences in income are required to stimulate workers to do certain types of work.

_____ 21. In real-life American markets, the number of producers is always so large that no firm has any control over price.

_____ 22. The United States, which is basically capitalistic, has adopted a mixed form of capitalism that combines the basic elements of capitalism with considerable government intervention.

_____ 23. The principle of consumer sovereignty is true because producers attempt to manipulate the tastes of consumers through advertising and other devices.

_____ 24. Under the price system, if plumbers are scarce relative to the demand for them, their price in the labor market—their wage—will be bid up, and they will tend to be used only in the places where they are productive enough so that their employers can afford to pay them the higher wages.

_____ 25. Consumer sovereignty does not extend—and cannot realistically be extended—to all areas of society. For example, many public services cannot be left to private enterprise.

_____ 26. Freedom of enterprise is involved in all economic production.

_____ 27. To maximize output, each person should try to be economically self-sufficient, like Henry David Thoreau at Walden Pond.

_____ 28. In drawing up a nation's production possibilities curve, one assumes that prices are held constant.

_____ 29. The price system is inherently in contradiction with anti-inflationary policies. To avoid inflation, all prices must remain constant, but such constancy of prices means that the price system cannot do its job of allocating resources.

_____ 30. It is irrational for any country to devote resources to research and development since it can obtain technology by imitating the advances made by other countries.

Multiple Choice

1. If economists could devise perfectly accurate models to describe the working of the economic system,

    a. this would insure the adoption of good economic policy.
    b. this would help promote the adoption of good economic policy.
    c. this would neither help nor hinder the adoption of good economic policy (since such policy is in the province of normative economics).
    d. this would hinder the adoption of good economic policy since, for good policies to take place, it is essential that there be uncertainty among firms and consumers concerning the effects of these policies.
    e. None of the above.

2. An economic model is *not*:

    a. a set of equations.
    b. a graph.
    c. a set of principles.
    d. a policy to help improve the well-being of this and other nations.
    e. a tool of analysis.

3. In choosing among alternative models, economists generally have the strongest preference for models that:

    a. have assumptions that are close to exact replicas of reality.
    b. predict better than any other that is available.
    c. have few assumptions and are as simple as possible, even if they cannot predict very well.
    d. are detailed and complex, with every available fact and figure included.
    e. all of the above.

4. If two points on a straight line are $(x, y) = (10, 10)$ and $(x, y) = (6, 8)$, the line will intersect the y-axis when y equals:

    a. −6.   d. 5.
    b. 6.   e. 8.
    c. −5.

5. Which of the following is *not* held constant in drawing up a nation's production possibilities curve?

    a. the nation's technology   d. the nation's money income
    b. the nation's labor resources   e. the nation's land
    c. the nation's capital resources

6. If a nation's production possibilities curve is as shown below, the opportunity cost of an extra gun:

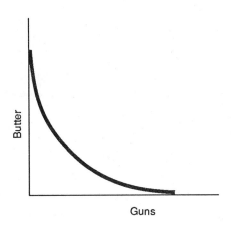

    a. increases as more guns are produced.
    b. increases and then decreases as more guns are produced.
    c. decreases as more guns are produced.
    d. decreases and then increases as more guns are produced.
    e. remains constant as more guns are produced.

7. Society will be at points inside the production possibilities curve when:

    a. resources are not used efficiently.
    b. there is full employment of resources.
    c. per capita income is increasing.
    d. income is distributed equally to all.
    e. all of the above.

8. An economy often can increase its output and its per capita income by:

    a. devoting more of its resources to the production of consumers' goods.
    b. cutting down on production of capital goods.
    c. pushing the production possibilities curve inward.
    d. investing in research and development.
    e. all of the above.

9. The price system:

    a. helps to determine how each good and service will be produced.
    b. helps to determine which goods and services each member of society receives.
    c. helps to determine the rate of growth of per capita income.
    d. all of the above.
    e. none of the above.

10. A purely capitalist system:

    a. has existed in the United States in the past, but no longer does.
    b. can be described as a useful model of reality, but not a description of it.
    c. emphasizes government control of capital.
    d. includes government provision of most goods and services, like transportation, power, and oil.
    e. all of the above.

11. A nation can produce 100 guns and 5 tons of butter or 80 guns and 6 tons of butter. (These are two points on this nation's production possibilities curve.) If the law of increased cost is valid in this case, which of the following *cannot* be a point on this nation's production possibilities curve?

    a. 90 guns and 5 2/3 tons of butter   d. 85 guns and 5 7/8 tons of butter
    b. 90 guns and 5 3/4 tons of butter   e. all of the above
    c. 90 guns and 5 1/4 tons of butter

Discussion and Extension Questions

1. A local movie theater has just initiated a "Dollar Night" program whereby all seats are $1 every Tuesday night. The price for any other time of the week remains $5. Explain how an economic model could be used to test the wisdom of that pricing scheme.

2. Individual states levy cigarette taxes (a certain amount per pack) to provide a source of revenue for the state. Suppose that New York were to propose a 2 cent per pack increase in its cigarette tax to reduce a deficit in the state budget. Under what conditions would you, as an economic consultant, advise the authorities to go ahead with the plan? How might the information that currently perhaps as many as half the cigarettes sold in New York City are illegal imports (from other states, mainly North Carolina and Virginia) that have been smuggled to avoid the New York tax affect your decision or advice?

3. Suppose you wanted to construct a model to explain the number of automobiles consumers would purchase in a given year. List twenty things which you feel might affect the demand for cars. Then reduce your list to just five. What criteria did you employ to pare the original list? Which is a better model? Why?

4. The text describes as the fourth function of any economic system the determination of the rate of economic growth. Could this mean that the society opts for the absence of economic growth?

5. "The fact that some countries—such as India or China—choose to carry on production with techniques that we would consider obsolete and with methods utilizing large amounts of labor and very little capital suggests that these economies are operating well inside their production possibilities curve." Comment.

6. "The production possibilities curve, while useful as a decision-making tool in a Communist economy, is not of use in a capitalistic economy, since no one knows what it looks like or can measure it. Another limitation of the production possibilities curve is that it only can be used when the law of increasing cost prevails." Do you agree with both of these criticisms? Do you agree with either of them? Explain.

7. "Specialization of labor results in alienation. Just look at the workers who are forced to work as half-human cogs in the capitalistic industrial machine. They are alienated from society and from one another!" Discuss and evaluate.

8. Economic moralists are fond of saying, "You can't get something for nothing." Is this always true? Under what circumstances, if any, is it not true?

9. "If the United States did not spend money on defense, we would suffer from widespread unemployment." Comment and evaluate.

Problems

1. Suppose that P represents the price of a pound of butter and Q represents the number of millions of pounds of butter demanded by American consumers. Suppose that the relationship between P and Q is as shown below:

P (dollar price of butter per pound)	Q (millions of pounds of butter)
1	300
2	200
3	100

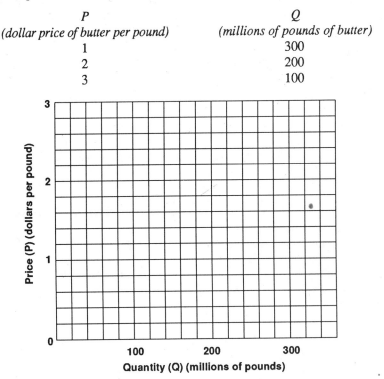

Plot the relationship in the preceding graph. What is the slope of the line connecting the points in this graph?

2. A metropolitan bus company is faced with the necessity of raising its fares due to increased operating costs. Based on estimates drawn from many sources, including other transit systems, the company determines how many tokens it can expect to sell at various prices. Suppose that the number of tokens sold by the company is Q, and the price per token is P.

P (cents)	Q (millions of tokens sold per day)
40	2.0
50	1.9
60	1.8
70	1.7
80	1.6

a. Using these data, plot the relationship between P and Q on the graph below.

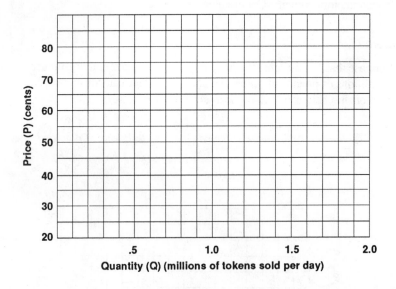

b. Is the relationship between P and Q direct or inverse? Does this seem realistic? Why or why not?

c. How many tokens would be sold if the price per token were set at $0.50? How many tokens would be sold if the price were set at $0.60? If the relationship is a straight line between these two prices ($0.50 and $0.60), how many tokens would be sold if the price were $0.55?

3. Suppose that we have data regarding the expenditures on food of 10 single, retired individuals in Altoona, Pa., in 1992, and that we also have data concerning their 1992 incomes. Suppose the data are as follows:

Individual	Income (dollars)	Food expenditure (dollars)
1	8,100	3,200
2	10,300	3,700
3	11,500	4,600
4	11,700	3,000
5	12,200	3,000
6	14,100	3,200
7	15,200	4,100
8	18,000	5,700
9	20,100	6,000
10	21,000	6,500

Plot the relationship between income and food expenditure in the graph below.

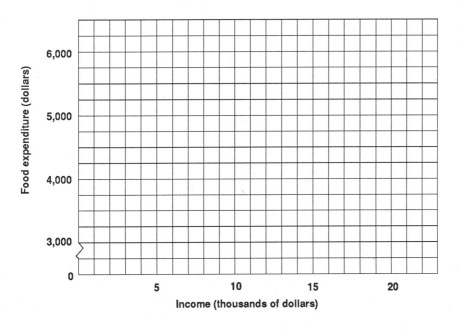

4. a. Using the data in problem 1 of Chapter 1, plot (in the diagram at the top of the next page) the costs due to crime when each proportion of criminals is caught and convicted.
   b. Is the resulting relationship direct or inverse?
   c. Connect the points you have plotted with straight lines. What is the slope of the line when the proportion caught and convicted is between 0.5 and 0.6?

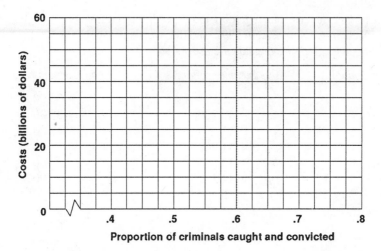

5. Provide the equations for the two lines shown in the graph below.

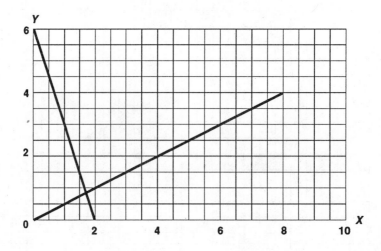

6. Solve each of the following equations for X. (That is, express X as a function of Y.)

   a. $Y = 4 + 7X$
   b. $Y = 2 - 10X$

7. In problem 8 of Chapter 1, we discussed the case of Mary Mineo who can devote a total of 8 hours per week to babysitting or writing stories.

a. If Y is the number of hours she spends per week on babysitting and X is the number of hours she spends per week on writing stories, plot the relationship between X and Y in the graph below.

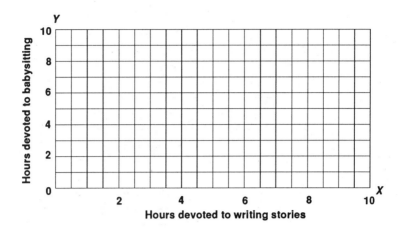

b. Suppose that Ms. Mineo decides to devote a total of 10, not 8, hours to babysitting or writing stories. Will the new relationship between X and Y have the same slope as the old relationship? Why or why not?

8. Suppose that a society's production possibilities curve is as follows:

Output (per year)

Possibility	Food (millions of tons)	Tractors (millions)
A	0	30
B	4	28
C	8	24
D	12	20
E	16	14
F	20	8
G	24	0

a. Is it possible for this society to produce 30 million tons of food per year?
b. Can it produce 30 million tractors per year?
c. Suppose this society produces 20 million tons of food and 6 million tractors per year. Is it operating on the production possibilities curve? If not, what factors might account for this?

d. Plot the production possibilities curve in the graph.

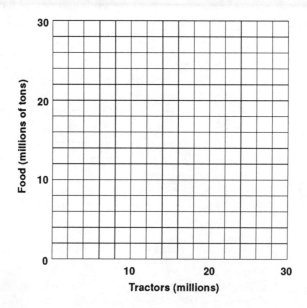

e. What is the cost to society if food output is increased from 12 to 16 million tons per year? If this increase occurs, what effect do you think it will have on this society's production possibilities curve next year?

f. Suppose that this society is governed by a dictator who feels that a tractor is worth infinitely more than a ton of food. What point on the production possibilities curve (of those presented in the table above) would the dictator choose? What problems would arise if he chooses this point?

9. Suppose that a government faces a choice among various levels of defense, represented by the production of missiles, and of food, represented by the production of corn. The following figures indicate the various combinations of missiles and corn that the country can produce:

Possibility	Missiles (number per year)	Corn (millions of bushels per year)
A	0	11
B	2	10
C	4	8
D	6	6
E	8	3
F	10	0

a. Plot the relevant production possibilities curve below.

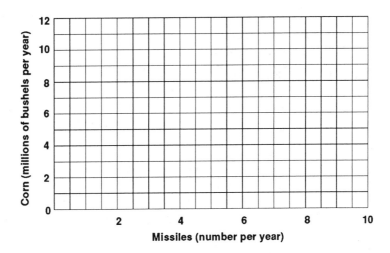

b. Can this country produce more than 12 million bushels of corn per year? Can it produce more than 10 million bushels per year? Can it produce more than 11 missiles per year? Can it produce more than 9 missiles per year?

c. Suppose that the government of this country decides that, in the interests of national security, it must produce 4 missiles per year. What is the maximum number of bushels of corn it can produce?

d. Measured in terms of corn, what is the cost of producing 4 missiles per year rather than 2 missiles per year?

e. Suppose that this country develops and obtains new technology that enables it to produce 50 percent more corn at each level of missile production shown in the table above. Will the new production possibilities curve be closer to, or farther from, the origin than the one graphed in part a?

f. Under the conditions described in part e, what is the cost of producing 4 missiles per year rather than 2 missiles per year?

10. An apple picker receives $2 per hour and can pick 2 bushels of apples per hour. Apples can also be picked by mechanical means, the cost being $1.25 per bushel.

a. If the price system is relied on completely, what proportion of apples will be picked by hand?

b. Suppose that the government institutes a minimum wage of $4 per hour for apple pickers. What will be the effect on the employment of apple pickers?

    c. What will be the effect of the minimum wage on the nation's production possibilities curve?

    d. Under what circumstances would the minimum wage have an effect on whether or not the nation produces at a point on (rather than inside) its production possibilities curve?

11. A nation's production possibility curve shifts from position 1 to position 2 in the graph below:

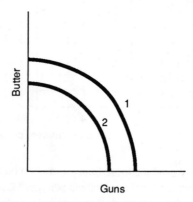

    a. Could this shift be due to a war? Why or why not?

    b. Could it be due to a natural disaster like an earthquake? Why or why not?

    c. Could it be due to technological change? Why or why not?

12. a. Using the data in problem 8 in Chapter 1, plot the amount of income that Mary Mineo will receive if she allocates 0, 5, or 7 hours to babysitting and the rest to story writing. Assume that she gets $15 per story.

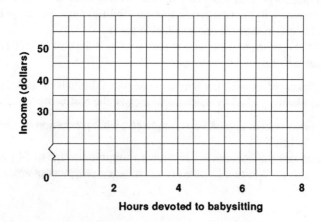

    b. Explain why the relationship you have drawn is *not* a production possibilities curve.

Answers

Matching Questions

1. C   2. B   3. D   4. F   5. E   6. A

Completion Questions

1. sale, not-for-profit, profit, 10 million, 9/10   2. firms, individuals, buy, sell, subset
3. explanation, prediction   4. model   5. predicts   6. Positive   7. normative
8. production possibilities curve   9. inverse   10. over-simplified, irrelevant,
variables   11. quantify, how much   12. 2   13. communism or socialism
14. price system   15. economic growth, less developed, per capita   16. level,
composition, production possibilities, good, good   17. production possibilities, inside,
unemployment, inefficiency   18. research and development, capital, consumers'
19. capitalistic, capital   20. business, perfect competition, price   21. corn, machine
tools, corn, machine tools   22. 500, .002, increasing cost   23. zero, zero   24. do not

True-False

1. False   2. False   3. False   4. True   5. False   6. True   7. False   8. True
9. True   10. True   11. True   12. False   13. False   14. False   15. False   16. True
17. False   18. False   19. True   20. True   21. False   22. True   23. False
24. True   25. True   26. False   27. False   28. False   29. False   30. False

Multiple Choice

1. b   2. d   3. b   4. d   5. d   6. c   7. a   8. d   9. d   10. b   11. c

Problems

1. a.

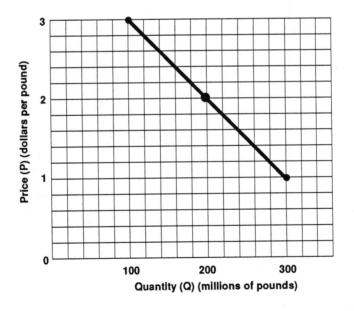

The slope is $-\dfrac{1}{100}$.

2. a.

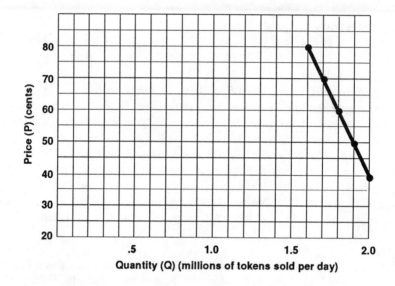

b. Inverse. Yes. Because one would expect a higher price to result in a smaller number of tokens sold.

c. 1.9 million. 1.8 million. 1.85 million.

3.

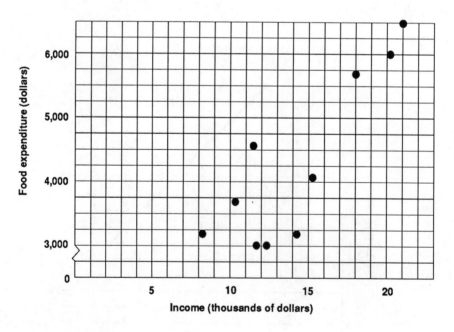

4. a.

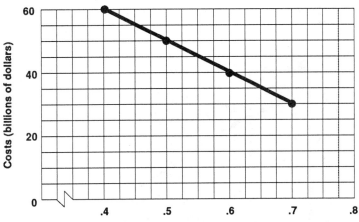

b. Inverse.
c. –$100 billion.

5. $Y = 6 - 3X$

    $Y = \frac{1}{2}X$

6. a. $X = -\frac{4}{7} + \frac{1}{7}Y$

   b. $X = 0.2 - 0.1Y$

7. a.

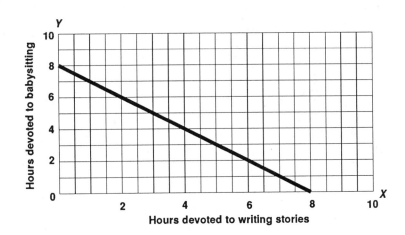

b. Yes, because under these new circumstances $X + Y = 10$, which means that $Y = 10 - X$. Thus, the slope will be -1, which is the same as in the graph in the answer to part a.

8. a. No.
   b. Yes.
   c. No. Inefficiency or unemployment of resources might account for this.
   d.

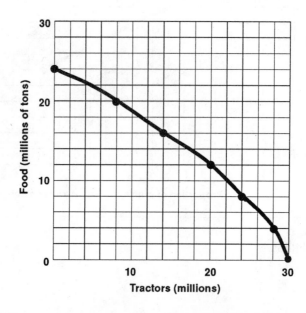

   e. Tractor output must be reduced from 20 million to 14 million. The production possibilities curve will not shift as far outward next year if this increase in food output occurs, because less tractors will be available then.
   f. 30 million tractors and no food. Mass starvation would be likely to result if such a (foolish) policy were adopted.

9. a.

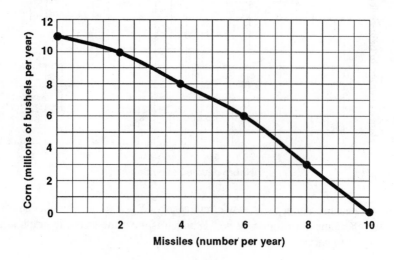

b. No. Yes. No. Yes.

c. 8 million bushels.

d. 2 million bushels of corn.

e. Farther from the origin.

f. 3 million bushels of corn.

10. a. 100 percent.

b. They will be replaced by mechanical pickers.

c. None.

d. If it changes the allocation of resources in such a way that the nation can not maximize output, the minimum wage results in the nation's producing at a point inside its production possibilities curve.

11. a. Yes, since the war could have reduced the nation's resources.

b. Yes, since this too could have reduced the nation's resources.

c. No, not so long as technology advanced, not regressed.

12. a.

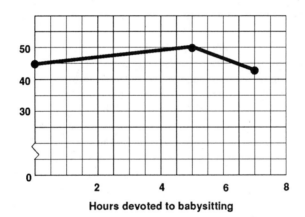

Hours devoted to babysitting

b. A production possibilities curve shows the various output combinations that can be produced with a given quantity of resources and given technology. The graph in part a does not show this so it is not a production possibilities curve.

CHAPTER 3

The Price System

Chapter Profile

There are two sides of every market: the demand side and the supply side. The demand side can be represented by the market demand curve, which almost always slopes downward to the right and whose location depends on consumer tastes, the number and income of consumers, and the prices of other commodities. The supply side of the market can be represented by the market supply curve, which generally slopes upward to the right and whose location depends on technology and resource prices. The equilibrium price and equilibrium quantity of the commodity are given by the intersection of the market demand and supply curves.

If conditions remain reasonably stable for a time, the actual price and quantity should move close to the equilibrium price and quantity. Changes in the position and shape of the demand curve—in response to changes in consumer tastes, income, population, and prices of other commodities—result in changes in the equilibrium price and equilibrium output of a product. Similarly, changes in the position and shape of the supply curve—in response to changes in technology and resource prices, among other things—also result in changes in the equilibrium price and equilibrium output of a product.

The price system sets up incentives for firms to produce what consumers want. To the extent that they produce what consumers want and are willing to pay for, firms reap profits; to the extent that they don't, they may experience losses.

The price system sets up strong incentives for firms to produce the goods consumers want at minimum cost. These incentives take the form of larger profits for firms that minimize costs and smaller profits (or losses) for firms that operate with relatively high costs.

The price system results in each person's receiving an income that depends on the quantity of resources he owns and the prices that they command. The price system also establishes incentives for activities that result in increases in a society's per capita income.

There are circular flows of money and products in a capitalist economy. In product markets, firms provide products to consumers and receive money in return. In resource markets, consumers provide resources to firms, and receive money in return.

The flow of resources and products is as follows: consumers provide resources to firms which in turn provide goods and services to consumers. The flow of money is as follows: firms pay money for resources to consumers who in turn use the money to buy goods and services from firms. Both flows go on simultaneously and repeatedly.

Behavioral Objectives

A. You should be able to define and explain the following key concepts in this chapter:

Demand	Market supply curve	Actual price
Market demand curve	Equilibrium	Product market
Supply	Equilibrium price	Resource market

B. Make sure that you can do each of the following:

1. Indicate the importance of a market demand curve, as well as the factors determining its position.

2. Indicate the importance of a market supply curve, as well as the factors determining its position.

3. Define what is meant by an equilibrium, and explain why the equilibrium price is at the point where the market demand and supply curves intersect.

4. Explain the effect on a commodity's equilibrium price of (a) a shift to the right in its demand curve, and (b) a shift to the left in its demand curve.

5. Explain the effect on a commodity's equilibrium price of (a) a shift to the right in its supply curve, and (b) a shift to the left in its supply curve.

6. Use supply and demand curves to analyze the exchange of goods in a prisoner-of-war camp, and to analyze the pricing practices of Broadway theaters.

7. Use supply and demand curves to explain why rent ceilings in New York City seem to have resulted in fewer resources being devoted to housing.

8. Describe the circular flows of money and products in our economy.

Getting Down to Cases: Meatless Fridays and the Price System

In February 1966, Pope Paul VI issued an apostolic decree that delegated power to national conferences of local bishops to decide whether to continue the rule, in effect for over 1,000 years, that members of the Catholic Church had to abstain from meat on Fridays. Based on this authority, the bishops of the United States terminated obligatory meatless Fridays (except during Lent), beginning in December 1966.

a. What effect do you think this decree of the Pope and the bishops had on the market demand curve for fish in New England?

b. This decree came during a period when there was a decline in commercial fishing in the United States. Both wages and the returns to capital invested in the commercial fishing industry were reported to be relatively low. What effect do you think this decree had on the amount of resources devoted to commercial fishing in the United States?

c. In what sense can it be argued that a movement of resources out of commercial fishing in response to this decree would be socially desirable?

d. Suppose that the government had decided to freeze the price of fish at the level that prevailed prior to this decree. Would this action have resulted in a surplus of fish, a shortage of fish, or neither a surplus nor a shortage of fish?

Matching Questions

_____	1.	Demand curve	A. No net tendency to change
_____	2.	Supply curve	B. Downward sloping to the right
_____	3.	Equilibrium	C. Upward sloping to the right
_____	4.	Equilibrium price	D. Coupons
_____	5.	Rationing	E. Intersection of demand and supply curves
_____	6.	Private sector	F. Consumers and firms

Completion Questions

1. Since wheat can be substituted to some extent for corn as livestock feed, the quantity of wheat demanded depends on the price of corn as well as on the price of wheat. If the price of corn is high, (more, less) _____ wheat will be demanded since it will be profitable to substitute _____ for _____. If the price of corn is low, (more, less) _____ wheat will be demanded since it will be profitable to substitute _____ for _____.

2. As technology progresses, it becomes possible to produce commodities more _____ , so that firms often are willing to supply a given amount of a product at a (lower, higher) _____ price than formerly. Thus, technological change often causes the supply curve to shift to the (left, right) _____.

3. The supply curve for a commodity is affected by the prices of the _____ (labor, capital, and land) used to produce it. Decreases in the price of these inputs make it possible to produce commodities more _____. Firms may then be willing to supply a given amount of a product at a(n) _____ price, thus causing the supply curve to shift to the (left, right) _____. On the other hand, increases in the price of inputs may cause it to shift to the (left, right) _____.

4. An equilibrium is a situation where there is no tendency for _____. In other words, it is a situation that can _____. Thus an equilibrium price is a price that can be _____.

5. When the actual price exceeds the equilibrium price, there will be (downward, upward) _____ pressure on price. Similarly, when the actual price is less than the equilibrium price, there will be a (downward, upward) _____ pressure on price. There is always a tendency for the actual price to move (toward, away from) _____ the equilibrium price, but it should not be assumed that this movement is always _____. Sometimes it takes a _____ time for the actual price to get close to the equilibrium price. Sometimes the actual price _____ gets to the equilibrium price because, by the time it gets close, the equilibrium price changes.

6. In general, a shift to the right in the demand curve results in a(n) (decrease, increase) _____ in the equilibrium price, and a shift to the left in the demand curve results in a(n) (decrease, increase) _____ in the equilibrium price. This conclusion depends on the assumption that the supply curve slopes upward to the (left, right) _____ , but this assumption is generally true.

7. In general, a shift to the right in the supply curve results in a(n) (decrease, increase) _____ in the equilibrium price, and a shift to the left in the supply curve results in a(n) (decrease, increase) _____ in the equilibrium price. Of course, this conclusion depends on the assumption that the demand curve slopes downward to the (left, right) _____ , but this assumption is generally true.

8. The demand curve for a product shows how much of that product consumers want at various _____. If consumers don't want much of a product at a certain price, its demand curve will indicate that fact by being positioned close to the _____ axis at that price. In other words, the demand curve will show that, at this price for the product, the amount consumers will buy is _____.

True-False

_____ 1. The demand curve for a free good (a good with a zero price) must be a horizontal line.

_____ 2. No equilibrium price or equilibrium quantity exists if a good's demand curve is a horizontal line and its supply curve is a vertical line.

_____ 3. As long as the actual price exceeds the equilibrium price, there ordinarily will be a downward pressure on price.

_____ 4. A shift to the left in the demand curve results in an increase in the equilibrium price.

_____ 5. The flow of money income from firms to consumers is exactly equal to the flow of expenditure from consumers to firms, so long as consumers spend all their income.

_____ 6. The price system results in each person's receiving an income that depends on the quantity of resources he or she owns and the prices they command.

_____ 7. The market supply curve depends on technology and the income of consumers.

_____ 8. One prerequisite for a perfectly competitive market is that the product sold by various producers be homogeneous.

_____ 9. A product's demand curve is an important determinant of how much firms will produce of the product, since it indicates the amount of the product that will be demanded at each price.

_____ 10. For the individual product, the question of who gets what is solved by the equality of the quantity demanded and quantity supplied.

_____ 11. The amount society invests in educating, training, and upgrading its labor resources is determined entirely outside the price system.

_____ 12. Many theater experts believe that the solution to Broadway's pricing problems lies in allowing the price system to work more effectively by permitting ticket prices to vary depending on a show's popularity.

_____ 13. During national emergencies, the government sometimes puts a lid on prices, not allowing them to reach their equilibrium levels.

_____ 14. Since a shift in demand for apples leads to a change in their supply, it is impossible to say anything about what happens to either equilibrium price or quantity sold.

_____ 15. Markets for individual commodities must always be in equilibrium since the amount actually sold is always equal to the amount actually bought.

_____ 16. The demand curve for coal in a 5-year period can be derived from the demand curve for coal in a 1-year period. At each price of coal, the quantity demanded in the 5-year period is 5 times the quantity demanded in the 1-year period.

Multiple Choice

1. If the supply of fishing licenses increases:

    a. the quantity of fishing poles demanded will probably decrease.
    b. the supply of fishing poles will probably decrease.
    c. the price of fishing licenses will probably increase.
    d. the demand for fishing poles will probably increase.
    e. none of the above.

2. Between 1974 and 1979 per capita coffee consumption fell in the United States while the price per pound of coffee more than doubled. One possible explanation is that:

    a. the supply of coffee decreased during this period.
    b. the demand for coffee increased during this period.
    c. both the demand and supply of coffee increased.
    d. coffee's supply curve is a vertical line.
    e. none of the above.

3. If the government were to announce that it would no longer allow private parties to buy uranium oxide (so the government would be the sole buyer), and if it were to announce that it would buy any and all uranium oxide at $20 per pound, which of the following diagrams would represent the demand curve for uranium oxide in the United States?

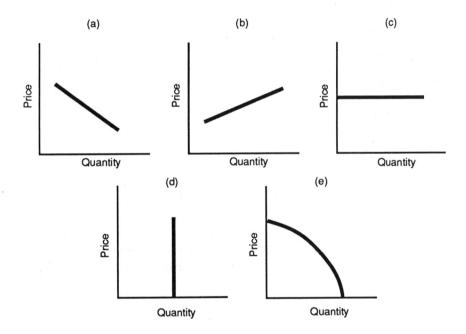

4. If people addicted to drug X must buy some given quantity of it (but not more than that quantity) and will pay whatever price is necessary (and if non-addicts do not buy drug X), which of the diagrams in the previous question represents the demand curve for drug X?

5. Which of the following will *not* affect the demand curve for fishing poles?

   a. pollution of local streams and rivers
   b. an increase in the price of fishing licenses
   c. an increase in the population
   d. an increase in the price of fish
   e. an increase in the price of a fishing pole

6. If the quantity supplied of gasoline exceeds the quantity demanded when gasoline is $1.10 a gallon, and the quantity demanded exceeds the quantity supplied at $1.00 a gallon, the equilibrium price of gasoline is:

   a. $1.00.
   b. $1.10.
   c. below $1.00.
   d. above $1.10.
   e. between $1.00 and $1.10.

7. The equilibrium price of a commodity is given by:

   a. the actual price minus the input costs.
   b. the intersection of market demand and supply curves.
   c. the first point at which market demand exceeds market supply.
   d. the actual price.
   e. none of the above.

8. The position of the supply curve is *not* directly affected by the:

   a. state of technology.
   b. prices of resources used.
   c. income level of consumers.
   d. all of the above.
   e. none of the above.

9. The price system:

   a. sets up incentives for firms to produce what consumers want.
   b. determines each person's income through the price of his or her resources.
   c. may result in unequal distribution of society's output.
   d. all of the above.
   e. none of the above.

10. The amount of new capital goods produced, the amount that society invests in education and training, and the rate of technological change are all influenced in the United States by:

    a. the price system.
    b. government action.
    c. neither a nor b.
    d. both a and b.

11. A perfectly competitive market does *not* require:

   a. a homogeneous product.
   b. so many buyers and sellers that none can influence price.
   c. a constant price.
   d. both a and b.
   e. none of the above.

Discussion and Extension Questions

1. In its 1988 Annual Report, the President's Council of Economic Advisers pointed to the serious congestion problems in the nation's airports. It pointed out that one way to improve the situation was to "set a price for takeoffs and landings that adequately reflects direct and indirect costs." How might such a system work? What sorts of costs would you want to consider? Would you favor such a system? Why or why not?

2. "The supply curve influences the demand curve, since the more that is produced of a commodity, the more people want of it (or the more producers convince them they want)." Discuss and evaluate.

3. When there was an increase in the demand for U.S. wheat from 1972 to 1974, what do you think happened in the corn market? The soybean market? The market for beef?

4. When we placed controls on gasoline prices in 1973–74 there still remained the problem of rationing a scarce good. How did we do it? Would you regard the mechanism we used as better or worse than alternative methods of rationing? Why?

5. The text mentions that more flexibility in prices for Broadway shows was achieved by allowing tickets to be sold at less than the stated price if a show was not sold out. If this innovation has worked well for the producers and the public, evaluate a proposal to create even more flexibility by allowing private individuals to come to the Times Square booth and offer to sell their tickets at prices above or below the original purchase price.

6. The discussion about an equilibrium point in the text focused on the equilibrium price and situations where the actual price was either above or below that equilibrium price. To see if you understand the argument, explain the adjustment mechanism in terms of equilibrium quantity. Begin with a quantity which is less than the equilibrium quantity; what pressures exist to move toward an equilibrium? When the price is too low for equilibrium we say that, at the prevailing price, the quantity people want to buy exceeds the amount suppliers want to sell. What is the counterpart if the quantity is too low for equilibrium?

7. What factors influence the position of the market demand curve for corn? What factors influence the position of the market supply curve for corn? What will happen to the equilibrium price of corn if the market demand curve shifts to the right? What will happen if it shifts to the left?

8. What will happen to the equilibrium price of corn if the market supply curve shifts to the right? What will happen if it shifts to the left?

Problems

1. Suppose that the market demand curve for corn is as follows:

Price of corn (dollars per bushel)	Quantity of corn demanded (millions of bushels per year)
0.50	100
1	80
2	60
3	40
4	30
5	20

a. How much corn would be demanded if the price were 50 cents? Plot the demand curve below:

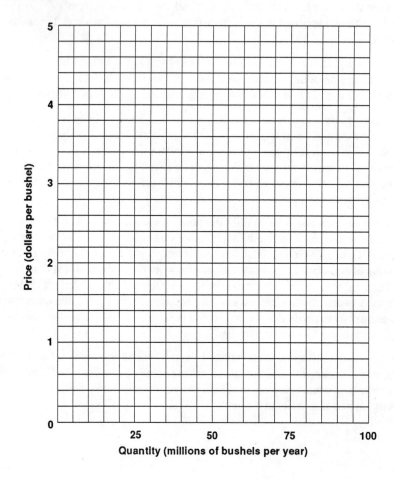

b. Suppose that the market supply curve for corn is as follows:

Price of corn (dollars per bushel)	Quantity of corn supplied (millions of bushels per year)
0.50	10
1	30
2	60
3	70
4	80
5	90

How much corn would be supplied if the price were 50 cents? $2? Plot the supply curve below:

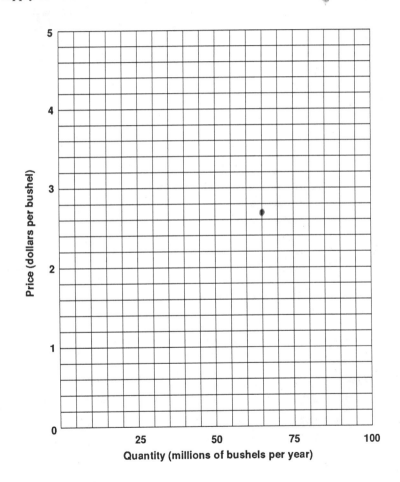

c. Using the data in part b, what is the equilibrium price for corn? Plot the demand and supply curves, and relate these curves to the equilibrium price.

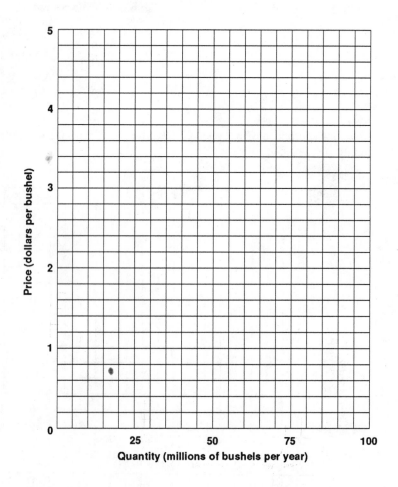

2. Suppose that the quantity of wheat that will be supplied at various prices is as shown below:

Quantity of wheat supplied (millions of bushels)	Price of wheat (dollars per bushel)
1,000	1
1,500	2
2,000	3
2,500	4

a. Plot the supply curve for wheat in the following graph. How much will be produced if the price is $3.50 per bushel (and if the supply curve is linear)?

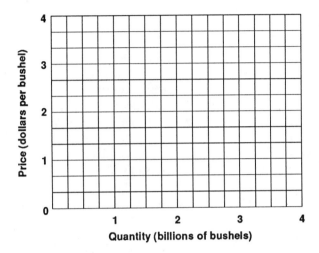

b. Suppose that, because of a technological change—a new, drought-resistant type of grain—farmers are willing to supply 20 percent more wheat at each price. Plot the new supply curve below.

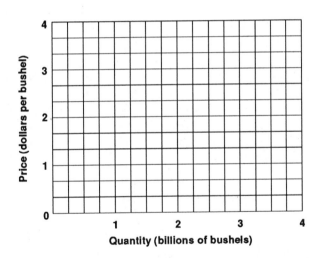

c. Suppose that the demand curve for wheat is as follows:

Quantity of wheat demanded (millions of bushels)	Price of wheat (dollars per bushel)
3,000	1
2,500	2
2,000	3
1,500	4

Plot this demand curve in the graphs in parts a and b above.
d. Under these new circumstances, will the equilibrium price be higher or lower than under the old circumstances, assuming that the demand curve remains constant?
e. Suppose that the demand curve in the new circumstances is unknown, but that the supply curve is as indicated in part b. If the equilibrium price under the new circumstances is $3 per bushel, at what point along the horizontal axis does the demand curve intersect the supply curve?

3. Suppose that the demand curve for tickets to the Metropolitan Opera for a performance of *Carmen* is as follows:

Price of a ticket (dollars)	Quantity demanded
56	3,000
60	2,800
64	2,600
68	2,400
72	2,200
76	2,000
80	1,800

a. If the Metropolitan Opera House has 2,400 seats, and if it sets a price of $72 per ticket, will the house be full? If not, how many seats will be vacant?
b. What is the equilibrium price of a ticket for this performance?
c. What is the shape of the supply curve for tickets?
d. Is there a "shortage" or "surplus" of tickets? In a free market, would the price of a ticket rise or fall?

4. The demand curve for fishing poles is $P = 50 - 10Q$, where P is the price of a fishing pole (in dollars) and Q is the quantity demanded per year (in millions).

a. If the government orders the producers of fishing poles to produce 1 million fishing poles per year, what will be the equilibrium price of a fishing pole?
b. If the current price of a fishing pole is $60, would you expect the price to rise or fall, once the government order occurs?
c. Suppose that after it issues the above order, the government sets a ceiling of $30 on the price of a fishing pole. Will a surplus or shortage result? How big will it be?

5. If supply and demand in a competitive market both increase, one can predict the direction of change of output but not of price. If supply increases but demand

decreases, one cannot, without further knowledge, be certain about the direction of either the price or the quantity change. Do you agree with this statement? Explain.

6. Use a diagram to show that a rise in the price of margarine could be a response to a rise in the price of butter.

7. According to *Business Week,* all major chocolate makers have shared a basic problem. Production costs have gone up, sales have gone down, and the price of a standard candy bar has risen. Depict this situation graphically and explain why a successful attempt to make candy appealing to more customers will only cause a further rise in price.

8. How do you reconcile the hypotheses that "the quantity demanded varies inversely with price" (law of demand), with the statement that "a rise in demand will lead to a rise in price, other things equal?"

9. It is impossible for the price of a commodity to fall at the same time the demand for the commodity is rising. Comment, using supply and demand curves.

10. Distinguish between a "change in demand" and a "change in quantity demanded."

11. "When it is said that there are shortages in some market, we know that that market is out of equilibrium. Take natural gas for instance. In the late 1970s there were shortages. Some people argued that they were due to the government price controls while others claimed that they were due to cold winters combined with the stock-piling of natural gas because firms and individuals feared a shortage might develop. The first group of people worried that releasing the controls would lead to very high prices, while the second group concluded that the shortage would disappear as soon as it warmed up and people became less worried." Explain the first group's argument using diagrammatic analysis.

Answers

Matching Questions
1. B   2. C   3. A   4. E   5. D   6. F

Completion Questions
1. more, wheat, corn, less, corn, wheat   2. cheaply, lower, right   3. resources, cheaply, lower, right, left   4. change, persist, maintained   5. downward, upward, toward, rapid, long, never   6. increase, decrease, right   7. decrease, increase, right   8. prices, vertical, small

True-False
1. False   2. False   3. True   4. False   5. True   6. True   7. False   8. True
9. True   10. True   11. False   12. True   13. True   14. False   15. False
16. False

Multiple Choice
1. d   2. a   3. c   4. d   5. e   6. e   7. b   8. c   9. d   10. d   11. c

Problems

1. a. 100 million bushels.

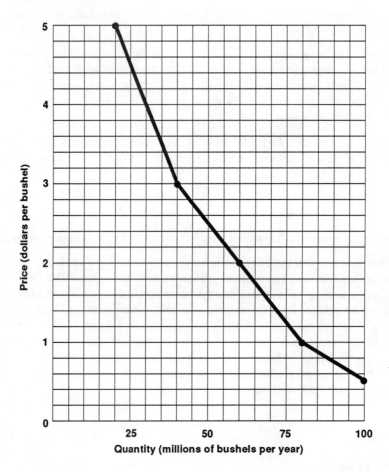

b. 10 million bushels, 60 million bushels.

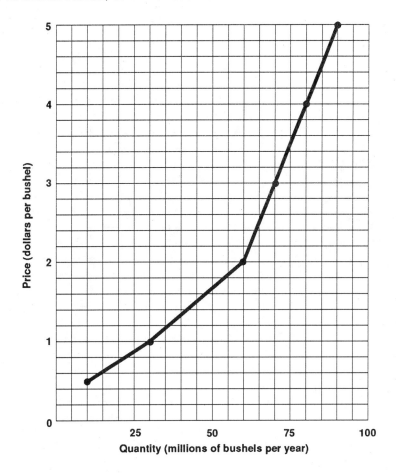

c. $2 a bushel.

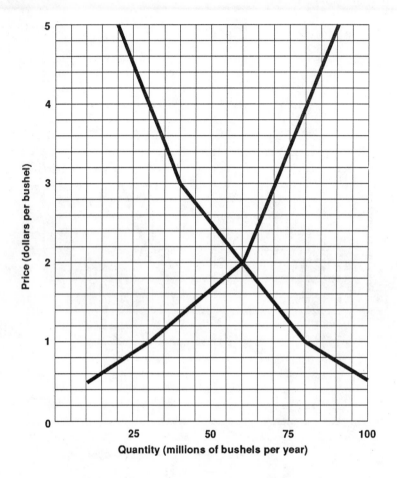

2. a. The graph is below. 2,250 million bushels.

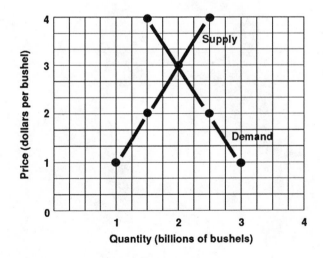

b.

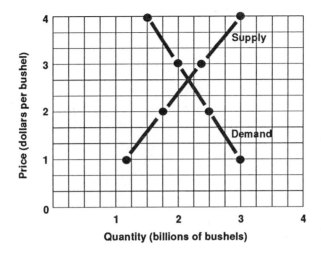

Quantity (billions of bushels)

c. The demands are plotted above.
d. Lower.
e. At 2,400 million bushels of wheat.
3. a. No. 200 seats.
b. $68.
c. A vertical line at 2,400 tickets.
d. Surplus. It would fall.
4. a. Since $50 - 10(1) = 40$, the answer is $40.
b. Fall.
c. Since $Q = 5 - 0.1P$, the quantity demanded equals $5 - 0.1(30) = 2$ million fishing poles when the price is at its ceiling of $30. Since the quantity supplied equals 1 million, there will be a shortage of 1 million fishing poles per year.
5. If the demand and supply curves both shift to the right, the equilibrium quantity must increase, but the equilibrium price may rise or fall. If the supply curve shifts to the right but the demand curve shifts to the left, the equilibrium price will fall, but the equilibrium quantity may rise or fall. The left-hand panel below shows a case where it falls (from Q_0 to Q_1); the right-hand panel below shows a case where it rises (from Q_0 to Q_2).

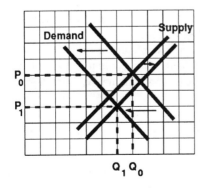

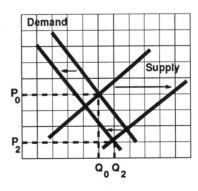

6. Butter and margarine are substitutes. An increase in the price of butter might shift the demand curve for margarine to the right, as shown below, the result being an increase (from P to P') in the price of margarine.

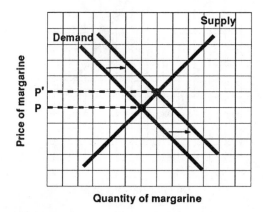

Quantity of margarine

7. These facts seem to suggest that the supply curve for candy bars has shifted to the left, as shown below.

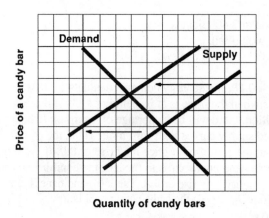

Quantity of candy bars

If candy is made appealing to more customers, this means that the demand curve shifts to the right, which causes a further rise in price.

8. The first hypothesis states that the demand curve slopes downward and to the right. The second hypothesis states that a shift of the demand curve to the right results in an increase in the equilibrium price. There is no contradiction between them.

9. If the supply of the commodity is rising at the same time that its demand is rising, the price may fall, as shown below:

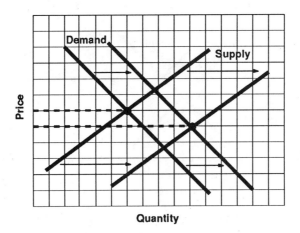

10. A change in demand is a shift in the demand curve, which is quite different from a change in the quantity demanded.
11. The first group felt that the price, P_c, was set below the equilibrium price by government controls, the situation being as shown below:

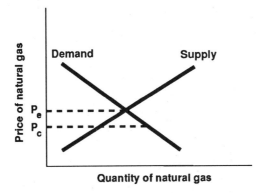

If the controls are released, the price will rise to P_e.

The second group felt that the demand curve had shifted to the right and that the price had not increased, so there was a shortage of $Q_D - Q_S$, as shown below:

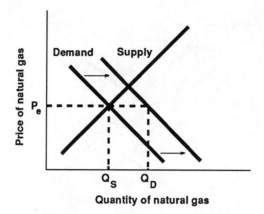

If the demand curve shifts back to its original position when the weather warms up and people become less worried, the shortage will disappear.

Market Demand and Price Elasticity

Chapter Profile

The market demand curve is the relationship between the price of a commodity and the amount of the commodity demanded in the market.

The price elasticity of demand measures the sensitivity of the amount demanded to changes in price. Whether a price increase results in an increase or decrease in the total amount spent on a commodity depends on the price elasticity of demand.

The income elasticity of demand measures the sensitivity of the amount demanded to changes in total income. A commodity's income elasticity of demand may be positive or negative. Luxury items are generally assumed to have higher income elasticities of demand than necessities.

The cross elasticity of demand measures the sensitivity of the amount demanded to changes in the price of another commodity. If the cross elasticity of demand is positive, two commodities are substitutes; if it is negative, they are complements.

The market demand curve for a commodity is not the same as the demand curve for the output of a single firm that produces the commodity, unless the industry is composed of only one firm. In general, the demand curve for the output of a single firm will be more elastic than the market demand curve for the commodity. If a great number of firms are selling a homogeneous commodity, the individual firm's demand curve becomes essentially horizontal.

There are many techniques for measuring demand curves, such as interview studies, direct experiments, and the statistical analysis of historical data.

Behavioral Objectives

A. You should be able to define and explain the following key concepts in this chapter:

Market demand curve	Price inelastic	Income elasticity of
Direct market experiment	Unitary elasticity	demand
Price elasticity of demand	Complement	Cross elasticity of demand
Arc elasticity of demand	Brannan plan	Substitute
Price elastic		

B. Make sure that you can do each of the following:

1. Indicate the significance of market demand curves, both for public policy and private decision making, and the principal ways that a market demand curve can be measured.

2. Calculate the price elasticity of demand, given a table showing the quantity demanded at various prices.

3. State the major determinants of whether the price elasticity of demand for a particular commodity is high or low.

4. Explain why, if the demand for a commodity is price elastic, reductions in price will increase the total amount spent on the commodity, whereas increases in price will reduce the total amount spent on the commodity.

5. Distinguish between the demand curve facing an entire industry and that facing an individual firm, and contrast the shapes of these demand curves.

6. Indicate the significance of the income elasticity of demand and how it is calculated.

7. Indicate the significance of the cross elasticity of demand and how it is calculated.

Getting Down to Cases: Price Elasticity Down on the Farm

Suppose that the market demand curve for beef at the retail level is as follows:

Price (dollars per pound)	Millions of pounds demanded per month
1.96	2,038
2.00	2,000
2.04	1,962
2.08	1,924

Because of transportation and distribution costs, assume that beef farmers receive $1 less than the retail price. For simplicity, suppose that the amount they sell equals the amount sold at the retail level.

a. What is the market demand curve for beef at the farm level?

b. What is the price elasticity of demand for beef at the retail level if the price is between $2.00 and $2.04 per pound?

c. What is the price elasticity of demand for beef at the farm level when the price is between $1.00 and $1.04 per pound?

d. According to a classic study published by Henry Schultz of the University of Chicago in 1938, the price elasticity of demand for beef at the retail level was about 0.49. What factors might result in a different value of this elasticity today?

e. According to some economists, the price elasticity of demand for farm products at the farm level is likely to be less than at the retail level. Using the above example of beef, can you explain why they believe this to be true?

Matching Questions

_____ 1. Price elasticity less than 1   A. Gin and tonic

_____ 2. Cross elasticity of demand   B. Potatoes
         is positive

_____ 3. Price elasticity equal to 1   C. Automobiles

_____ 4. Income elasticity greater   D. Unitary elasticity
         than 1

_____ 5. Cross elasticity of demand is   E. Butter and margarine
         negative

_____ 6. Horizontal demand curve   F. Firm under perfect competition

Completion Questions

1. When income increases from $80 billion to $81 billion, the quantity demanded of good X increases from 3,000 to 3,050. The income elasticity of demand for good X equals _____. When computing the income elasticity of demand, the price of good X is held _____.

2. The total amount spent on a good is not affected by its price if the price elasticity of demand equals _____. The total quantity demanded of a good is not affected by its price if the price elasticity of demand equals _____.

3. If the government imposes a $1 tax on a commodity, it will obtain the most revenue from the tax if the commodity's price elasticity of demand equals _____. The largest burden of the tax is borne by consumers if the price elasticity of demand equals _____.

4. Whether a price cut results in an increase in the total amount spent on a commodity depends on the _____.

5. The total amount spent on a commodity is the _____ times _____.

6. If the demand for a commodity is price inelastic, then the price elasticity of demand is _____.

7. The income elasticity of demand is the percentage change in the quantity demanded resulting from _____ increase in total _____.

8. If the cross elasticity of demand is positive, two commodities are _____.

9. The demand for a commodity is _____ when the price increase or decrease results in no difference in the total amount spent on the commodity.

10. The _____ is the percentage change in quantity demanded resulting from a 1 percent change in price.

11. During a (long, short) _____ period, demand for a nondurable good is likely to be more sensitive to price than over a (long, short) _____ one. The longer the period, the (easier, harder) _____ it is for consumers and business firms to substitute one good for another.

12. The demand curve for the output of a particular firm is generally (less, more) _____ price elastic than the market demand curve for the commodity, because the products of other firms in the industry are close (substitutes, complements) _____ for the product of this firm.

13. According to an early study by Roos and von Szeliski, the _____ _____ for automobiles is about 2.5: in other words, a 1 percent increase in income will result in about a(n) _____ percent increase in the quantity demanded of automobiles. In later studies by Atkinson, Chow, and Suits, the income elasticity of demand is about 3.0: in other words, a 1 percent increase in income will result in about a(n) _____ percent increase in the quantity demanded of automobiles.

True-False

_____ 1. An increase in the price of fishing licenses will reduce the total amount spent on fishing poles.

_____ 2. Holding constant the demand curve of a perfectly competitive firm, the total amount spent on the firm's product is proportional to the number of units of output it produces and sells.

_____ 3. The demand for an appendectomy is likely to be less price elastic than the demand for aspirin.

_____ 4. If the price elasticity of demand of product Y equals infinity, and if the government imposes a tax of $1 per unit of product Y, none of the tax will be shifted to consumers.

_____ 5. If the quantity demanded of product Z falls by 5 units whenever the price of product Z increases by 1 dollar, the price elasticity of demand for product Z is 5.

_____ 6. The consumer almost always responds to an increase in a commodity's price by reducing the amount of it he or she consumes.

_____ 7. If the demand for a commodity is price elastic, an increase in its price will lead to an increase in the total amount spent by consumers on the commodity.

_____ 8. A commodity's income elasticity of demand may be positive or negative.

_____ 9. The income elasticity of demand for food is very high.

_____ 10. The price elasticity of demand is expressed in terms of relative, not absolute, changes in price and quantity demanded.

_____ 11. The price elasticity of demand is a measure of the sensitivity of quantity demanded to the price of other commodities.

_____ 12. Since the market demand curve reflects what consumers want and are willing to pay for, when the market demand curve for wheat shifts upward to the right, this indicates that consumers want more wheat at the existing price.

_____ 13. The demand for a particular brand of oil is more price elastic than the demand for fuel as a whole.

_____ 14. The demand for a commodity is price elastic if the price elasticity of demand is less than 1.

_____ 15. If the demand for the commodity is price elastic, an increase in its price will lead to a decrease in the total amount spent by consumers on the commodity.

_____ 16. The demand for a commodity is price inelastic if the price elasticity of demand is greater than 1.

Multiple Choice

1. A representative of organized labor says that an increase in the wage rate would have no effect on the total amount of wages paid to labor. If this is true, the price elasticity of demand for labor is:

   a. less than 1.   d. more than 2.
   b. 1.   e. none of the above.
   c. 2.

2. The supply curve for product Q is a vertical line. The government establishes a floor under the price of product Q, this floor being $1 above the equilibrium price. The surplus of product Q will be greatest if the price elasticity of demand of product Q is:

   a. 0.25.   d. 2.50.
   b. 1.   e. 3.00.
   c. 1.25.

3. The amount of strawberries available on any given day is 3 tons in Baltimore and 5 tons in Philadelphia. The equilibrium price is the same in both cities, but the government establishes a price ceiling that is 50¢ per box below the equilibrium price of both cities. The price elasticity of demand for strawberries is 2 in Baltimore and 3 in Philadelphia. The size of the shortage in Baltimore is:

   a. .50 tons.   d. zero.
   b. (1 − .50) ÷ 2 = .25 tons.   e. indeterminate from the information
   c. 2 ÷ (1 − .50) = 4 tons.   given.

4. In the previous question, the size of the shortage in Baltimore:

    a. will exceed that in Philadelphia.
    b. will equal that in Philadelphia.
    c. will be less than that in Philadelphia.
    d. will be less than or equal to that in Philadelphia.
    e. may or may not be greater than that in Philadelphia.

5. (Advanced.) Along any straight-line demand curve, the price elasticity of demand:

    a. increases as price falls.
    b. decreases as price falls.
    c. remains constant as price falls.
    d. equals the slope of the line.
    e. first increases and then decreases as price falls.

6. The quantity of Velasquez paintings increases by 2 percent because a number of such paintings is discovered in a cave by Basque revolutionaries. If the price elasticity of demand for Velasquez paintings is 0.3, the result will be a reduction in the price of Velasquez paintings of:

    a. 0.3 percent.
    b. 0.6 percent.
    c. $3^1/_3$ percent.
    d. $6^2/_3$ percent.
    e. none of the above.

7. A 1 percent increase in the price of good X results in a 2 percent increase in the quantity demanded of good Y. A 1 percent increase in the price of good Y will result in an increase in the quantity demanded of good X that is:

    a. 2 percent
    b. $^1/_2$ percent.
    c. more than 2 percent.
    d. less than $^1/_2$ percent.
    e. indeterminate from the information given.

8. If two goods are substitutes, a decrease in the price of one of them will result in:

    a. a shift to the right in the other good's supply curve.
    b. a shift to the left in the other good's supply curve.
    c. a shift to the right in the other good's demand curve.
    d. a shift to the left in the other good's demand curve.
    e. an increase in the quantity demanded of the other good.

9. If two goods are complements, a decrease in the price of one of them will result in:

    a. a shift to the left in the other good's demand curve.
    b. a shift to the right in the other good's demand curve.
    c. a decrease in the quantity demanded of the other good.
    d. no change in the quantity demanded of the other good.
    e. none of the above.

10. In general, the individual demand curve will not remain fixed if there is a change in:

    a. preferences.
    b. income.
    c. prices of other goods.
    d. any of the above.
    e. none of the above.

11. If there are a great many firms selling a homogeneous product, an individual firm's demand curve becomes:

    a. of unitary elasticity.
    b. price inelastic.
    c. cross elastic.
    d. close to horizontal.
    e. income elastic.

12. If the cross elasticity of demand is negative, two commodities are:

    a. complements.
    b. substitutes.
    c. positive elastomers.
    d. negative elastomers.
    e. none of the above.

13. If the income elasticity of demand for a product is zero and incomes increase considerably during a 10 year period, then the effect of this change in income on the product's sales should be:

    a. positive.
    b. negative.
    c. impossible to predict.
    d. none of the above.
    e. infinite.

14. The income elasticity of demand:

    a. must always be negative.
    b. must always be positive.
    c. can be positive or negative.

Discussion and Extension Questions

1. According to the *New York Times*, "Coffee drinking, drip or perk, isn't as popular as it once was. Per capita consumption has dropped from 3.12 cups a day in 1962 to 2.2 cups. . . . The decline hasn't kept prices down, though." Does the information given here prove that there has been a shift to the left in the demand curve for coffee? Would such a shift necessarily result in a decrease in the price of coffee? Why or why not?

2. In one year there was talk of a beef shortage; in the next year there was talk of a gasoline shortage. Why did government officials talk more about rationing gasoline to solve the latter problem than about rationing beef to solve the former?

3. If a family budgets a fixed amount of money for certain expenditures during the coming year, such as $200 a month for food and $100 a month for clothing purchases, what is that family's price elasticity of demand for food? Clothing? Be careful!

4. How could a state government use the information that the price elasticity of demand for cigarettes is about 0.4 when considering an increase in the state cigarette tax as a means of providing additional revenue for the state? How might the information that New Hampshire has a per capita sales of cigarettes that is twice that of any neighboring state affect your decision to use the number 0.4 as your estimate of price elasticity in your calculations?

CHAPTER FOUR

5. "If the demand curve for coffee is linear, the price elasticity of demand for coffee is the same at all prices." Discuss and evaluate.

6. "The theory of demand is based entirely on the supposition that individualism should reign supreme. Yet it is obvious that people often do not know what is good for them. Consequently, the state should play a greater role in determining what consumers should have." Comment and evaluate.

7. What are some ways that market demand curves can be measured? According to results obtained by Professor William Vickrey, the demand for passenger service on the New York subways is price inelastic. Does this mean that fare increases would result in greater revenues for the New York subways?

8. According to estimates made by agricultural economists, the price elasticity of demand for cotton is about 0.12. If this is the case, to what extent will the quantity demanded of cotton increase if the price of cotton is reduced by 1 percent?

9. What is meant by a market? How can one derive the market demand curve from the demand curves of the individuals comprising the market?

10. According to the Department of Agriculture, the income elasticity of demand for coffee is about 0.23. If incomes rose by 1 percent, what effect would this have on the quantity demanded of coffee?

11. Based on the information in Question 8 above, would you expect that the price elasticity of demand for the output of a single cotton producer is 0.12? If not, what would you guess its value to be?

Problems

1. Suppose that the relationship between the price of aluminum and the quantity of aluminum demanded is as follows:

Price (dollars)	Quantity
1	8
2	7
3	6
4	5
5	4

What is the arc elasticity of demand when price is between $1 and $2? Between $4 and $5?

2. Suppose that the price elasticity of demand for gasoline is 0.50. About how big a price increase will be required to reduce the consumption of gasoline by 1 percent?

3. Suppose that the income elasticity of demand for automobiles is 2.5 in the United States and 3.0 in the United Kingdom. If incomes in the United States rise by 2 percent next year and incomes in the United Kingdom rise by 1 percent, what will be the effect in each country on the quantity of automobiles purchased?

4. If a 1.5 percent reduction in the price of Nike running shoes results in a 3.0 percent reduction in the quantity demanded of New Balance running shoes, what is the cross elasticity of demand for these two commodities? Are they substitutes or complements?

5. Suppose that the market demand curve for mink coats is as follows:

Price (dollars)	Quantity of mink coats
500	500
1,000	300
1,500	200
2,000	100

   a. What is the price elasticity of demand for mink coats when the price is between $1,500 and $2,000?
   b. What is the price elasticity of demand when the price is between $500 and $1,000?
   c. According to the text, an increase in price results in increased total expenditures on a product if its price elasticity of demand is less than 1, and less total expenditure on a product if its price elasticity of demand is greater than 1. Show that this proposition is true if the price of mink coats is raised from $500 to $1,000.
   d. Show that the proposition in part c is true if the price of mink coats is raised from $1,500 to $2,000.

6. Suppose that there are only 3 people in the market for sable coats—Mrs. Smith, Mrs. Kennedy, and Mrs. Jones. Suppose that their demand curves are as given below. Fill in the blank spaces for the market demand curve for sable coats.

Price of a sable coat (dollars)	Quantity demanded Smith	Kennedy	Jones	Market demand
500	3	2	5	_____
1,000	2	1	4	_____
1,500	2	1	3	_____
2,000	1	0	2	_____

7. (Advanced) Prove that the price elasticity of demand at any price less than $5.00 will always be the same on D_1 as on D_2. (Both D_1 and D_2 are shown below.)

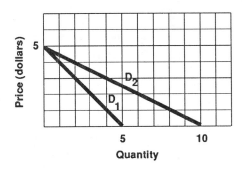

8. Every time the price of a sixpack falls by a dime, Tom runs out and buys three more sixpacks per week, but Jean runs out and buys five more. The price is now $1.00, and we observe Tom buying twenty-five sixpacks per week while Jean is buying ten sixpacks.

   a. Draw each person's demand curve for beer.

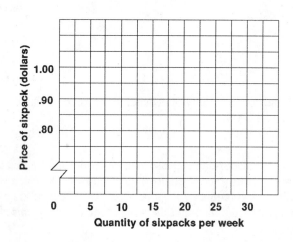

   b. Whose price elasticity of demand for beer is higher at the current price of a sixpack?

9. Suppose the price elasticity of demand for zambowies is unity when the price is $40. Suppose further that when the price is $40, 100 zambowies are sold each week in Sommersville. Assuming no change in the elasticity for a small rise in zambowie prices, how many will be sold next week if price should rise to $42 per zambowie?

10. Suppose that the Brazilian government destroys a substantial portion of its coffee harvest in order to increase its revenue from coffee exports. What conditions are essential in order to make this type of policy economically beneficial for the country? Why would the conditions you identify increase export revenues?

11. a. Based on the diagram on the next page, which would be more expensive for the government?

   (1) set minimum wages at $2.50 per hour and hire all the people the market will not hire at that wage or;

   (2) let the market determine an equilibrium wage ($1.50 per hour in the diagram) and pay everyone who works a subsidy of $1.00 to make up the difference between what the market will pay and what is deemed a fair wage ($2.50 per hour)?

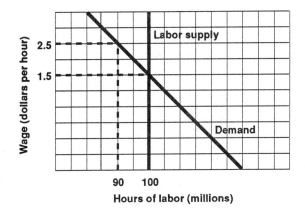

b. Would the answer be different if the demand for labor were price elastic with the result that an increase in the wage rate to $2.50 cut the quantity of labor demanded to a greater extent than shown above? Why or why not?

12. A firm estimates that the demand curves for its two products are given by

$$Q_1 = 200 - 2P_1 - 3P_2 \text{ and } Q_2 = 450 + 6P_1 - 2P_2,$$

where Q_1 is the quantity demanded of the first product, P_1 is its price, Q_2 is the quantity demanded of the second product, and P_2 is its price. Compute the following elasticities at $P_1 = \$2$ and $P_2 = \$2$:

a. Price elasticity of demand for the first product.
b. Cross elasticity of demand for the second product with respect to variation in the price of the first product.

Answers

Matching Questions
1. B   2. E   3. D   4. C   5. A   6. F

Completion Questions
1. 1.3, constant   2. 1, zero   3. zero, zero   4. price elasticity of demand
5. quantity demanded, price   6. less than 1   7. a 1 percent, money income
8. substitutes   9. of unitary elasticity   10. price elasticity of demand   11. long,
short, easier   12. more, substitutes   13. income elasticity of demand, 2.5, 3.0

True-False
1. True   2. True   3. True   4. True   5. False   6. True   7. False   8. True
9. False   10. True   11. False   12. True   13. True   14. False   15. True
16. False

Multiple Choice

1. b   2. e   3. e   4. c   5. b   6. d   7. e   8. d   9. b   10. d   11. d   12. a
13. d   14. c

Problems

1. $-\dfrac{(Q_2-Q_1)}{\dfrac{Q_1+Q_2}{2}} \div \dfrac{(P_2-P_1)}{\dfrac{P_1+P_2}{2}} = -\dfrac{(7-8)}{\dfrac{8+7}{2}} \div \dfrac{(2-1)}{\dfrac{1+2}{2}} = \dfrac{3}{15} = 0.20$

$-\dfrac{(Q_2-Q_1)}{\dfrac{Q_1+Q_2}{2}} \div \dfrac{(P_2-P_1)}{\dfrac{P_1+P_2}{2}} = -\dfrac{(4-5)}{\dfrac{5+4}{2}} \div \dfrac{(5-4)}{\dfrac{4+5}{2}} = \dfrac{9}{9} = 1.00$

2. 2 percent.
3. The quantity of automobiles demanded will increase by 3 percent in the United Kingdom and by 5 percent in the United States (assuming other factors are constant).
4. Plus two. Substitutes.
5. a. $-\dfrac{200-100}{150} \div \dfrac{1,500-2,000}{1,750} = \dfrac{100}{150} \div \dfrac{500}{1,750}$

   $= \dfrac{2}{3} \div \dfrac{2}{7} = \dfrac{2}{3} \times \dfrac{7}{2} = \dfrac{7}{3} = 2\frac{1}{3}$

   b. $-\dfrac{500-300}{400} \div \dfrac{500-1,000}{750} = \dfrac{200}{400} \div \dfrac{500}{750} = \dfrac{1}{2} \div \dfrac{2}{3} = \dfrac{1}{2} \times \dfrac{3}{2} = \dfrac{3}{4}$

   c. As indicated in part b, the price elasticity of demand is less than 1 in this range. Thus, an increase in price should increase the total expenditure on the product. Looking at the figures, this is the case. When the price is $500, total expenditure is $250,000; when it is $1,000, total expenditure is $300,000.

   d. As indicated in part a, the price elasticity of demand is greater than 1 in this range. Thus, an increase in price should decrease the total expenditure on the product. Looking at the figures in the table, this is the case. When the price is $1,500, total expenditure is $300,000; when it is $2,000, total expenditure is $200,000.

6. *Market demand*
   10
   7
   6
   3

7. Expressed in terms of calculus, the price elasticity of demand is $-\dfrac{dQ}{dP} \cdot \dfrac{P}{Q}$. If the demand curve is D_1, $\dfrac{dQ}{dP} = -1$; thus $-\dfrac{dQ}{dP} \cdot \dfrac{P}{Q} = \dfrac{P}{Q} = \dfrac{P}{5-P}$. If the demand curve is D_2, $\dfrac{dQ}{dP} = -2$; thus, $-\dfrac{dQ}{dP} \cdot \dfrac{P}{Q} = \dfrac{2P}{Q} = \dfrac{2P}{10-2P} = \dfrac{P}{5-P}$. Since the price elasticity of demand equals $\dfrac{P}{5-P}$ in each case, it must be the same for both demand curves if the price is the same.

8. a.

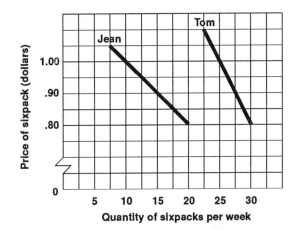

b. For each person we can compute the arc elasticity of demand between $1.00 per sixpack and $0.90. For Tom it is $- \left(\dfrac{28 - 25}{26.5} \right) \div \left(\dfrac{90 - 100}{95} \right) = 1.08$. For Jean it is $- \left(\dfrac{15 - 10}{12.5} \right) \div \left(\dfrac{90 - 100}{95} \right) = 3.8$. Thus Jean's is higher.

9. About 95.

10. The price elasticity of demand must be less than one. Export revenue would increase because, if the price elasticity of demand is less than one, increases in price (and reductions in quantity) will increase revenue.

11. a. The cost of the first alternative would be 10 million × $2.50, or $25 million. The cost of the second alternative would be 100 million × $1, or $100 million. Thus, the second alternative would be more expensive.

b. If the demand for labor were price elastic, the answer would be the opposite. Let Q_1 be the quantity of labor demanded (in millions of hours) when the wage is $2.50. Under the first alternative, the cost to the government is $2.5 × (100 − Q_1)$. Under the second alternative, the cost is $100 million. If $2.5 × (100 − Q_1) > 100$, the cost under the first alternative would be higher. In other words, if $Q_1 < 60$, this is the case. If the demand for labor is price elastic, Q_1 will be less than 60, because an increase in the wage rate will reduce the total amount spent on labor.

12. a. If $P_2 = 2$, $Q_1 = 194 − 2P_1$. Thus, if $P_1 = 2$, $Q_1 = 190$. And if $P_1 = 2.02$, $Q_1 = 189.96$. Consequently, a 1 percent increase in price (from 2 to 2.02) results in about a .02 percent decrease (from 190 to 189.96) in quantity demanded so the price elasticity of demand is about 0.02.

b. If $P_2 = 2$, $Q_2 = 446 + 6P_1$. Thus, if $P_1 = 2$, $Q_2 = 458$. And if $P_1 = 2.02$, $Q_2 = 458.12$. Consequently, a 1 percent increase in price (from 2 to 2.02) results in about a .03 percent increase (from 458 to 458.12) in quantity demanded, so the cross elasticity of demand is about + 0.03.

Getting behind the Demand Curve: Consumer Behavior

Chapter Profile

Consumer wants and desires are a basic determinant of the nature and quantity of the goods and services produced in our economic system. Recent government figures show that consumers spend about 79 percent of their income on goods and services; the rest goes for taxes and saving (and interest). Much of their expenditures for goods and services go for housing, food and drink, and transportation.

The model of consumer behavior explains how an individual consumer allocates his or her income among various commodities. This model assumes that the consumer's preferences are transitive and that commodities are defined so that more of them is preferred to less.

Given these assumptions, the consumer's preferences can be represented by a utility index. Utility is a number that indexes the level of satisfaction derived by the consumer from a particular market basket. Market baskets with higher utilities are preferred over market baskets with lower utilities.

The model of consumer behavior recognizes that preferences alone do not determine the consumer's actions. Given the consumer's preferences, as reflected in his or her utility index, the choices open to the consumer are dictated by the size of his or her money income and the nature of commodity prices. The consumer is assumed to choose the market basket that maximizes his or her utility.

If the consumer maximizes utility, his or her income is allocated among commodities so that, for every commodity he or she buys, the marginal utility of the commodity is proportional to its price. In other words, the marginal utility of the last dollar spent on each commodity is made equal for all commodities.

An individual demand curve shows the quantity of a commodity that a consumer will buy at various prices, when other prices and the consumer's tastes and income are held constant. Individual demand curves almost always slope downward to the right because of the so-called law of decreasing marginal utility. One can explain this same phenomenon in terms of the substitution and income effects of a price change.

Behavioral Objectives

A. You should be able to define and explain the following key concepts in this chapter:

Model of consumer behavior	Law of diminishing marginal utility	Individual demand curve
Utility	Equilibrium market basket	Consumer's surplus
Marginal utility	Income effect	Substitution effect

B. Make sure that you can do each of the following:

1. State the three principal assumptions underlying the economist's model of consumer behavior.

2. Explain why, if the consumer maximizes utility, his or her income must be allocated among commodities so that, for every commodity purchased, the marginal utility of the commodity is proportional to its price.

3. Give some real-life examples where the budget allocation rule (described in the previous sentence) can be of use.

4. State the factors influencing the position of a consumer's demand curve for a particular commodity.

5. Explain why individual demand curves almost always slope downward and to the right.

* 6. Demonstrate that two indifference curves cannot intersect.

* 7. Indicate how, given a consumer's money income and the prices of two commodities, you can construct the consumer's budget line.

* 8. Show how, given a consumer's indifference curves and budget line, you can determine his or her equilibrium market basket.

* 9. Explain why the utility index attached to higher indifference curves is greater than that attached to lower indifference curves.

*10. Indicate the difficulties in measuring utility in practical situations.

Getting Down to Cases: The Allocation of Study Time

Suppose that professors in three of your courses (economics, English, and chemistry) announce that they will give examinations the day after tomorrow. You figure that the total amount of time you can devote to these three exams is 10 hours. For each examination, the relationship between the number of hours you spend studying and the grade you think you'll get is shown on the next page:

---

* Pertains to chapter appendix.

Number of hours spent studying	Grade		
	Economics	English	Chemistry
0	55	50	55
1	65	60	70
2	75	69	80
3	80	74	85
4	83	79	89
5	85	83	93
6	87	85	95
7	88	86	96
8	89	87	96
9	89	88	96
10	89	89	96

a. If you want to maximize the sum of your scores on the three exams, how many hours should you devote to each exam?

b. Suppose that the sum of your scores on the three exams can be used as a measure of the total utility you derive from the work you put in on them. If so, what is the marginal utility of the first hour spent studying economics? What is the marginal utility of the second hour spent studying English? What is the marginal utility of the third hour spent studying chemistry?

c. Can the budget allocation rule discussed in this chapter be adapted to determine how many hours you should devote to each exam? If so, how?

d. Suppose that your roommate faces the same problem and that he decides to allocate his time so that he will get at least a 75 on each exam. Is this a rational way to maximize the sum of the scores he gets on the three exams?

e. Because of unforeseen circumstances it turns out that you have only 5 hours, rather than 10, to study for all three exams. How many hours should you devote to each exam?

Matching Questions

_____ *1. Indifference curve   A. Connects points of equal desirability

_____ 2. Utility   B. Must be equal (for goods consumed) if consumer is maximizing utility

_____ *3. Budget line   C. Higher for preferred market baskets

_____ 4. Equilibrium market basket   D. Extra utility from an extra unit of commodity

_____ 5. Marginal utility divided by price   E. Slope equals –1 times price ratio

_____ 6. Marginal utility   F. One that maximizes utility

---

* Pertains to chapter appendix.

Completion Questions

1. If the price of good X falls, this will (decrease, increase) _____ the real income of the consumer. The effect of this change in real income on the quantity demanded of good X is likely to be (positive, negative, zero) _____ if good X is a luxury item.

2. Holding the consumer's real income constant, the quantity demanded of good X will (sometimes, usually, always) _____ increase in response to a decrease in the price of good X. The consumer's demand curve (does, does not) _____ hold the consumer's real income constant.

3. If the income effect of a price decrease is a(n) (decrease, increase) _____ in the quantity demanded, it is possible that a commodity's demand curve does not slope downward and to the right. Whether or not this is true depends on the size of the _____ effect as compared with the _____ effect.

4. All other things being equal, it is assumed that the consumer always prefers _____ of a commodity to _____ of a commodity.

5. Economists assume that the consumer attempts to _____ utility.

6. It is frequently assumed that, as a person consumes more and more of a particular commodity, there is a (decrease, increase) _____ in the commodity's marginal utility.

7. For the equilibrium market basket, the consumer's income is allocated among commodities so that, for every commodity purchased, the _____ utility of the commodity is proportional to its _____.

8. In allocating a budget, the amount spent on each of two items should be set so that the marginal utility of the _____ dollar spent on each item is _____.

9. The concept of _____ is used to measure the additional satisfaction derived from an additional unit of a commodity.

10. The consumer, when confronted with two alternative _____ , can decide which he prefers or whether he or she is _____ between them.

11. If one market basket has more of one commodity than a second market basket, it must have (less, more) _____ of the other commodity than the second market basket—assuming that the two market baskets are to yield equal _____ to the consumer.

12. Besides knowing the consumer's preferences, we must also know his or her
_____ and the _____ of commodities to predict
which market basket he or she will buy.

*13. Every indifference curve must slope (downward, upward) _____ and
to the right, to reflect the fact that commodities are defined so that (less, more)
_____ of them are preferred to (less, more) _____.

*14. Since market baskets on higher indifference curves are given (higher, lower)
_____ utilities, and since market baskets on higher indifference
curves are always (preferred, not preferred) _____ to market baskets
on lower indifference curves, the consumer will always choose a market basket with
a (higher, lower) _____ utility over a market basket with a (higher,
lower) _____ utility.

*15. The consumer's _____ show what he or she wants, and the
consumer's _____ shows which market baskets his or her income
and prices permit him or her to buy.

*16. An increase in money income means that the budget line (falls, rises)
_____ , and a decrease in money income means that the budget line
(falls, rises) _____.

*17. Commodity prices affect the budget line: a decrease in a commodity's price causes
the budget line to cut this commodity's axis at a point (closer to, farther from)
_____ the origin.

True-False

_____ 1. If the total utility from consuming hot dogs is proportional to the number
of hot dogs consumed, the law of diminishing marginal utility may or may
not be violated, depending on the number of utils received per hot dog.

_____ 2. If the total utility from consuming hot dogs is 3 times the number of hot
dogs consumed and the total utility from consuming hoagies is 4 times the
number of hoagies consumed, the consumer should buy hoagies, not hot
dogs.

_____ 3. If a consumer buys 3 pieces of pizza on August 1 when the price per piece
is 70 cents, and if she buys 4 pieces on September 3 when the price per
piece is 60 cents, a change in her demand for pizzas must have occurred
between August 1 and September 3.

---

* Pertains to chapter appendix.

_____ 4. If the consumer's tastes were transitive, the consumer would have inconsistent or contradictory preferences.

_____ 5. According to the theory of consumer behavior, the consumer's equilibrium market basket is the one which yields maximum utility, given the constraints imposed on the consumer by his or her income and by prices.

_____ 6. The law of diminishing marginal utility states that, beyond a point, extra satisfaction from consuming an extra unit of a commodity declines.

_____ 7. The best way to allocate the military budget is to spend it all on the highest priority item of each service.

_____ 8. Though misleading advertising and fraud are bad for the consumer, the price system works about as well under these circumstances as without them.

_____ 9. A utility is a number that represents the level of satisfaction the consumer derives from a particular market basket.

_____ 10. In the nineteenth and early twentieth centuries, economists believed that utility was cardinally measurable, in the same sense as a person's height or weight.

_____ 11. The marginal utility derived from a certain amount of food is the extra utility derived from this amount of food over and above the utility derived from one less pound of food.

_____ *12. Indifference curves cannot intersect.

_____ *13. Market baskets on higher indifference curves must have lower utilities than market baskets on lower indifference curves.

_____ *14. The consumer's budget line shows the market baskets that can be purchased, given the consumer's income and prevailing commodity prices.

_____ *15. The higher the consumer's money income, the lower the budget line.

_____ *16. A consumer buys two goods, U and V. If the price of a unit of U is equal to the price of a unit of V, the slope of the consumer's budget line is –1.

_____ *17. Two consumers buy two goods, U and V. The first consumer is located in a region where the price of U is higher than in the region where the second consumer is located. The price of V is the same in both regions. Nonetheless, if the first consumer's income is higher than the second consumer's, it is possible for the two consumers' budget lines to be parallel.

---

* Pertains to chapter appendix.

Multiple Choice

1. Suppose that Mary Murphy's total utility from various quantities of good X and good Y are as follows:

	Good X		Good Y
Quantity	Total Utility	Quantity	Total Utility
0	0	0	0
1	10	1	30
2	30	2	50
3	40	3	60
4	45	4	65
5	48	5	67
6	50	6	68

   For good X, diminishing marginal utility occurs:

   a. at some, but not all quantities consumed.
   b. at quantities exceeding 2.
   c. at larger quantities than those where increasing marginal utility occurs.
   d. all of the above.
   e. none of the above.

2. In the previous question, the price of good X equals the price of good Y, and Ms. Murphy's income allows her to buy 6 units of good X. Under these circumstances, her optimal market basket is:

   a. 4 units of good X and 2 units of good Y.
   b. 3 units of good X and 3 units of good Y.
   c. 2 units of good X and 4 units of good Y.
   d. 5 units of good X and 1 unit of good Y.
   e. none of the above.

3. In question 1, if good X's price is $5, the marginal utility of the last dollar spent on good X is 4 if Ms. Murphy consumes:

   a. 1 unit of good X and 1 unit of good Y.
   b. 2 units of good X and 2 units of good Y.
   c. 3 units of good X and 3 units of good Y.
   d. all of the above.
   e. none of the above.

4. In question 1, if good X's price is $5 and good Y's price is $10, and Ms. Murphy has $35 to spend on good X and good Y combined, she should purchase:

   a. a market basket where the marginal utility of the last dollar spent on good X equals 2.
   b. 2 units of good Y and 3 units of good X.
   c. a market basket where the marginal utility of the last dollar spent on good Y equals 2.
   d. all of the above.
   e. none of the above.

5. John Jones has 8 hours to spend during which he can either play tennis or read. The marginal utility he obtains from an hour of reading is 8 utils. The total utility he obtains from 1, 2, 3, 4, and 5 hours of tennis is as follows:

Hours	Total utility
1	20
2	33
3	40
4	40
5	35

If he maximizes utility (and if he can allocate only an integer number of hours to each activity), he will spend:

a. 3 hours playing tennis and 5 hours reading.
b. 2 hours playing tennis and 6 hours reading.
c. 4 hours playing tennis and 4 hours reading.
d. 1 hour playing tennis and 7 hours reading.
e. none of the above.

6. Modern economists regard utility as:

a. easily measurable.
b. constant over time.
c. independent of tastes.
d. all of the above.
e. none of the above.

7. The equilibrium market basket is the one where a product's marginal utility is:

a. lowest.
b. median.
c. highest.
d. proportional to price if it is consumed.
e. none of the above.

8. The model of consumer behavior assumes that a consumer's preferences:

a. may vary between two market baskets and at times he or she may not come to a decision.
b. are transitive.
c. are always for more of a commodity rather than less.
d. b and c above.
e. all of the above.

9. American consumers spend about what percent of their pretax income (net of interest payments) on goods and services?

a. 60
b. 70
c. 80
d. 90
e. 95

Discussion and Extension Questions

1. Do you think the law of diminishing marginal utility applies to income as well as to specific goods like pizzas and shirts?

2. Apply the principles in this chapter to the expressions: (a) "Anything worth doing is worth doing well," and (b) "The more the merrier."

3. Do you think it is in a firm's best interest purposefully to deceive consumers? Can you think of factors which affect the amount of deception a firm would consider?

4. "Since no one can measure a person's utility, the theory of consumer behavior cannot provide an adequate basis for decision-making. Furthermore, since a person cannot tell whether he or she will like something until he or she has bought and tried it, no one knows what utility to attach to a good until it is too late to be of any use in decision making." Discuss and evaluate.

5. "Although the total utility of a particular commodity may be great, its marginal utility may be small. This is equally true of air, water, diamonds, and sable coats." Discuss and evaluate.

6. If the marginal utility of one good is 3 and its price is $1, while the marginal utility of another good is 6 and its price is $3, is the consumer maximizing his or her satisfaction, given that he or she is consuming both goods? Why or why not?

7. If the marginal utility of one good is 3 and its price is $1, while the marginal utility of another good is 6 and its price is $2, is this in keeping with the maximization of the consumer's satisfaction? Why or why not?

8. In what respect can the model of consumer behavior be used to aid decision makers in allocating a government agency's budget?

Problems

1. Suppose that Bill Smith's utility can be regarded as measurable, and that the utility he gets from the consumption of various numbers of hot dogs per day is as shown below:

Hot dogs consumed per day	Total utility (utils)
0	0
1	5
2	11
3	16
4	20
5	23

   a. What is the marginal utility of the third hot dog per day to Bill Smith? What is the marginal utility of the fourth hot dog?

b. Plot Bill Smith's total utility curve for hot dogs in the graph below:

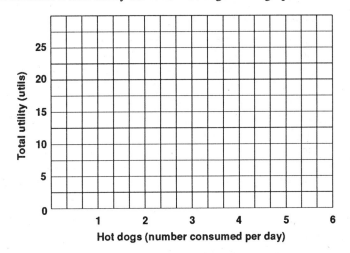

c. Suppose that Bill Smith divides his income entirely between hot dogs and Hershey bars—on the advice of his (incompetent) physician. He allocates his income between these two commodities in such a way as to maximize his satisfaction. His marginal utility from an extra Hershey bar is 2 utils, and the price of a Hershey bar is 80 cents. If the price of a hot dog is $1.60, how many hot dogs does he consume per day?

d. In part c how many hot dogs would be consumed per day if the price of a hot dog were $1.20?

e. In part c how many hot dogs would he consume per day if the price of a hot dog were $2.00?

2. The fact that each individual consumes many different goods supports the theory of diminishing marginal utility. Use an example to show that without diminishing marginal utility, we would allocate our incomes very differently than we do with this phenomenon.

3. "The markets for some goods must be truly strange! Why, just the other day I heard that some people actually buy more hamburger at $1.00 per pound than others do at $.75 per pound. Surely this violates the law of downward sloping demand curves." Explain why it does or does not.

4. You are given the following information about Sue, who buys only clothing and food with her income of $700.

Food price (dollars per unit)	Quantity (units)	
	Food	Clothing
40	5	_____
30	10	_____
10	20	_____

a. Fill in the last column of the table. (Clothing costs $50 per unit.)
b. Diagram three points on Sue's demand curve for food.

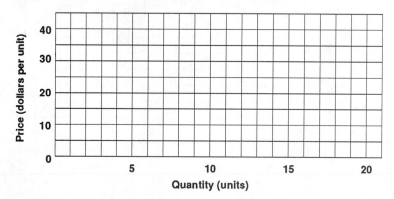

*5. Suppose Sandy gets the same utility from each of the 6 combinations of goods Z and W shown below. Good Z costs $10.00 per unit and good W costs $4.00 per unit.

	Commodity Combination					
	1	2	3	4	5	6
Amount of good W (units)	1	2	4	7	11	16
Amount of good Z (units)	10	9	8	7	6	5

a. What is the minimum income she must have to achieve the level of utility associated with these commodity combinations?
b. If she has the income you found in part a, draw her budget line.

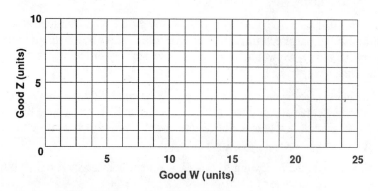

c. Draw her indifference curve.

*6. Draw the indifference curve that includes the following market baskets in the graph on the next page. Each of these market baskets gives the consumer equal satisfaction.

---

* Pertains to chapter appendix.

Market basket	Meat (pounds)	Potatoes (pounds)
A	1	9
B	2	8
C	3	7
D	4	6
E	5	5
F	6	4
G	7	3
H	8	2

Meat (pounds) / Potatoes (pounds)

*7. a. Suppose that the consumer has an income of $10 per period and that he or she must spend it all on meat or potatoes. If meat is $1 a pound and potatoes are 10 cents a pound, draw the consumer's budget line.

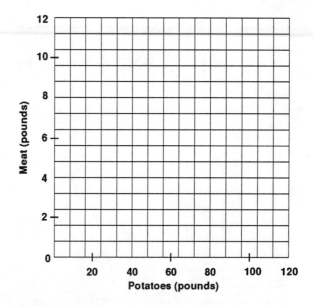

b. What will be the budget line if the consumer's income increases to $12? What will be the budget line if the consumer's income is $10, but the price of meat increases to $2 per pound? What will be the budget line if the consumer's income is $10, and the price of meat is $1 per pound, but the price of potatoes increases to 20 cents per pound?

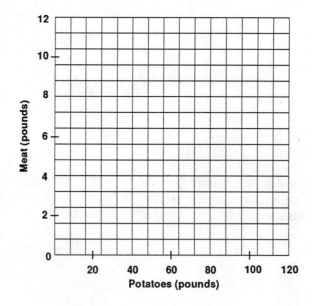

*8. a. Suppose that John Jones has a money income of $100 per week, and that he spends it all on nails and fertilizer. Suppose fertilizer is $2.50 per pound and nails are $1.00 per pound. Draw John Jones's budget line on the graph below:

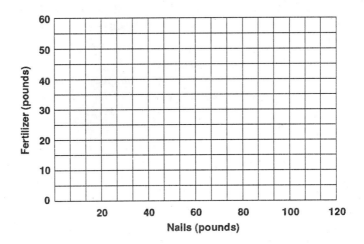

b. Suppose that John Jones has the following set of indifference curves:

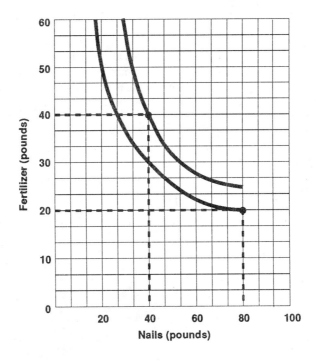

Does John Jones prefer 40 pounds of fertilizer and 40 pounds of nails to 20 pounds of fertilizer and 80 pounds of nails? Why or why not?

---

c. Suppose that John Jones's money income is $100 per week and that fertilizer is $1.67 per pound and nails are $1.25 per pound. Based on the information in part b, what (approximately) is his equilibrium market basket?

*9. Sally spends all her $100.00 income on two goods, X and Z, whose prices are $1.00 and $2.00 respectively. She is currently spending half her income on each good and is maximizing her utility.

a. How much of each good is she consuming?
b. Represent Sally's utility-maximizing consumption of each good, given her tastes, income, and the prices of each good in the graph below.

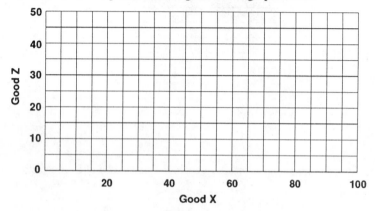

c. Draw her budget line in the graph above.
d. Using your diagram, show that if she is now offered a choice of 10 additional units of goods X for free or $10 extra income, she cannot be worse off, and may be better off, by taking the $10. Explain why this is true.

*10. The straight lines shown below are budget lines. The curved lines are indifference curves of Mr. William White. The budget lines assume that Mr. White's income is $100 per week.

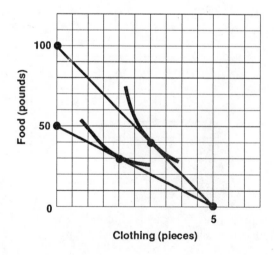

---

a. What is the price of a piece of clothing? Explain your reasoning.
b. Specify two points on Mr. White's demand curve for food.

Answers

Matching Questions

1. A   2. C   3. E   4. F   5. B   6. D

Completion Questions

1. increase, positive   2. always, does not   3. decrease, income, substitution
4. more, less   5. maximize   6. decrease   7. marginal, price   8. last, equal
9. marginal utility   10. market baskets, indifferent   11. less, satisfaction
12. income, prices   *13. downward, more, less   *14. higher, preferred, higher, lower
*15. indifference curves, budget line   *16. rises, falls   *17. farther from

True-False

1. False   2. False   3. False   4. False   5. True   6. True   7. False   8. False
9. True   10. True   11. True   *12. True   *13. False   *14. True   *15. False
*16. True   *17. False

Multiple Choice

1. d   2. b   3. b   4. d   5. b   6. e   7. d   8. d   9. c

Problems

1. a.   5 utils, 4 utils.
   b.

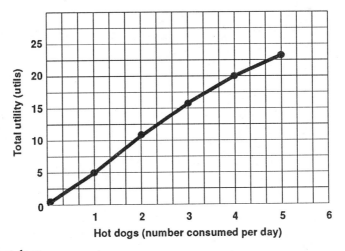

   c.   4 hot dogs.
   d.   5 hot dogs.
   e.   3 hot dogs.

---

* Pertains to chapter appendix.

2. If the consumer received increasing marginal utility from good X, he or she might spend all of his or her income on good X.

3. It does not, because not all people have the same demand curve for hamburger.

4. a.

Clothing (dollars per unit)

$$500 \div 50 = 10$$
$$400 \div 50 = 8$$
$$500 \div 50 = 10$$

b.

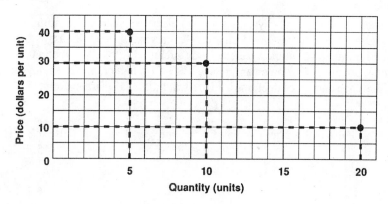

* 5. a. $96

b. and c.

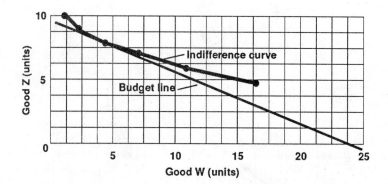

* 6.

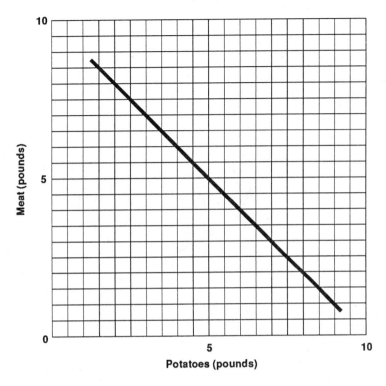

* 7. a. The consumer's budget line is drawn below.

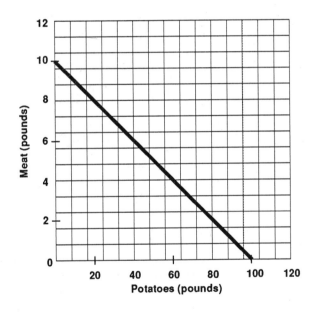

---

* Pertains to chapter appendix.

CHAPTER FIVE

b. Under the first set of circumstances the budget line is *A*. Under the second set of circumstances it is *B*. And under the third set of circumstances it is *C*.

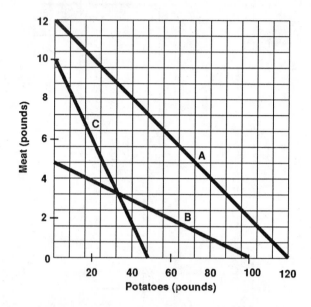

* 8. a.

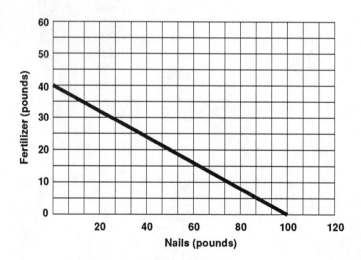

b. Yes. Because it is on the higher indifference curve.
c. It is difficult to tell from the diagram exactly what the equilibrium market basket will be but it will contain about 25 to 40 pounds of nails and about 30 to 40 pounds of fertilizer.

---

* Pertains to chapter appendix.

* 9. a. Quantity of $X = 50$, quantity of $Z = 25$.
  b. and c.

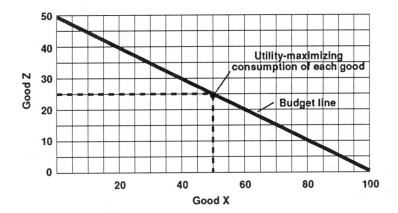

  d. If she takes $10 extra income, her budget line shifts to the right and goes through the point corresponding to her consuming the same amount of Z and 10 additional units of X. Thus, she can consume 10 extra units of X if she likes. However, she may be able to attain a higher indifference curve by spending some of the extra $10 on Z.
*10. a. The price must be $20 per piece since the budget line (which pertains to an income of $100) intersects the horizontal axis at 5 pieces.
  b. At $2 per pound he consumes 30 pounds of food. At $1 per pound he consumes 40 pounds of food.

CHAPTER 6

A Guided Tour of the Business Firm

Chapter Profile

There are three principal types of business firms: proprietorships, partnerships, and corporations. The corporation has many advantages over the other two—limited liability, unlimited life, and greater ability to raise large sums of money.

The corporation raises money by issuing various kinds of securities, of which three kinds—common stock, preferred stock, and bonds—are particularly important.

A relatively small number of giant corporations control a very substantial proportion of the total assets and employment in the American economy.

As a first approximation, economists generally assume that firms attempt to maximize profits.

In the model of the profit-maximizing firm, the economist must somehow include the state of technology. To do so he or she uses the concept of the production function, which shows the maximum output rate of a given commodity that can be achieved from any specified set of usage rates of inputs.

The balance sheet shows the nature of the firm's assets and liabilities at a given point in time. The difference between its assets and its liabilities is its net worth, which is the value of the firm's owners' claims against its assets.

A firm's income statement shows its sales during a particular period, its costs incurred in connection with these sales, and its profits during the period.

Economists define profits somewhat differently than accountants do. The economist excludes from profit the value of the capital and labor provided by the owners, and he is interested in longer periods than those to which accounting statements apply.

Behavioral Objectives

A. You should be able to define and explain the following key concepts in this chapter:

Proprietorship	Capital gain	Balance sheet
Partnership	Preferred stock	Current assets
Corporation	Bonds	Fixed assets
Board of directors	Profits	Net worth
Liability	Input	Income statement
Common stock	Production function	Depreciation
Dividends		

86

B. Make sure that you can do each of the following:

1. Explain the advantages and disadvantages of a proprietorship, partnership, and corporation.

2. Explain the differences between common stock, preferred stock, and bonds, and the advantages and disadvantages to the investor of each one.

3. Describe how the stock market works, and give various theories concerning the factors determining common stock prices.

4. Explain why, in many large corporations, there is a separation of ownership from control, and show why this separation is of social significance.

5. Indicate the reasons why firms may not maximize profits—and the reasons why economists nevertheless use models that assume that they do.

6. Indicate how the production function represents the state of technology.

7. Describe a firm's balance sheet and income statement, indicate what each item on such statements means, and explain the uses of the balance sheet and income statement.

8. Explain the difference between accounting and economic profits, and the circumstances when economic profits are a more appropriate concept than accounting profits.

Figuring Out Exxon's Financial Condition: A Case Study

Each year, the Exxon Corporation issues an annual report to its stockholders, which includes its balance sheet and income (profit and loss) statement. These are a bit more detailed than the hypothetical statements of the Milwaukee Machine Company, but they are constructed on the same principles. Exxon's balance sheet, as of December 31, 1990, was as follows:

Assets (millions of dollars)		Liabilities and net worth (millions of dollars)	
Cash	1,322	Accounts payable	15,611
Marketable securities	47	Long-term liabilities	17,447
Accounts receivable	9,574	Other liabilities	21,594
Inventories	6,386	Net worth	33,055
Plant and equipment	62,688		
Other assets	7,690		
Total	87,707		87,707

Exxon's income statement, for the year ended on December 31, 1990, was as follows (all figures in millions of dollars):

Net sales (and other income)	115,794
Manufacturing cost of goods sold (other than depreciation)	62,741
Depreciation	5,545
Selling and administrative expenses	38,902
Net earnings (before taxes)	8,606
Income taxes	3,170
Other items	426
Net earnings after taxes	5,010

a. How much of Exxon's assets (as of December 31, 1990) was obtained through borrowing? How much were contributed by the stockholders?

b. About how much of Exxon's assets were current assets? About how much were fixed assets? Why would a financial analyst be interested in how much of a company's assets are current assets?

c. According to the above figures, Exxon incurred depreciation costs of $5,545 million in 1990. Did Exxon have to pay out this amount in cash? Why or why not?

d. Can you determine how much Exxon earned per share of common stock? Financial analysts pay close attention to how much a firm earns per share of common stock. Why is this of relevance in determining how much a share of the firm's common stock is worth?

Matching Questions

_____	1. Proprietorship	A.	IOU
_____	2. Corporation	B.	Relation between input and output
_____	3. Bond	C.	Fictitious person
_____	4. Partnership	D.	Relation between income and outgo
_____	5. Production function	E.	Many law firms
_____	6. Income statement	F.	One owner

Completion Questions

1. The production function is the relationship between the amount of

   _____ and the amount of _____ during a

   given period of time.

2. The corporation permits people to assemble the large quantities of

   _____ required for efficient production in many industries. Without limited _____ and other such advantages of the corporation, it is doubtful that the opportunities and benefits of _____ production could have been reaped.

3. A disadvantage of the corporation is _____ taxation of income, since corporations pay income taxes and so do the _____.

4. Common stock is the ordinary certificate of _____ of the corporation. A holder of common stock is an _____ of the firm. He shares in the firm's _____—and in its losses as well.

5. Bonds are _____ of the firm. In contrast to stockholders, the bondholders are its (owners, creditors) _____ , and receive (interest, dividends) _____ , not (interest, dividends) _____.

6. Because of the wide diffusion of _____ , working control of a large corporation can often be maintained by a group with _____ or even less of all the voting stock. The result is a separation of _____ from _____. In other words, the owners _____ the firm in only a limited sense.

7. Economists generally assume that firms attempt to maximize _____ which are defined as the difference between the firm's _____ and its _____.

8. Because of risk and uncertainty, it is difficult to know exactly what profit maximization means, since the firm cannot be sure that a certain level of _____ will result from a certain _____. The best the firm can do is to estimate that a certain _____ of profit levels will result from a certain action. Under these circumstances, the firm may choose less _____ actions, even though they have a lower expectation of large profit than other actions.

9. If a taxi company buys a new taxi for $20,000 and estimates that it will be worn out in 5 years (when it will have no scrap value), the amount of depreciation charged each year will be _____ if straight-line depreciation is used.

10. In the previous question, accountant John Lloyd mistakenly underestimates the scrap value of the taxi when it is worn out in 5 years. This mistake will result in an (underestimate, overestimate) _____ of the taxi company's profits next year.

True-False

_____ 1. The stock market contributes to the prosperity of the United States by channeling savers' funds into capital formation.

_____ 2. Both the income statement and the balance sheet generally pertain to a period of one year, although firms sometimes issue them for quarterly periods.

_____ 3. No dividends can be paid on the common stock unless the dividends on the preferred stock are paid in full.

_____ 4. In the largest corporations often a minority of the shareholders have working control.

_____ 5. A firm must pay the interest on the bonds and the principal when it is due, or it can be declared bankrupt.

_____ 6. The tendency for the price level in the United States to increase over time has meant that owners of common stocks have reaped substantial capital gains, while bondholders have been paid off with dollars that were worth less than those they lent.

_____ 7. Just as the consumer is limited by his or her income, the firm is limited by the current state of technology.

_____ 8. Some of the inputs of a farm producing corn might be seed, land, labor, water, fertilizer, various types of machinery, as well as the time of the people managing the farm.

_____ 9. The production function summarizes the characteristics of existing technology at a given point in time. It shows the technological constraints the firm must reckon with.

_____ 10. The sum of the items on the left-hand side of the balance sheet must equal the sum of the items on the right-hand side because of the way we define net worth.

_____ 11. A firm's income statement shows its assets during a particular period, its costs incurred in connection with these assets, and its profits during this period.

_____ 12. The cost of manufacturing the items made during a period always equals the cost of manufacturing the items sold during the period.

_____ 13. If a firm's economic profits promise to be at least zero, the firm should continue in existence; otherwise, it should not.

_____ 14. A firm is the same as a plant.

_____ 15. George Johnson and Eli Scott each put up $25,000 to start a restaurant. Since they establish a partnership, the most that each of them can lose if the restaurant fails is $25,000.

_____ 16. Only in capitalist societies do specialization, division of labor, capital, and money exist.

_____ 17. In socialist economies like China, ownership of the means of production is divided equally among the nation's citizens, each citizen being given the same amount of stocks and bonds as the next citizen.

_____ 18. Within a firm the price system generally is used as the sole means of communication and source of information and incentives. Just as in the economy as a whole, the price system results in order not chaos, and there is little or no need for direct central control.

_____ 19. There is no way that a firm can influence its production function, since the production function is a reflection of the state of the engineering art.

_____ 20. The production function of an electronics firm in Japan is the same as the production function of an electronics firm in Mexico, since all firms must become acquainted with the latest technology in order to remain competitive.

Multiple Choice

1. Which of the following is *not* found in a balance sheet?

   a. cash
   b. inventories
   c. accounts receivable
   d. accounts payable
   e. none of the above

2. Which of the following is true of a bond?

   a. It offers maximum probability of a capital gain.
   b. It is issued by every corporation.
   c. Its price never varies.
   d. Its due date is generally 3 years or less from its date of issue.
   e. None of the above.

3. Which of the following is true of the corporation income tax?

   a. It is imposed only on a firm's retained earnings.
   b. It is imposed only on a firm's dividends.
   c. It is imposed on the difference between a firm's sales and its manufacturing cost of goods sold.
   d. It is imposed only on preferred stock dividends.
   e. None of the above.

4. The owner(s) have unlimited liability for debts of the business in a:

   a. proprietorship.
   b. partnership.
   c. corporation.
   d. a and b above.
   e. all of the above.

5. The type of certificate that pays a specified dividend is:

   a. common stock.
   b. preferred stock.
   c. bond.
   d. IOU.
   e. all of the above.

6. Anything the firm uses in its production process is called:

   a. technology.
   b. production function.
   c. input.
   d. all of the above.
   e. none of the above.

7. If a firm is deciding whether to stay in business, the most relevant concept of profits should be those of the:

   a. economist.
   b. accountant.
   c. consumers' union.
   d. chamber of commerce.

8. One of the main advantages of the corporation over the partnership or proprietorship is:

   a. the large number of owners who share liability though it is still unlimited.
   b. double taxation of income.
   c. that it permits assembling large quantities of capital required for efficiency in many industries.
   d. all of the above.
   e. none of the above.

9. In the last 25 years, common stocks:

   a. have performed less well, on the average, than bonds or preferred stocks.
   b. have performed better, on the average, than bonds or preferred stocks.
   c. have become much easier to predict.
   d. have no longer been affected by psychological considerations.
   e. all of the above.

Discussion and Extension Questions

1. Many large corporations make substantial contributions to charity, sponsor programs on public television stations, and fund educational and outside research projects. Are such actions inconsistent with a profit-maximization hypothesis?

2. One prominent economist has said that the only social responsibility of business is to make profits for its stockholders. Comment on that assertion.

3. "If I can unload a share of stock in the Bugsbane Music Box Corporation for $10 in a year or so, I'm more than willing to pay $8 for it now. What do I care what its earnings per share will be in the long run?" Comment and evaluate.

4. Suppose that you are thinking of lending some money to a firm. Why would you be interested in its balance sheet and its income statement?

5. The balance sheet of the Ford Motor Company, as of December 31, 1990, was as follows:

Assets *(billions of dollars)*		*Liabilities and net worth* *(billions of dollars)*	
Cash and marketable		Accounts payable	7.2
securities	4.5	Other current liabilities	13.7
Accounts and notes		Long-term debt	4.6
receivable	3.9	Other long-term	
Inventories	7.1	liabilities	124.2
Other current assets	3.9	Shareholders' equity	24.0
Fixed assets	154.2		
Total	173.7	*Total*	173.7

(Note: Figures may not add to totals because of rounding errors.)

If you had been thinking of investing in Ford, of what use would this be?

6. The income statement of the Ford Motor Company for 1990 was as follows (all figures in billions of dollars):

Sales (and other income)	97.7
Cost of goods sold	86.5
Selling, administrative, and general expenses	8.6
Other expenses and taxes	0.8
Depreciation	0.9
Net income	0.9

If you had been thinking of investing in Ford, of what use would this be?

7. "Managers of large corporations have little or no incentive to fight for the principles of capitalism since they do not own more than a very small amount of stock in the companies they manage. If these companies were to be taken over by the government, the managers would keep the same jobs and would not be affected much." Do you agree? Why or why not?

Problems

1. The Harrington department store is owned by Sophie Harrington, whose profits after taxes were $50,000 in 1992.

   a. If the firm's total assets were $2 million and its liabilities were $1 million, how much profit did Ms. Harrington receive in 1992 for every dollar she had invested in the business?

b. If Ms. Harrington could obtain 6 percent interest from alternative uses of her money, how much did she make or lose in 1992, based on the economist's concepts of profit or loss?

c. If the Harrington department store's cost of goods sold in 1992 was $150,000, its other costs were $80,000, and its taxes were $60,000, how much were its sales?

2. The Uphill Corporation is a small firm manufacturing bicycle pedals. Suppose that its production function is as follows:

Number of workers hired per month	Number of bicycle pedals produced per month
0	0
1	200
2	400
3	600
4	700
5	800

a. How many additional pedals can be manufactured when the company increases its work force from 3 to 4 members? Does the addition of each extra worker result in the same addition to output?

b. Suppose that all workers at the Uphill Corporation are paid $500 a month. At what level of employment is the labor cost per unit of output highest?

c. Plot the production function of the Uphill Corporation in the graph below.

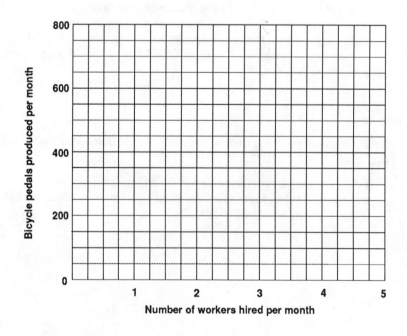

3. The balance sheet of the Uphill Corporation, as published in its 1991 annual report, is shown below:

Assets (hundreds of thousands of dollars)		Liabilities and net worth (hundreds of thousands of dollars)	
Cash	1	Accounts payable	2
Inventory	4	Bonds	4
Equipment	8	Common stock	8

After the annual report was published, it was discovered that the inventory figure was printed incorrectly, but that all the other numbers were right. What is the correct figure for inventory?

4. a. Suppose that the Uphill Corporation purchases a machine tool for $100, 000 and that it expects the tool to last 15 years, at which time its scrap value will be 10 percent of its original price. How much will the company charge each year for the depreciation of this asset, if it uses straight-line depreciation?

   b. An error is made in the Uphill Corporation's income statement. In computing its profits, the firm uses a figure of $7,000 for the depreciation of the asset discussed in part a, rather than the correct figure. Will this error result in an underestimate or overestimate of the firm's profits? How big is the error in profits?

5. Construct a balance sheet from the following items:

	(dollars)
Cash	100
Notes payable	200
Accounts payable	200
Long-term debt	200
Other liabilities	200
Net worth	1,000
Other assets	200
Securities	100
Inventories	400
Plant and equipment	1,000

6. According to a line on the stock market page of the June 25, 1991, *New York Times,*

   $61^3/_8$ $46^3/_4$ Exxon 2.68 8179 $58^3/_4$ 58 $58^1/_8$ $-^3/_8$

   a. What was the highest price that Exxon's common stock achieved in the previous 12 months?
   b. What was the lowest price that it achieved in the previous 12 months?
   c. What was the closing price on June 24, 1991?
   d. What was the change in price on June 24, 1991, over the day before?

7. Suppose that you have decided to buy a General Motors bond yielding 10 percent. (That is, you will receive 10 cents per year for every dollar you invest.) After deciding this, you watch a television newscast saying that the price level in the United States is increasing at a rate of 12 percent per year. Would you reconsider your decision? Why or why not?

8. According to Lee J. Seidler, professor of accounting at New York University, the SCM Corporation's accounting statements for a particular year exaggerated the firm's operating earnings. In particular, he said that, "The sharp decline in depreciation appears to have had the . . . effect of making the business equipment group show profits for the first time in five years." How can this occur? Explain in detail.

9. The Grotesk Company's president receives the following information from the firm's accountants regarding its 1991 operations (all figures in millions of dollars):

Sales	120	Selling and administrative costs	20
Materials costs	10	Fixed interest charges	10
Labor costs	15	State and local taxes	8
Depreciation	9	Beginning inventory	40
Other operating costs	8	Closing inventory	35
Cash (as of 1/1/91)	7	Equipment (as of 1/1/91)	10

  a. How much were the firm's accounting profits in 1991?
  b. What was the firm's ratio of profits to sales in 1991? Of what use might this ratio be to management?
  c. Can you tell from these figures whether it is socially optimal for the resources used by the Grotesk Company to be used in this rather than some alternative way? If so, how? If not, why not?

10. Over a decade ago, *Fortune* magazine printed an interview with W. Michael Blumenthal, then President Carter's Secretary of the Treasury. Before going to Washington, Blumenthal had been chairman and chief executive officer of the Bendix Corporation. In the interview, Blumenthal pointed out many differences between problems faced by a cabinet member and problems faced by the head of a major corporation.

  a. According to Blumenthal, "the head of a government department or agency is not like the chief executive of a large corporation who has control over the personnel system, who can change it, . . . who can hire and fire." Should each cabinet member have these powers? Why or why not? Is a cabinet member really analogous to the head of a firm?
  b. Blumenthal said that, "If you wish to make substantive changes . . . and the departmental employees don't like what you're doing, they have ways of frustrating you . . . that do not exist in private industry." In particular, they go to Congress and to the press. Do employees in private industry have ways of frustrating their bosses? What are they? Do government employees have a responsibility to make their views known to Congress? Why or why not?
  c. According to Blumenthal, ". . . the tests of efficiency and cost-effectiveness, which are the basic standards of business, are in government not the only—and frequently not even major—criteria." Should efficiency be the sole test of performance of government agencies? Why or why not?
  d. According to Blumenthal, "In business, the directors and the shareholders essentially have a common interest. . . . The Congress's interests are much more diverse." Is this because the problems faced by a business are simpler than those faced by the government? Is this because citizens differ a great deal in their beliefs concerning what should be the objectives of the government, whereas the directors and shareholders of a firm generally agree that the firm should maximize its profits? Explain.

Answers

Matching Questions
1. F   2. C   3. A   4. E   5. B   6. D

Completion Questions
1. inputs used, output produced   2. capital, liability, large-scale   3. double, stockholders   4. ownership, owner, profits   5. debts, creditors, interest, dividends
6. ownership, $\frac{1}{5}$, ownership, control, control   7. profits, revenue, costs
8. profit, action, probability distribution, risky   9. $4,000   10. underestimate

True-False
1. True   2. False   3. True   4. True   5. True   6. True   7. True   8. True
9. True   10. True   11. False   12. False   13. True   14. False   15. False
16. False   17. False   18. False   19. False   20. False

Multiple Choice
1. e   2. e   3. e   4. d   5. b   6. c   7. a   8. c   9. b

Problems
1. a. 5 cents.
    b. She lost $10,000, since she could have earned $60,000 on her $1 million investment.
    c. $340,000.
2. a. 100 units of output per month. No.
    b. 5 workers per month.
    c.

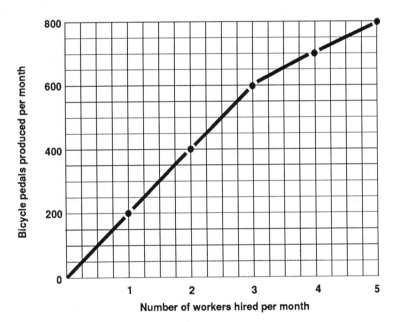

3. $500,000, since the total assets must equal $1,400,000, which is the sum of the liabilities and net worth.
4. a. $6,000.
   b. Underestimate. $1,000.
5.

Assets		Liabilities and net worth	
Cash	100	Accounts payable	200
Inventories	400	Notes payable	200
Securities	100	Long-term debt	200
Plant and equipment	1,000	Other liabilities	200
Other Assets	200	Net worth	1,000
Total	1,800	Total	1,800

6. a. $61.375 per share.
   b. $46.75 per share.
   c. $58.125 per share.
   d. The price fell by $.375 per share.
7. If the price level is increasing at 12 percent per year, the interest you receive each year is less than the amount that you lose in real terms, if you sell or cash in the bond at what you paid for it. Under these circumstances, you would be well advised to see if better investments could be found.
8. If depreciation declines, this tends to increase profit because depreciation is deducted to obtain profit.
9. a. $35 million.
   b. About 29 percent. This ratio might be compared with other firms in the same industry, or it might be compared with previous years for this firm, in order to see how the firm's profitability stacks up against that of other firms and against its own past performance.
   c. No, because these figures do not tell us what are the opportunity costs of using these resources in this way.
10. a. Since a department (Treasury, Commerce, Defense, etc.) is only part of the executive branch of the federal government, not a separate entity like a private corporation, a cabinet member's power to hire and fire must be limited by the president's wishes. Also, Congress and the courts have relevant responsibilities.
    b. Yes. Employees in private industry join unions and do other things to limit their bosses' power. Government employees have a responsibility to make known improper actions or policies.
    c. Efficiency should be one test, but it is also important that government agencies have the proper goals.
    d. Yes, at least in some respects. Yes.

CHAPTER 7

Optimal Input Decisions by Business Firms

Chapter Profile

The production function shows the maximum output rate that can be derived from each combination of input rates. A fixed input is one whose quantity cannot change during the period of time under consideration. A variable input is one whose quantity can be changed during the relevant period. The short run is defined as a period of time in which at least one of the firm's inputs is fixed. The long run is the period of time in which all inputs are variable.

The law of diminishing marginal returns states that, if equal increments of an input are added, the quantities of other inputs held constant, the resulting increments of product will decrease beyond some point; that is, the marginal product of the input will diminish.

The marginal product of an input is the addition to total output due to the addition of the last unit of the input, the amount of other inputs used being held constant. An input's average product is the firm's total output divided by the amount of the input used to produce this amount of output.

To minimize its cost (and maximize its profits) a firm must choose its input combination so that the marginal product of a dollar's worth of any one input equals the marginal product of a dollar's worth of any other input used. Or, stated differently, the firm should combine inputs so that, for every input used, the marginal product of the input is proportional to its price.

Behavioral Objectives

A. You should be able to define and explain the following key concepts in this chapter:

Production function	Short run	Law of diminishing
Fixed input	Long run	marginal returns
Variable input	Average product	Marginal product

B. Make sure that you can do each of the following:

1. Define a firm's production function and indicate how it can be estimated from engineering, experimental, and historical data.

2. Distinguish between fixed and variable inputs, and give examples of each.

3. Distinguish between the short run and the long run, and give examples of each.

4. Calculate the marginal product and average product of an input, given the production function.

5. Explain why a firm will minimize cost by combining inputs in such a way that the marginal product of a dollar's worth of any one input equals the marginal product of a dollar's worth of any other input used.

Getting Down to Cases: The Production of Health Services

For many years it was argued that the United States had a shortage of physicians. For this reason the federal government enacted the Health Professions Educational Assistance Act to subsidize the training of more physicians. According to some observers such as Princeton's Uwe Reinhart, one way to expand the effective supply of health services is to use more aides (registered nurses, medical technicians, and clerical staff) per physician. These observers argue that it would be economical to substitute the time of aides for that of physicians in handling many relatively routine cases. Suppose that the following table shows the number of patients' visits that can be taken care of each week, if various amounts of a physician's time are combined with various amounts of aides' time:

Hours (per week) of a physician's time	Hours of aides' time (per week)		
	40	60	80
	(Number of visits per week)		
30	200	300	360
40	400	550	600
50	550	700	750

a. Is this table a production function? If so, what is output? What are the inputs?

b. What is the average product of an hour of aides' time if 30 hours of a physician's time are combined with 40 hours of aides' time per week?

c. What is the marginal product of an hour of aides' time if a physician works 40 hours per week and an aide works between 40 and 60 hours per week?

d. Do diminishing marginal returns exist in this case?

e. If the hourly wage of a physician is 5 times that of an aide, does it make sense for a physician to work 50 hours per week and hire an aide to work 40 hours per week? Why or why not?

Matching Questions

_____ 1. Average product
_____ 2. Long run
_____ 3. Marginal product
_____ 4. Short run

_____ 5. Fixed input
_____ 6. Variable input

A. Planning horizon

B. Output ÷ quantity of input

C. 1 year for General Motors

D. Increase in output due to extra unit of input

E. None in long run

F. Water at a car wash

Completion Questions

1. The _____ of an input is the addition to total output due to the addition of the last unit of input.

2. A firm will minimize cost by combining inputs so that, for every input used, the _____ of the input is proportional to the input's _____.

3. Marginal product must exceed average product when the latter is (decreasing, increasing) _____ , it must equal average product when the latter reaches a (maximum, minimum) _____ , and it must be less than average product when the latter is (decreasing, increasing) _____.

4. An inefficient combination of inputs is one that includes (less, more) _____ of at least one input, and as much of other inputs, as some other combination of inputs that can produce the same _____. Inefficient combinations generally (can, cannot) _____ minimize costs or maximize profits.

5. The firm will minimize cost by combining inputs in such a way that the (average product, marginal product) _____ of a dollar's worth of any one input equals the (average product, marginal product) _____ of a dollar's worth of any other input used.

6. If the marginal product of the first unit of labor equals 2 units of output, and if the marginal product of the second unit of labor equals 3 units of output, the total output produced with 2 units of labor equals _____ units of output.

This answer will remain valid only if the quantities of other _____ are held constant and if there is no change in _____.

7. If the marginal product of the eighth unit of labor equals the marginal product of the ninth unit of labor, and if total output with 7 units of labor is 80 and total output with 9 units of labor is 90, the marginal product of the eighth unit of labor equals

   _____.

8. The average product of labor equals $3L$, where L is the number of units of labor employed per day. The total output produced per day if 4 units of labor are employed per day is _____. The total output produced per day if 5 units of labor are employed per day is _____. The marginal product of the fifth unit of labor employed per day is _____.

True-False

_____ 1. If the average product of labor equals $6/L$, where L is the number of units of labor employed per day, total output is the same regardless of how much labor is used per day.

_____ 2. If the average product of labor equals 4 when the number of units of labor employed per day is between 1 and 6, the marginal product of labor also equals 4 when the amount of labor used is within this range.

_____ 3. If the average product of labor equals $5L$, where L is the number of units of labor employed per day, the law of diminishing marginal returns is violated.

_____ 4. In production processes, both the average product of the variable input and the marginal product usually rise, fall, and then rise again to infinity.

_____ 5. The law of diminishing marginal returns indicates that, if equal increments of an input are added (and quantities of others are held constant), the marginal product of the input will diminish beyond some point.

_____ 6. The long run refers to a period when all inputs are variable and none is fixed.

_____ 7. The average product of an input is the addition to total output due to the addition of the last unit of input, the quantity of other inputs used being held constant.

_____ 8. The marginal product curve intersects the average product curve when the latter is a maximum.

_____ 9. If technology changes, the law of diminishing marginal returns can predict the effect of an additional unit of input.

_____ 10. The law of diminishing marginal returns is not applicable to cases where there is a proportional increase in all inputs.

_____ 11. If the price of a unit of capital is equal to the price of a unit of labor, a cost-minimizing firm will choose a combination of inputs where the marginal product of capital minus the marginal product of labor equals zero.

_____ 12. If a nonzero amount of output results when no labor is used, this violates the law of diminishing marginal returns.

_____ 13. If the price of a unit of capital is double the price of a unit of labor, a cost-minimizing firm will choose a combination of inputs where the marginal product of capital minus the marginal product of labor equals the marginal product of labor.

_____ 14. If labor can be obtained free, a cost-minimizing firm will choose a combination of inputs where the marginal product of capital minus the marginal product of labor equals the marginal product of capital.

Multiple Choice

1. If the marginal product of capital is negative:
   a. more capital results in less output.
   b. more capital does not affect output.
   c. more capital increases output but at a decreasing rate.
   d. more capital increases output at an increasing rate.
   e. none of the above.

2. If labor is the only input, a cost-minimizing firm, if it can hire all the labor it wants at $8 per hour, and if it must produce 10 units of output per day, will:
   a. maximize the amount of output from the labor it hires.
   b. minimize the amount of labor used to produce the 10 units per day.
   c. operate at a point on the production function.
   d. all of the above.
   e. none of the above.

3. Between 1 and 2 person-years of labor, what is the marginal product of labor, if the average product of labor is 20 bushels for 1 person-year and 25 bushels for 2 person-years?
   a. 20 bushels   d. 40 bushels
   b. 25 bushels   e. 50 bushels
   c. 30 bushels

4. Which of the following statements about the law of diminishing marginal returns is *not* true?
   a. It is an empirical generalization.
   b. It assumes that technology remains fixed.
   c. No inputs are fixed in quantity.
   d. It must be possible to vary the proportions in which various inputs are used.
   e. It holds in both agriculture and industry.

5. Based on its production function alone, a firm can determine:

   a. what input combination to use.   d. all of the above.
   b. what amount of output to produce.   e. none of the above.
   c. what price to charge.

6. Firm A is run by a big-time spender who wants to maximize the amount that he produces, regardless of the amount that it costs. Firm A should:

   a. increase its employment of labor indefinitely.
   b. increase its employment of capital indefinitely.
   c. increase its employment of labor until the marginal product of labor is zero.
   d. increase its employment of capital until the marginal product of capital is zero.
   e. both (a) and (b).
   f. both (c) and (d).

7. If the average product of labor equals $4 \div \sqrt{L}$, where L is the amount of labor employed per day:

   a. labor always is subject to diminishing marginal returns.
   b. labor is subject to diminishing marginal returns only when L is greater than 4.
   c. labor is not subject to diminishing marginal returns.
   d. labor is not subject to diminishing marginal returns when L is greater than 4.
   e. none of the above.

Discussion and Extension Questions

1. Distinguish between diminishing marginal returns and decreasing returns to scale.

2. "Any fool knows that a firm should not operate at a point where there are rising marginal returns." Comment and evaluate.

3. Suppose that capital and labor are a firm's only inputs. If the price of capital is held constant, how can we determine how many units of labor the firm will hire at various prices of labor, if the output of the firm is held constant? Show that the amount of labor that the firm will hire is inversely related to the price of labor.

4. Is the production function for an auto firm the same in the long run as in the short run? Why or why not?

5. Is General Motors' production function the same as Ford's? Is General Motors' production function the same as the production function of an automobile manufacturer in Argentina? Explain.

6. Do firms have detailed and reliable information concerning the quantity of output that they will receive from each and every combination of inputs? Or do they have such information only concerning those input combinations that are close to those that they have used or experimented with? Explain.

7. Do firms take their production functions as given, or do they engage in various kinds of activities to alter their production functions? If the latter is the case, what are some names commonly used to designate activities of this sort? Give some examples of cases where firms altered their production functions.

8. Is it commonly true that activities carried out by one firm alter another firm's production function? If so, is this commonly true even though the firms are in different industries? Explain, and give examples to buttress your answer.

Problems

1. Suppose that the production function for a 1-acre wheat farm is as follows:

Number of person-years of labor	Bushels of wheat produced per year
1	50
2	90
3	120
4	145
5	165

   a. What is the average product of labor when 1 person-year of labor is used?
   b. What is the marginal product of labor when between 2 and 3 person-years of labor are used?
   c. Does the law of diminishing marginal returns seem to hold? Why or why not?

2. Suppose that the production function for a car wash is as follows:

Hours of labor per day	Cars washed per day	Average product of labor		Marginal product of labor
0	0	_____		
1	2	_____		_____
2	5	_____		_____
3	7	_____		_____
4	8	_____		_____

   a. Fill in the blanks in the table above.
   b. Why don't we compute the average product of labor when there are zero hours of labor?

3. Suppose that the marginal product of labor is as shown below:

Quantity of labor per day		Marginal product of labor	Total output per day
0			0
1		3	–
2		5	–
3		8	–
4		–	23
5		2	–

    a. Fill in the blanks.
    b. Does this case conform to the law of diminishing marginal returns? Why or why not?

4. Suppose that the average product of capital is as shown below:

Quantity of capital used per day	Average product of capital	Marginal product of capital
1	3	_____
2	8	_____
3	8	_____
4	6	_____
5	4	

    a. Fill in the blanks.
    b. What is the maximum amount of capital that this firm will use per day? Why?

5. The average product of labor equals 6, regardless of how much labor is used.

    a. What is the marginal product of the first unit of labor?
    b. What is the marginal product of the fiftieth unit of labor?
    c. By how much will output increase if labor is increased by 200 units?
    d. By how much will output fall if labor is reduced by 100 units?
    e. Does this case conform to the law of diminishing marginal returns? Why or why not?
    f. Does this case seem realistic? Why or why not?

6. A firm uses two inputs, labor and capital. The price of capital is $5 per unit; the price of labor is $7 per unit; and the marginal product of capital is 15.

    a. Is the firm minimizing cost if the marginal product of labor is 20? Why or why not?
    b. If the firm is not minimizing cost, should it use more or less labor relative to capital? Why?
    c. If the marginal product of labor is 23, is the firm minimizing cost? Why or why not?
    d. If the firm is not minimizing cost, should it use more or less labor relative to capital? Why?
    e. If the marginal product of labor is 21, is the firm minimizing cost? Why or why not?

7. A firm has two plants, A and B. Both produce the same product. The price of capital is the same at both plants, and the price of labor is the same at both plants. The marginal product of labor is 6 at plant A and 15 at plant B.

    a. Can you tell whether each plant is minimizing cost? Why or why not?
    b. If the marginal product of capital is 20 at plant A and 40 at plant B, is each plant minimizing cost? Why or why not?

c. If the marginal product of capital is 40 at plant A, what must the marginal product of capital be at plant B, if each plant is minimizing cost?

d. If the marginal product of capital is 40 at plant A, and each plant is minimizing cost, can you tell what the price of capital and the price of labor are?

e. If the marginal product of capital is 40 at plant A, what is the ratio of the price of labor to the price of capital?

Answers

Matching Questions

1. B   2. A   3. D   4. C   5. E   6. F

Completion Questions

1. marginal product   2. marginal product, price   3. increasing, maximum, decreasing
4. more, output, cannot   5. marginal product, marginal product   6. 5, inputs, technology   7. 5   8. 48, 75, 27

True-False

1. True   2. True   3. True   4. False   5. True   6. True   7. False   8. True
9. False   10. True   11. True   12. False   13. True   14. True

Multiple Choice

1. a   2. d   3. c   4. c   5. e   6. f   7. a

Problems

1. a. 50 bushels of wheat per person-year of labor.
   b. 30 bushels of wheat.
   c. Yes, because as more labor is used, the marginal product of labor declines.

2. a.

Average product of labor	Marginal product of labor
—	
	2
2	
	3
$2\frac{1}{2}$	
	2
$2\frac{1}{3}$	
	1
2	

   b. Because it would mean dividing zero by zero, since both output and labor are zero.

3. a.

Marginal product of labor	Total product per day
	0
3	
	3
5	
	8
8	
	16
7	
	23
2	
	25

b. Yes, because marginal product eventually falls as more labor is applied.

4. a.

Marginal product
of capital

13
8
0
−4

b. 3 units, because capital's marginal product is not positive when more capital is used.

5. a. 6.
   b. 6.
   c. 1,200.
   d. 600.
   e. No, because the marginal product of labor is the same regardless of how much labor is used.
   f. No, because it violates the law of diminishing marginal returns.

6. a. No, because the ratio of the marginal product of capital to its price does not equal the ratio of the marginal product of labor to its price.
   b. It should use less labor because the ratio of labor's marginal product to its price is lower than the ratio of capital's marginal product to its price.
   c. No, for the same reason as in part a.
   d. It should use more labor because the ratio of labor's marginal product to its price is higher than the ratio of capital's marginal product to its price.
   e. Yes, because the ratio of labor's marginal product to its price equals the ratio of capital's marginal product to its price.

7. a. You cannot tell because not enough information is given.
   b. No, because, since the prices of capital and labor are the same at both plants, the ratio of the marginal product of labor to the marginal product of capital must be the same at both plants, if each plant is minimizing cost.
   c. 100.
   d. No.
   e. 3/20.

Cost Analysis

Chapter Profile

The cost of a certain course of action is the value of the best alternative course of action that could have been pursued instead. This is the doctrine of opportunity, or alternative, cost.

Cost functions play an important practical role in economics and management. Three kinds of total cost functions are important in the short run—total fixed cost, total variable cost, and total cost. Corresponding to each of the total cost functions are three kinds of average cost functions—average fixed cost, average variable cost, and average total cost.

Marginal cost is the addition to total cost due to the addition of the last unit of output. Because of the law of diminishing marginal returns, marginal cost tends to increase beyond some output level.

The firm's long-run average cost curve shows the minimum average cost of producing each output level when any desired type or scale of plant can be built. The shape of the long-run average cost curve is determined partly by whether there are increasing, decreasing, or constant returns to scale.

Behavioral Objectives

A. You should be able to define and explain the following key concepts in this chapter:

Opportunity cost	Average variable cost	Long-run average cost
Alternative cost	Average total cost	function
Implicit cost	Marginal cost	Increasing returns to
Cost functions	Total cost function	scale
Fixed cost	Average total cost	Decreasing returns to
Variable cost	function	scale
Total cost	Marginal cost function	Constant returns to
		scale

B. Make sure that you can do each of the following:

1. Define cost, and indicate why implicit costs must be included in the economist's cost concept.

2. Indicate the nature of a firm's total cost, total fixed cost, and total variable cost, and how one can draw the firm's total cost function, total fixed cost function, and total variable cost function.

3. Explain the shape of a firm's average total cost function, average fixed cost function, and average variable cost function.

4. Indicate how marginal cost is calculated, and explain the shape of a firm's marginal cost function.

5. Show how the long-run average cost function is important in determining whether competition in a particular industry is feasible.

6. Explain the reason why increasing returns to scale prevail in some industries, whereas decreasing (or constant) returns to scale prevail in others.

7. Describe how a firm's cost functions can be estimated, and describe the sorts of results obtained in statistical studies of cost functions.

8. Indicate how break-even charts can be of practical use to firms.

Getting Down to Cases: The Cost of Air Transportation

According to George Douglas and James Miller, the cost per passenger of flying between two cities (call them A and B) depends in the following way on the load factor: the load factor is defined to be the percent of available seats that are filled with passengers.

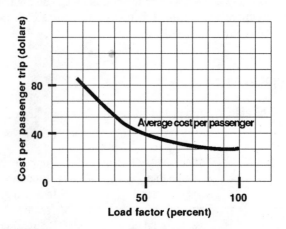

a. If the price of a ticket between points A and B is $40, about how great must the load factor be for the flight to make any profit?

b. Do you think that the marginal cost of adding another passenger to this flight (up to the capacity number of passengers) is high or low? Why?

c. Is the average cost function shown above a long-run or short-run function? Why?

d. Suppose that an economist says that the above graph proves that there are increasing returns to scale in domestic air transportation. Does this follow from this graph? Why or why not?

e. Suppose that all of the costs of the trip are fixed. What then would be the marginal cost of carrying an additional passenger?

Matching Questions

_____	1. Opportunity cost	A. Constant ÷ output
_____	2. Break-even point	B. Alternative cost
_____	3. Total fixed cost curve	C. Output level that must be reached to avoid loss
_____	4. Average fixed cost	D. Horizontal line
_____	5. Average total cost minus average fixed cost	E. Declines with increase in output
_____	6. Average fixed cost curve	F. Average variable cost

Completion Questions

1. If average fixed cost is triple average variable cost, and if average total cost is $40, average fixed cost equals _____ and average variable cost equals _____. If marginal cost equals $20, average variable cost is (rising, falling) _____ , and average total cost is (rising, falling) _____.

2. Total cost at a given output is the sum of _____ and _____.

3. Average fixed cost is the firm's total fixed cost divided by its _____.

4. The addition to total cost resulting from the addition of the last unit of output is called _____.

5. To construct a break-even chart, the firm's total revenue must be plotted on the same chart with its _____.

6. Social costs of producing a given commodity do not always equal the _____ costs. That is, the costs to _____ do not always equal the costs to the individual producer.

7. Total fixed cost is the total expenditure per period of time by the firm for _____ inputs. Since the quantity of the _____ inputs is unvarying (by definition), the total fixed cost will be (the same, different) _____ for various levels of the firm's output. Among the firm's fixed costs in the short run are _____ taxes and _____ on bonds issued in the past.

8. Total variable cost is the total expenditure per period of time on _____ inputs. Due to the law of diminishing marginal returns, total variable cost (decreases, increases) _____ first at a(n) (decreasing, increasing)

_____ rate, then at a(n) (decreasing, increasing)

_____ rate.

9. Average total cost is total cost divided by _____. It equals average _____ cost plus average _____ cost; and beyond a point, it increases as output _____ because of the law of diminishing marginal returns.

10. Marginal cost is the addition to total cost resulting from the _____ of the last unit of output. Beyond a point, it _____ as output increases because of the law of diminishing marginal returns.

11. If the marginal cost of producing the first unit of output is $20, if the marginal cost of producing the second unit of output is $25, and if the marginal cost of producing the third unit of output is $30, the total variable cost of producing 3 units of output is _____. The average variable cost of producing two units of output is _____. Average variable cost (rises, falls) _____ when output increases from 1 to 3 units.

12. If the average fixed cost of producing 10 units of output is $10, the average fixed cost of producing 20 units is _____. If the marginal cost of each of the first 20 units of output is $5, the average variable cost of producing 20 units is _____. And the average total cost of producing 20 units is _____.

True-False

_____ 1. If there are diminishing marginal returns from the variable input, total variable cost will ultimately increase at an increasing rate.

_____ 2. If average variable cost always equals $10 when output is less than 100 units, marginal cost is less than $10 when output is in this range.

_____ 3. There is sometimes a marked difference between social and private costs of producing a given commodity.

_____ 4. Average fixed cost must increase in the short run with increases in output.

_____ 5. Since price is not usually influenced by amount sold, total revenue is equal to output.

_____ 6. Average cost is at a minimum only when it is lower than marginal cost.

_____ 7. If a payment is made to a supplier (other than the firm's owner), this is an explicit cost.

_____ 8. The total cost curve differs by a constant amount (equal to total fixed cost) from the total variable cost curve.

_____ 9. Break-even charts are used very extensively by firms and other groups to estimate the effect of the sales rate on costs, receipts, and profits.

_____ 10. One of the principal determinants of the shape of the long-run average cost function is the law of diminishing marginal returns.

_____ 11. In the long run a firm's fixed costs in industries like steel and autos may amount to tens of millions of dollars per year.

_____ 12. When a firm is experiencing diminishing marginal returns to its variable input, marginal cost is increasing.

Multiple Choice

1. Suppose that firm C's total costs per month equal $50,000 + \$10Q$, where Q is the number of units of output produced per month. If firm C produces 100 units of output per month, its average fixed cost and average variable cost are:

   a. $500 and $20.
   b. $510 and $10.
   c. $490 and $10.
   d. $500 and $10.
   e. none of the above.

2. Under the circumstances described in the previous question, increases in output result in:

   a. decreases in average total cost and no change in marginal cost.
   b. decreases in average variable cost and no change in average total cost.
   c. decreases in average fixed cost and increases in average variable cost.
   d. decreases in average fixed cost and increases in marginal cost.
   e. none of the above.

3. If marginal cost is less than average cost, then with increased inputs the average cost of production will tend to:

   a. rise.
   b. drop.
   c. stay the same.
   d. none of the above.
   e. all of the above.

4. In measuring long-run cost functions, it has generally been found that in most industries for which we have data:

   a. the long-run average cost curve tends to be L-shaped.
   b. the marginal cost tends to be constant at all output levels above zero.
   c. the total, average total, and marginal cost functions tend to be w-shaped.
   d. the shape of the long-run average cost curve is influenced by fixed costs.
   e. long-run average costs increase at all output levels.

5. An example of a fixed cost for a firm would be:

   a. expenditures on variable inputs.
   b. labor.
   c. property taxes.
   d. all of the above.
   e. none of the above.

6. A firm can build a plant of three different sizes. The short-run average cost curves of each are as follows:

Plant X		Plant Y		Plant Z	
Output	Average total cost (dollars)	Output	Average total cost (dollars)	Output	Average total cost (dollars)
1	20	20	30	50	20
5	18	40	20	200	5
10	15	60	10	400	3
20	20	80	20	600	8
25	40	100	50	800	20

The long-run average cost of producing 20 units of output is:

a. $15.
b. $20.
c. $25.

d. $30.
e. none of the above.

7. Under the circumstances described in the previous question, the output at which long-run average cost is a minimum is:

a. 10.
b. 60.
c. 200.

d. 400.
e. 600.

8. Firm R's average total cost per month equals $3 \times Q$, where Q is the number of units of output produced per month. The marginal cost of the fourth unit of output produced per month is:

a. zero.
b. $3.
c. $9.

d. $21.
e. none of the above.

9. Under the circumstances described in the previous question, firm R's total fixed costs per month are:

a. zero.
b. $3.
c. $9.

d. $21.
e. none of the above.

Discussion and Extension Questions

1. The state of Virginia reimburses its employees when their personal cars are used for state business; they receive a stipulated amount per mile. The rationale for this mileage rate is that it costs about that much to own and operate an automobile. What costs should the state be considering as the relevant ones? Why?

2. Universities frequently ask for student opinion about instructors and courses. The usual method is to distribute a questionnaire in class toward the end of a term. What are the costs of such programs? Be sure to think through what economists mean by costs. Try to formulate an actual dollar cost at your institution. Do you think such surveys are worth the costs?

3. If a large increase in the demand for economists by business firms and governmental agencies increases the salaries of such people, how can one also say that it has increased the cost of having an economist at a university?

4. "Statistical studies have shown that total cost is generally a linear function of output. This has embarrassed some economists, who insist that marginal cost must rise. In fact, marginal cost does not rise as output increases." Discuss and evaluate.

5. Consulting firm X claims that the minimum point on the long-run average cost curve occurs at an output level of 1,000 tons of output per week in a certain industry. As evidence for this claim, they say that firms of this size reap the biggest profits. Is this conclusive evidence? Why or why not?

6. "The concept of marginal cost is a purely academic concept. In the real world, no one can possibly tell what the value of marginal cost is." Comment and evaluate.

7. What is the cost of a certain course of action? Be specific. How do firms use break-even charts? What is the break-even point?

8. Why does the marginal cost curve intersect both the average variable cost curve and the average total cost curve at their minimum points? Can there be cases where this is not true?

9. Suppose that two firms have exactly the same marginal cost curve, but their average fixed cost curve is not the same. Will their average variable cost curve be the same?

10. According to the *New York Times*, the cost of producing a barrel of oil from shale was thought by experts to be about $4.40 in 1972, about $10 in 1978, and about $25 in 1979. What factors can account for such great increases? Did productivity decrease in the industry? Did input prices change?

Problems

1. Suppose that the Chicago plant of the Bolton Press Company has the following cost structure: (1) its fixed costs are $1,000 per month; (2) its variable costs are shown below.

   a. Fill in the blanks indicated below:

Output (presses per month)	Total fixed cost (dollars)	Total variable cost (dollars)	Total cost (dollars)
0	_____	0	_____
1	_____	500	_____
2	_____	1,000	_____
3	_____	2,000	_____
4	_____	3,500	_____
5	_____	5,000	_____

b. Fill in the blanks below. These blanks indicate the average cost functions of the Chicago plant of the Bolton Press Company.

Output (presses per month)	Average fixed cost (dollars)	Average variable cost (dollars)	Average total cost (dollars)
1	_____	_____	_____
2	_____	_____	_____
3	_____	_____	_____
4	_____	_____	_____
5	_____	_____	_____

c. Fill in the blanks below:

Output (presses per month)	Marginal cost (dollars)
0 to 1	_____
1 to 2	_____
2 to 3	_____
3 to 4	_____
4 to 5	_____

2. Suppose that the Wilson Press Company's short-run total cost function is as follows:

Output (number of units per year)	Total cost (dollars per year)
0	20,000
1	20,100
2	20,200
3	20,300
4	20,500
5	20,800

a. What are the firm's total fixed costs?
b. What are its total variable costs when it produces 4 units per year?
c. What is the firm's marginal cost when between 4 and 5 units are produced per year?
d. Does marginal cost increase beyond some output level? Why?

3. Farm A is a profit maximizing, perfectly competitive producer of wheat. It produces wheat using 1 acre of land (price = $1,000) and varying inputs of labor (price = $500 per person-month). The production function is as follows:

Number of person-months (per month)	Output per month (in truckloads)
0	0
1	1
3	2
7	3
12	4
18	5
25	6

Show that the production of Farm A is subject to increasing marginal cost.

4. Suppose that firm B makes rugs, and that its fixed costs are $10,000 a month, while its average variable cost is $100 per rug. Suppose that it gets a price of $500 per rug.

 a. Present the firm's break-even chart below:

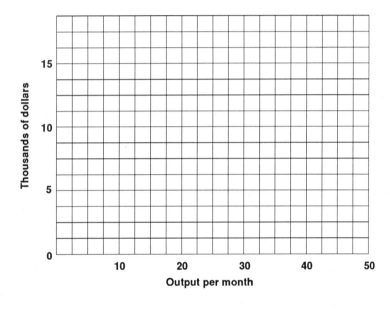

 b. What is the firm's break-even point?

5. Suppose that you are given the production function, the price of the variable input, and the total fixed costs of the ABC Company. These data are shown below. Fill in the blanks.

Number of units of variable input	Number of units of output produced	Average product	Marginal product	Price of unit of variable input	Total variable cost	Average variable cost (dollars)	Total fixed cost	Total cost	Average total cost	Marginal cost
0	0	____		2	____	____	100		____	____
			>——							>——
1	4	____		2	____	____	100		____	____
			>——							>——
2	9	____		2	____	____	100		____	____
			>——							>——
3	15	____		2	____	____	100		____	____
			>——							>——
4	22	____		2	____	____	100		____	____
			>——							>——
5	30	____		2	____	____	100		____	____
			>——							>——
6	37	____		2	____	____	100		____	____
			>——							>——
7	43	____		2	____	____	100		____	____
			>——							>——
8	48	____		2	____	____	100		____	____
			>——							>——
9	52	____		2	____	____	100		____	____

6. A firm can build plants of three types: D, E, and F. The short-run average cost curve with each type is given below:

Type D		Type E		Type F	
Output	Average cost (dollars)	Output	Average cost (dollars)	Output	Average cost (dollars)
20	10	80	6	140	3.00
40	8	100	4	160	2.00
60	6	120	2	180	0.50
80	4	140	1	200	0.40
100	6	160	1	220	0.75

a. Draw the firm's long-run average cost curve in the graph below.

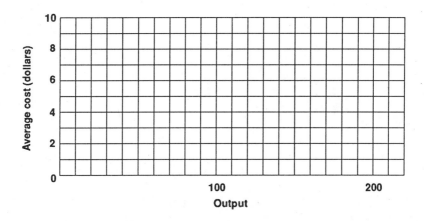

b. What is the minimum price at which the firm will stay in the industry?

7. Firm S hires a consultant to estimate its long-run total cost function. The consultant, after a long study, concludes that for firm S long-run total cost equals $2 million + $4 × Q, where Q is annual output.

   a. What does this equation imply about the long-run total cost of producing nothing? Is this reasonable? Why or why not?
   b. What is the minimum value of long-run average cost?
   c. What size of plant results in the minimum value of long-run average cost? Is this reasonable? Why or why not?

8. Firm P's total cost curve is shown below:

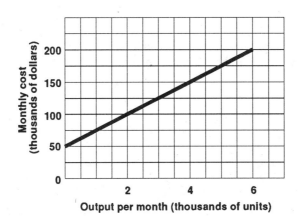

a. Draw the firm's marginal cost function in the graph below.

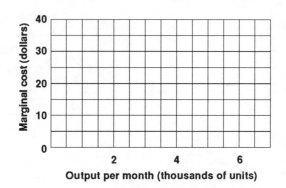

Output per month (thousands of units)

b. Suppose that it is impossible for firm P to produce more than 6,000 units of output per month. What is marginal cost at outputs above 6,000?

9. Based on the graph in the previous problem, fill in the blanks in the table below for firm P.

Output (thousands)	Average fixed cost (dollars)	Average variable cost (dollars)	Average total cost (dollars)
1	_____	_____	_____
2	_____	_____	_____
3	_____	_____	_____
4	_____	_____	_____
5	_____	_____	_____
6	_____	_____	_____

10. Suppose that firm P (in problems 8 and 9) is a perfectly competitive firm. What is its break-even point if the price of a unit of its product is:

a. $75? c. 37\frac{1}{2}$?

b. $50? d. 33\frac{1}{3}$?

Answers

Matching Questions
1. B   2. C   3. D   4. A   5. F   6. E

Completion Questions
1. $30, $10, rising, falling   2. total fixed cost, total variable cost   3. output
4. marginal cost   5. total costs   6. private, society   7. fixed, fixed, the same, property, interest   8. variable, increases, decreasing, increasing   9. output, fixed, variable, increases   10. addition, increases   11. $75, $22.50, rises   12. $5, $5, $10

True-False

1. True   2. False   3. True   4. False   5. False   6. False   7. True   8. True
9. True   10. False   11. False   12. True

Multiple choice

1. d   2. a   3. b   4. a   5. c   6. b   7. d   8. d   9. a

Problems

1. a.

Total fixed cost (dollars)	Total cost (dollars)
1,000	1,000
1,000	1,500
1,000	2,000
1,000	3,000
1,000	4,500
1,000	6,000

b.

Average fixed cost (dollars)	Average variable cost (dollars)	Average total cost (dollars)
1,000	500	1,500
500	500	1,000
333	667	1,000
250	875	1,125
200	1,000	1,200

c.

Marginal cost (dollars)
500
500
1,000
1,500
1,500

2. a. $20,000.
   b. $500.
   c. $300.
   d. Yes. The law of diminishing marginal returns.

3. Since the services of each laborer cost $500 per month, the total variable cost of each output level is (per month):

Output	Total variable cost (dollars)
0	0
1	500
2	1,500
3	3,500
4	6,000
5	9,000
6	12,500

Thus, marginal cost is $500 between 0 and 1 units of output, $1,000 between 1 and 2 units of output, and so forth. Clearly, marginal cost increases as output increases.

4. a.

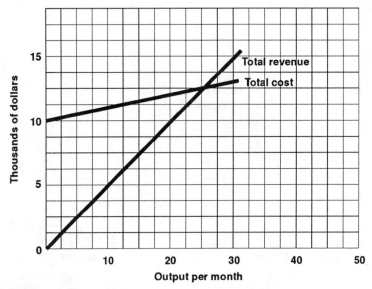

b. $10,000 + 100X = 500X$
$10,000 = 400X$
$25 = X$
The break-even point is 25 rugs per month.

5.

Average product	Marginal product	Total variable cost	Average variable cost	Total cost (dollars)	Average total cost	Marginal cost
—		0	—	100	—	
	4					0.50
4		2	$1/2$	102	$25^{1}/_{2}$	
	5					0.40
$4^{1}/_{2}$		4	$4/9$	104	$11^{5}/_{9}$	
	6					0.33
5		6	$6/15$	106	$7^{1}/_{15}$	
	7					0.29
$5^{1}/_{2}$		8	$8/22$	108	$4^{10}/_{11}$	
	8					0.25
6		10	$1/3$	110	$3^{2}/_{3}$	
	7					0.29
$6^{1}/_{6}$		12	$12/37$	112	$3^{1}/_{37}$	
	6					0.33
$6^{1}/_{7}$		14	$14/43$	114	$2^{28}/_{43}$	
	5					0.40
6		16	$1/3$	116	$2^{20}/_{48}$	
	4					0.50
$5^{7}/_{9}$		18	$18/52$	118	$2^{14}/_{52}$	

6. a.

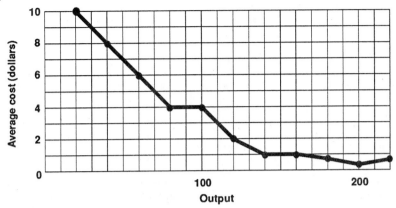

b. $0.40.
7. a. It implies it equals $2 million. No, because there are no fixed costs in the long run.
   b. $4.
   c. An infinite size of plant. No, because one would expect that eventually the long-run average cost function would turn up.

8. a.

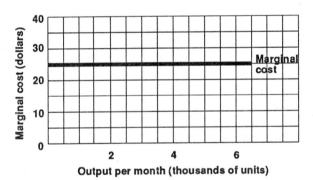

b. Infinite.

9.

Average fixed cost (dollars)	Average variable cost (dollars)	Average total cost (dollars)
50	25	75
25	25	50
$16^2/_3$	25	$41^2/_3$
$12^1/_2$	25	$37^1/_2$
10	25	35
$8^1/_3$	25	$33^1/_3$

10. a. 1,000 units.
    b. 2,000 units.
    c. 4,000 units.
    d. 6,000 units.

CHAPTER 9

Perfect Competition

Chapter Profile

Economists generally classify markets into four types: perfect competition, monopoly, monopolistic competition, and oligopoly.

Perfect competition requires that the product of any seller be the same as the product of any other seller, that no buyer or seller be able to influence the price of the product, and that resources be able to switch readily from one use to another.

The basic rules the firm must follow to maximize profits, if it takes as given the price of its product and it can sell all it wants at that price, are: (1) the firm should set its output rate in the short run at the level where marginal cost equals price, so long as price exceeds average variable cost; (2) if there is no output rate at which price exceeds average variable cost, the firm should discontinue production.

From these basic rules it follows that the firm's supply curve coincides with its marginal cost curve for prices exceeding the minimum value of average variable cost. For prices that are less than or equal to the minimum value of average variable cost, the firm's supply curve coincides with the price axis.

As a first approximation, the market supply curve can be viewed as the horizontal summation of the supply curves of all of the firms producing the product. This assumes that increases or decreases in output by all firms simultaneously do not affect input prices—a strong assumption.

In general, the market supply curve of a product is determined by the size of the firms' plants, the level of input prices, the nature of technology, and the other factors determining the shape of the firms' marginal cost curves, as well as by the effect of changes in the industry output on input prices and by the number of firms producing the product.

The sensitivity of the quantity supplied to changes in price is measured by the price elasticity of supply, defined as the percentage change in quantity supplied resulting from a 1 percent change in price. In general, the price elasticity of supply is greater if the time interval is long rather than short.

Price and output under perfect competition are determined by the intersection of the market supply and demand curves. In the market period, supply is fixed; thus price, which is determined by demand alone, plays the role of the allocating device. In the short run, price influences as well as rations the amount supplied.

In the long run, equilibrium is achieved under perfect competition when enough firms—no more, no less—are in the industry so that economic profits are eliminated. In other words, the long-run equilibrium position of the firm is at the point where its long-run average cost equals price. But since price must also equal marginal cost (to maximize profit), it follows that the firm must be operating at the minimum point on the long-run average cost curve.

Behavioral Objectives

A. You should be able to define and explain the following key concepts in this chapter:

Perfect competition	Oligopoly	Price elasticity of supply
Monopoly	Firm's supply curve	Market period
Monopolistic competition	Market supply curve	Economic profits

B. Make sure that you can do each of the following:

1. State how perfect competition differs from monopoly or oligopoly or monopolistic competition.

2. Indicate how equilibrium price and quantity are determined in a competitive industry in the market period and the short run.

3. Indicate how equilibrium price and quantity are determined in a competitive industry in the long run.

4. Explain how, under perfect competition, resources are reallocated if a change in tastes occurs, product A becoming more popular, product B becoming less popular.

5. Explain why a competitive firm will set its output so that price equals marginal cost.

6. Explain why a competitive firm will shut down if price never exceeds average variable cost.

7. Derive a competitive firm's supply curve from its marginal cost curve (and average variable cost curve).

8. Derive a competitive industry's supply curve from the supply curves of the individual firms.

9. Describe how market supply curves are estimated, and how their shape varies with the length of the relevant time period.

10. Calculate the price elasticity of supply, given a table showing the quantity supplied at various prices.

Getting Down to Cases: The Supply of Corn

Agriculture has many of the characteristics of perfect competition. According to Daniel Suits, the average total cost curve (ATC), average variable cost curve (AVC), and marginal cost curve (MC) of a typical corn producer in the early 1970s were as follows:

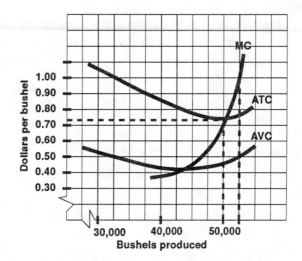

a. Assuming perfect competition, how many bushels of corn would this farmer produce if the price of corn were $1.00 per bushel?

b. Assuming perfect competition, how many bushels would this farmer produce if the price were 40 cents per bushel?

c. If the price were 70 cents per bushel, would this farmer be making a profit or a loss?

d. Suppose that every corn producer has the cost functions shown above, and that perfect competition prevails. If there are 100,000 corn producers, what would be the total supply of corn if the price were $1 per bushel?

e. If the price were $1 per bushel, would long-run equilibrium prevail? Why or why not?

Matching Questions

_____ 1. Supply curve in the market period

_____ 2. Price elasticity of supply

_____ 3. Firm's supply curve

_____ 4. Short run

_____ 5. Long run

_____ 6. Oligopoly

A. No fixed inputs

B. Vertical line

C. Measure of sensitivity of quantity supplied to price variation

D. Fixed plant and equipment

E. Marginal cost curve, above minimum value of average variable cost

F. Few firms

Completion Questions

1. If a perfectly competitive firm's marginal cost of producing the Qth unit of output per month equals $5Q$ dollars, and if the price of a unit of output is $30, the firm, if it maximizes profit, should produce _____ units of output per month. If it does so, its profits per month will equal _____ if its fixed costs per month equal $100. If its fixed costs were $300 per month, the firm (would, would not) _____ be better off to shut down in the short run.

2. If a firm cannot affect the price of its product and it can sell any amount that it wants, the firm is said to be _____.

3. Maximum profit under perfect competition is achieved usually at the output rate where _____ equals _____.

4. A firm's _____ shows how much it will desire to produce at each price.

5. The _____ is the horizontal summation of the supply curves of all the firms producing the product, assuming that industry output does not influence input prices.

6. If there is an output rate where price exceeds average _____ cost, it will pay the firm to produce, even though price does not cover average _____ cost. If there is no such output rate, the firm is better off to produce _____.

7. Under perfect competition the firm's supply curve is exactly the same as the firm's _____ cost curve for prices above the minimum value of average _____ cost. For prices at or below the minimum value of average _____ cost, the firm's supply curve corresponds to the _____ axis, the desire to supply at these prices being uniformly _____.

8. The _____ of an item is the percentage change in quantity supplied as a result of a 1 percent change in _____. For instance, suppose that a 1 percent reduction in the price of an item results in a 1.3 percent reduction in the quantity supplied. The price elasticity of supply for that item, at approximately the existing price, is _____.

9. Market supply curves, like many market demand curves, tend to be (less, more) _____ price elastic if the time period is long rather than short.

For instance, estimates of the short-run price elasticities of supply are about 0.2 for cotton and about 0.1 for corn; but in the long run, Marc Nerlove estimates the price elasticity of supply to be about _____ for cotton and about _____ for corn.

10. In perfect competition, each firm has (no, little, much) _____ control over the price of its product.

11. The _____ is the time during which the supply of a good is fixed.

12. In the short run, _____ determines the amount of a product supplied. For instance, according to Hubert Risser of the University of Kansas, the short-run supply curve for bituminous coal is very price (elastic, inelastic) _____ when output is within the range of existing capacity. In other words, if output is less than existing capacity, small variations in price will result in (large, small) _____ variations in output.

13. Under perfect competition, long-run equilibrium requires that price equals the (highest, lowest) _____ value of long-run average total costs. In other words, firms must be producing at the (maximum, minimum) _____ point on their long-run average cost curves, because to maximize their _____ they must operate where price equals long-run (average, marginal) _____ cost. Also, they must operate where price equals long-run _____ cost. But if both these conditions are satisfied, long-run _____ cost must equal long-run _____ cost—since both equal price. And we know that long-run _____ cost equals long-run _____ cost only at the point at which long-run average cost is a (maximum, minimum) _____.

14. Firm X is a perfectly competitive firm that is in long-run equilibrium. The price of its product is $10 more than the value of its economic profit, which means that the price of its product equals _____. Its long-run average cost (equals, exceeds, is less than) _____ $10. Its short-run marginal cost (equals, exceeds, is less than) _____ $10. In this situation firm X's economic profit (does, does not) _____ equal its accounting profit.

True-False

_____ 1. If the short-run marginal cost curve of each and every firm in an industry slopes upward and to the right, the industry's long-run supply curve must slope upward and to the right.

_____ 2. At all points where the total revenue curve lies below the total cost curve, profits will be negative.

_____ 3. If price is fixed, then increases in output will have little effect on the firm's profits.

_____ 4. Market supply curves tend to be more price elastic if the time period is short rather than long.

_____ 5. The Golden Rule of Output Determination for a perfectly competitive firm is: Choose the output rate at which marginal cost is equal to price.

_____ 6. The firm will maximize profits by producing nothing if there is no output rate at which price exceeds average variable cost.

_____ 7. If we are dealing with a very short period, the supply of a product may be fixed; that is, the market supply curve may be perfectly inelastic. The price elasticity of supply will be zero, because the period is too short to produce any more of the product or transport it to the market.

_____ 8. No industry, now or in the past, has met all of the requirements of perfect competition.

_____ 9. In the market period, output is set by demand alone.

_____ 10. Under perfect competition the product of any one seller must be the same as the product of any other seller.

_____ 11. A perfectly competitive firm in long-run equilibrium is earning normal profits (that is, profits equal to those obtainable elsewhere).

_____ 12. If firm X's marginal cost curve intersects its average variable cost curve at $4 per unit of output, firm X will shut down in the short-run if the price of its product falls below $4 per unit.

Multiple Choice

1. The output of industry S does not affect input prices in the industry. There are 1,000 firms in the industry, and for each firm the marginal cost of producing 5 units per month is $2, the marginal cost of producing 6 units per month is $3, and the marginal cost of producing 7 units per month is $5. If the price per unit of the industry's product is $3, the industry output will be:

   a. no more than 5,000 units per month.
   b. 5,000 units per month.
   c. 6,000 units per month.
   d. 7,000 units per month.
   e. at least 7,000 units per month.

2. In the previous question if the price per unit of the industry's product is $6, the industry output will be:

   a. no more than 5,000 units per month.
   b. 5,000 units per month.
   c. 6,000 units per month.
   d. 7,000 units per month.
   e. not less than 7,000 units per month.

3. If a firm has no fixed costs, it follows that:

    a. the firm would cease production if price were less than average total cost.
    b. average variable cost equals average total cost.
    c. average variable cost achieves a minimum at the same point that average total cost achieves a minimum.
    d. all of the above.
    e. none of the above.

4. If marginal cost exceeds average total cost at its profit-maximizing output, a competitive firm:

    a. will make positive profits.
    b. will operate at a point to the right of the minimum point on the average total cost curve.
    c. will not discontinue production.
    d. all of the above.
    e. none of the above.

5. A firm is better off in the short run to produce when the:

    a. loss from production is less than fixed costs.
    b. fixed costs are less than the loss from production.
    c. average total cost minus price is greater than average fixed cost.
    d. average total cost is greater than average fixed cost plus price.
    e. none of the above.

6. The simultaneous expansion or contraction of output by all firms is likely to alter for an individual firm:

    a. input prices.
    b. cost curves.
    c. supply curve.
    d. all of the above.
    e. none of the above.

7. The shape of the short-run market supply curve may be influenced by:

    a. changes in input prices.
    b. number of firms in the industry.
    c. size of the firm's plants.
    d. the nature of technology.
    e. the type of product.
    f. all of the above.

8. The graph at the top of the next page shows the total revenue and total cost of a firm. Based on this graph, it appears that:

    a. the firm is perfectly competitive.
    b. the firm's fixed costs equal $2,000 per month.
    c. the firm will maximize its profit if it produces about 4 units of output per month.
    d. all of the above.
    e. only a and b are true.

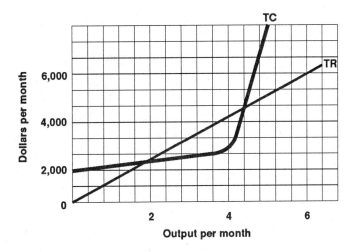

9. Based on the graph in the previous question, it is clear that:

    a. marginal cost is less than marginal revenue when output is less than 3 units per month.

    b. marginal cost is greater than marginal revenue when output is greater than 5 units per month.

    c. there is only one output rate at which average total cost equals average revenue. (Average revenue is total revenue divided by output.)

    d. all of the above.

    e. only a and b are true.

10. Oligopoly is a kind of market where there is/are _____ seller(s).

    a. one   d. no

    b. few   e. too many

    e. many

11. If the demand curve shifts to the right (and if the supply curve is upward-sloping), equilibrium price will:

    a. decrease.   d. be impossible to determine.

    b. increase.   e. none of the above.

    c. stay the same.

* 12. The market demand curve for product R is as follows:

Price (dollars)	Quantity demanded
30	200
20	300
10	400
5	600
3	800

---

* Pertains to chapter appendix.

The industry producing product R is a constant cost industry, and each firm has the following long-run total cost curve:

Output	Total cost (dollars)
1	10
2	12
3	15
4	30

The total number of firms in the industry in the long run will be approximately:

a. 100.

b. 200.

c. 300.

d. 400.

e. none of the above.

13. In the previous question the price of product R in the long run will be approximately:

a. $10.

b. $12.

c. $15.

d. $30.

e. none of the above.

Discussion and Extension Questions

1. In the *New York Times*, the late Henry Ford II wrote that, "The main reason more oil hasn't been found is that, with a 34-year inventory on hand, there has been little incentive to look farther or deeper for still more. . . . As the easily recovered supply of petroleum is depleted, the cost of finding and extracting new supplies will go up and up." Based on this statement, what, according to Mr. Ford, is the shape of the long-run supply curve for oil? Do you agree? Why or why not?

2. Suppose you are currently enrolled for five courses this term. Use the principles presented in this chapter (and the previous one; maybe even Chapter 5) to illustrate how much time you will devote to studying for the final exam in each course. What is the cost to you of an hour's study for your economics final exam? Under what circumstances would it pay you not to study at all for a particular course, and what is the counterpart for the competitive firm?

3. Suppose the Pentagon is interested in expanding our military force by 10 percent. We currently operate under a system called a volunteer army, whereby ordinary market forces are used to help raise our army. Describe why it is important for the Pentagon and other government agencies to have some idea of the elasticity of supply of military personnel when contemplating an increase in their numbers.

4. "There is a learning curve in many industries; that is, unit costs go down as more units are produced. This is a major reason why supply curves slope downward to the right." Comment and evaluate.

5. Suppose that the quantity supplied of left-handed monkey wrenches equals $500P$, where P is the price (in dollars) of a left-handed monkey wrench. What is the price elasticity of supply? Explain.

6. "Higher prices don't result in greater supplies; they result in higher profits." Comment and evaluate.

7. Show why a firm will continue to produce in the short-run so long as price exceeds average variable cost, even if price is smaller than average total cost.

8. What is the effect of the length of the time period on the price elasticity of supply?

*9. Distinguish between (a) diminishing marginal returns, (b) diseconomies of scale, and (c) increasing cost industries.

10. According to Kenneth Boulding, "From the point of view of society as a whole, the inability of agriculture to reduce output in a depression is an almost unmixed blessing." Why can't agriculture reduce output? Why is this a blessing, and why is this blessing not quite unmixed? What are the effects of government farm programs on the validity of this statement?

11. "Competition is all very well in theory, but in practice it generally is a disaster, leading to low profits and eventual government intervention. Agriculture is a case in point." Comment and evaluate.

12. Explain why equilibrium in the long run under perfect competition requires that price must be equal to the lowest value of long-run average total cost.

*13. What does the long-run supply curve of a constant cost industry look like? How does it differ from the long-run supply curve of an increasing cost industry?

Problems

1. Suppose that the total costs of a perfectly competitive firm are as follows:

Output rate	Total cost (dollars)
0	40
1	60
2	90
3	130
4	180
5	240

Assume that the output rate can only assume integer values.

a. If the price of the product is $50, what output rate should the firm choose?
b. Draw on the following graph the short-run supply curve of the firm.
c. Draw the firm's demand curve.
d. Draw the firm's average total cost curve.

---

* Pertains to chapter appendix.

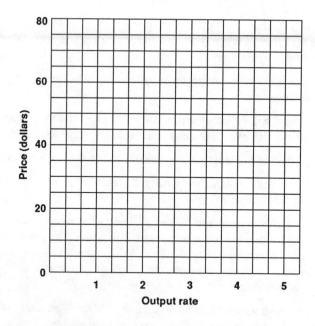

e. What will be the firm's total profit?

2. Suppose that the price elasticity of supply of crude oil is 0.3. How much of a price increase will be required to obtain a 3 percent increase in the quantity supplied of crude oil?

3. You are the owner of a firm that is currently losing $1,000 per month, with fixed costs per month of $800. A management consultant advises you to cease production. Should you accept the advice? Why or why not?

4. Suppose that the total cost curve of the Rem Sofa Company is as follows:

Output (sofas per month)	Total cost (dollars per month)
1	1,000
2	1,100
3	1,200
4	1,300
5	1,500
6	1,700
7	2,000
8	2,500

Assume that the output rate must be an integer amount per month.

a. If the price of a sofa is $300, how many sofas should Rem produce per month?
b. Suppose that Rem's fixed costs increase by $100 per month. What effect will this have on the optimal output?
c. If its fixed costs increase by $100 per month, what will be the maximum profit rate that the Rem Sofa Company can earn?

d. Does the Rem Sofa Company exhibit increasing marginal cost? What is the value of marginal cost when between 7 and 8 units of output are produced per month?

5. Data are provided below concerning the Allied Peanut Company, a firm producing peanut brittle.

a. Supposing that this firm is a member of a perfectly competitive industry, complete the table below:

Output of peanut brittle per day by Allied (tons)	Price of a ton of peanut brittle	Total cost	Revenue (dollars)	Profit	Marginal cost
0	200	100	_____	_____	
					_____
1	_____	200	_____	_____	
					_____
2	_____	310	_____	_____	
					_____
3	_____	500	_____	_____	
					_____
4	_____	700	_____	_____	
					_____
5	_____	1,000	_____	_____	

Assume that the output rate must equal an integer number of tons per day.

b. If the price of a ton of peanut brittle falls to $50, will Allied continue producing it, or will it shut down?
c. What is the minimum price at which Allied will continue production (assuming that it cannot produce fractions of tons of output)?
d. If the price of a ton of peanut brittle is $200, what output rate will Allied choose? Does price equal marginal cost at this output rate?

6. The following graph shows the total cost and total revenue curves of a hypothetical competitive firm:

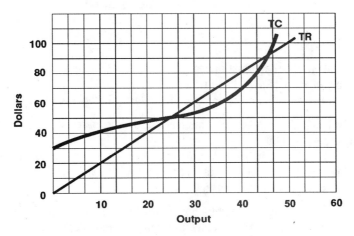

135

    a. How much is the price of the firm's product?
    b. How much is the firm's total fixed cost?
    c. At what output levels will the firm's profit be zero?
    d. At what output level will the firm's profit be a maximum?

7. Suppose that a perfectly competitive firm has the short-run total cost function shown below:

Output	Total cost (dollars)
0	10
1	12
2	16
3	22
4	30
5	40

    a. If the firm can produce only integer amounts of output, what output level will it choose when the price of its product is (1) $3, (2) $5, (3) $7, (4) $9?

    b. What will be the firm's profits when the price of its product is (1) $3, (2) $5, (3) $7, (4) $9?

    c. If there are 1,000 firms in this industry, and all have the cost function shown above, the market supply curve is given below. Fill in the blanks.

Price (dollars)	Quantity demanded
3	_____
5	_____
7	_____
9	_____

    d. If the market demand curve is as shown below, what will be the equilibrium price of the product?

Price (dollars)	Quantity demanded
3	3,000
5	2,000
7	1,500
9	1,000

    e. What will be the output of each firm?

    f. How much profit will each firm make?

    g. Will firms tend to enter or leave this industry in the long run?

8. As of midnight, December 13, American Agriculture, a recently formed farmers' lobby group, is calling for a nation-wide strike by farmers. The goal is to raise the price of the crops enough to cover production costs and to provide some profit. Suppose that the current price of wheat is $1.50 per bushel, which is about one-half of the cost of growing that bushel.

    a. Depict the current plight of a typical wheat farmer graphically. (Treat her as a perfect competitor.) Your diagram should correctly depict both variable and total costs relative to the assumed market price given the fact that the typical farmer is choosing to continue producing even while making losses.

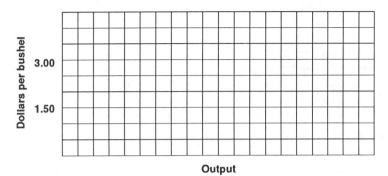

b. In perfect competition no single firm has any market power. Suppose that by such an organization as American Agriculture all farmers could coordinate the selling of their produce. What would be the effect on the price of their produce? What would be the effect on the amount they would sell?

9. Assume that perfect competition exists. Assume that marginal cost increases with increases in output. In the table below you are to fill in all spaces which do not contain a number. An asterisk in a space means that ATC or AVC is at a minimum level at that output. *Treat each horizontal row in the table as a separate problem.* Enter in the last column one of the following responses:

Number	Response
1	Firm now at correct output
2	Firm should increase price
3	Firm should decrease price
4	Firm should increase output
5	Firm should decrease output
6	Firm should shut down operations

The symbols are as follows: P = Price, Q = Quantity, TR = Total Revenue, TC = Total Cost, TFC = Total Fixed Cost, TVC = Total Variable Cost, ATC = Average Cost, AVC = Average Variable Cost, MC = Marginal Cost.

P	Q	TR	TC	TFC	TVC	ATC	AVC	MC	Response
10	----	800	----	500	----	10	----	----	1
----	----	400	----	100	----	2	1	5	----
----	10	30	----	20	----	----	.30	.25	----
10	100	----	----	200	----	----	10	----	----
----	50	300	----	----	----	7	5	----	----

Answers

Matching Questions

1. B   2. C   3. E   4. D   5. A   6. F

Completion Questions

1. 6, –$25, would not   2. perfectly competitive   3. price, marginal cost   4. supply curve   5. market supply curve   6. variable, total, nothing   7. marginal, variable, variable, price, zero   8. price elasticity of supply, price, 1.3   9. more, 0.7, 0.2   10. no   11. market period   12. price, elastic, large   13. lowest, minimum, profits, marginal, average, marginal, average, marginal, average, minimum   14. $10, equals, equals, does not

True-False

1. False   2. True   3. False   4. False   5. True   6. True   7. True   8. True   9. False   10. True   11. True   12. True

Multiple Choice

1. c   2. e   3. d   4. d   5. a   6. d   7. f   8. d   9. e   10. b   11. b   12. b   13. e

Problems

1. a.   3 or 4 units of output per period of time.

   b., c., and d.

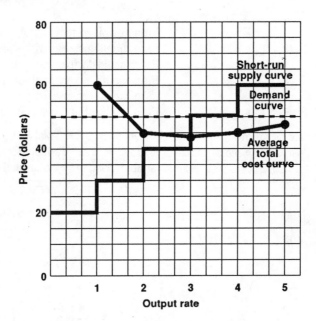

   e. $20.

2. 10 percent price increase.
3. Yes. Because you will lose less money ($800 rather than $1,000) if you cease production than at present.
4. a.   6 or 7 units per month.
   b.   No effect.
   c.   Zero profits.
   d.   Yes. $500.
5. a.

Price of a ton of peanut brittle	Total revenue (dollars)	Profit	Marginal cost
	0	−100	
			100
200	200	0	
			110
200	400	90	
			190
200	600	100	
			200
200	800	100	
			300
200	1,000	0	

   b.   It will shut down.
   c. $100.
   d.   Either 3 or 4 tons per day. Yes; as shown in the answer to part a, marginal cost is $200 when output is between 3 and 4 tons per day. Price too equals $200.
6. a. $2 per unit of output.
   b. $30.
   c.   25 and 45 units of output.
   d.   About 35 units of output.
7. a.   1, 2, 3, 4
   b.   −$9, −$6, −$1, +$6
   c.

   Quantity supplied

   1,000
   2,000
   3,000
   4,000

   d. $5
   e.   2
   f.   −$6
   g.   They will leave it.

8. a.

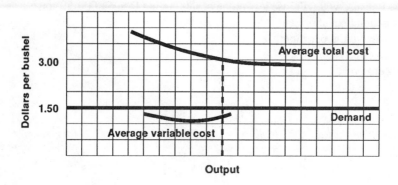

b. Price would increase, and quantity would decrease.

9.

P	Q	TR	TC	TFC	TVC	ATC	AVC	MC	Response
10	80	800	800	500	300	10	$3^3/_4$	10	1
4	100	400	200	100	100	2	1	5	5
3	10	30	23	20	3	2.3	.30	.25	4
10	100	1,000	1,200	200	1,000	12	10	10	6
6	50	300	350	100	250	7	5	7	5

Monopoly and Its Regulation

Chapter Profile

A pure monopoly is a market with one, and only one, seller. Monopolies may occur because of patents, control over basic inputs, and government action, as well as because of decreasing average costs up to the point where the market is satisfied. If average costs reach their minimum at an output rate large enough to satisfy the entire market, perfect competition cannot be maintained, and the public often insists that the industry (a natural monopoly) be regulated by the government.

Since the monopolist is the only seller of the product, the demand curve facing the monopolist is the market demand curve, which slopes downward (rather than being horizontal as in perfect competition). The unregulated monopolist will maximize profit by choosing the output where marginal cost equals marginal revenue, marginal revenue being defined as the addition to total revenue attributable to the addition of one unit of sales. This rule for output determination also holds under perfect competition, since price equals marginal revenue under perfect competition.

If the monopolist cannot prevent losses from exceeding fixed costs, he, like a perfect competitor, will discontinue production. In contrast to the case in perfect competition, the long-run equilibrium of a monopolistic industry may not be marked by the absence of economic profits.

The output of a perfectly competitive industry tends to be greater and the price tends to be lower than under monopoly. Under certain circumstances, it can be shown that society would be better off if more resources were devoted to the production of the good than under monopoly, the competitive output being best.

One way that society has attempted to reduce the harmful effects of monopoly is through public regulation. Commissions often set price at the level at which it equals average total cost, including a fair rate of return on the firm's investment. Regulatory commissions try to prevent a monopoly from earning excessive profits; the firm is allowed only a "fair" rate of return on its investment. One difficulty with this arrangement is that, since the firm is guaranteed this return regardless of how well or poorly it performs, there is no incentive for the firm to increase its efficiency. Although regulatory lag results in some incentives of this sort, they often are relatively weak. In some industries, like airlines, trucking, and railroads, there was a noteworthy trend toward deregulation in the past 20 years.

Behavioral Objectives

    A. You should be able to define and explain the following key concepts in this chapter:

Monopoly	Marginal revenue	Reproduction cost
Natural monopoly	Regulation	Regulatory lag
Total revenue	Historical cost	

    B. Make sure that you can do each of the following:

1. State the principal characteristics of monopoly, and give examples of industries that are close to being monopolies.

2. Indicate the major reasons for monopoly.

3. Indicate how marginal revenue can be calculated, given the demand curve facing the monopolist.

4. Explain why a monopolist will choose the output where marginal revenue equals marginal cost.

5. Explain why economists generally feel that the allocation of resources under perfect competition is socially more desirable than under monopoly.

6. Describe the public regulation of monopoly in the United States.

7. Discuss the effects of regulation on the efficiency of the regulated industries.

Getting Down to Cases: Marginal Costs and Peak Loads in Electric Power

    In this chapter, we have seen that the output rate that will result in an optimal allocation of resources (under the assumptions made here) is the one where price equals marginal cost. Economists have suggested that public utilities set their prices equal to their marginal costs. (See the Appendix to this chapter.) By so doing, it is argued that the allocation of resources will be improved. For example, consider an electric power plant which has the marginal cost curve shown below. Suppose that this plant's demand curve varies over time. For simplicity, assume that there is a peak period (when air conditioners are running and lights are on) and an off-peak period. The demand curve during each period is shown below:

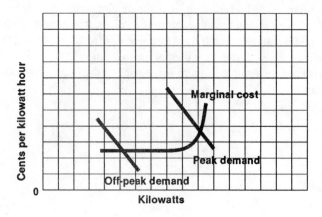

a. Should the electric power plant charge a higher price during the peak period than during the off-peak period? Why or why not?

b. Would such a price differential help to even out the amount of electricity utilized at various times of day? Explain.

c. A number of regulatory commissions have instituted higher rates for electric utilities during the summer than during the winter. Is this sensible, based on your answers to parts a and b?

d. A number of commissions have introduced experiments with meters that record electricity use at different times of day. Such meters are costly. How would you determine whether their introduction and utilization by residential customers is worthwhile?

e. When AT&T established lower telephone rates during the off-peak night hours than during business hours, the result was that there was a large number of calls in the early evening. Indeed, the peak was shifted to the early evening. To correct this, AT&T changed its rates once again. Can you guess what changes it made in the rates during the day, the early evening, and late at night?

Matching Questions

_____ 1. Marginal revenue

_____ 2. Airlines

_____ 3. Average revenue

_____ 4. Patents

_____ 5. Marginal cost

_____ 6. Natural monopoly

A. Same as price

B. One cause of monopoly

C. Deregulated

D. Less than price under monopoly

E. Average cost decreases as output rises

F. Equals marginal revenue if profits are maximized (and the monopolist does not shut down)

Completion Questions

1. If the marginal revenue from the first unit of output is $5 and the marginal revenue from the second unit of output is $4, the total revenue from the first two units of output is _____. The average revenue when 1 unit of output is produced and sold equals _____. The average revenue when 2 units of output are produced and sold equals _____.

2. A monopolist can sell 12 units of output when it charges $10 a unit, 11 units of output when it charges $11 a unit, and 10 units of output when it charges $12 a unit. The marginal revenue from the eleventh unit of output equals _____. The marginal revenue from the twelfth unit of output equals _____.

3. For the monopolist, if demand is price _____ , marginal revenue is positive; if demand is price _____ , marginal revenue is negative.

4. The output of a perfectly competitive industry tends to be _____ and the price tends to be _____ than under monopoly.

5. Commissions often set price at the level at which it equals _____ including a fair return.

6. A firm's _____ is the addition to total revenue attributable to the addition of one unit of the quantity sold.

7. The firm under _____ has no direct competitors at all; it is the sole _____. However, such a firm is not entirely free of rivals but is affected by certain indirect and potential forms of _____.

8. A firm may become a monopolist because it is awarded a(n) _____ by a government agency. The government may give a particular firm the franchise to sell a particular product in a(n) _____ or the right to provide a(n) _____ , such as telephone service, to people in a particular area. In exchange for this right, the firm agrees to allow the government to _____ certain aspects of its operations.

9. A firm may become a monopolist because the average costs of producing the product reach a(n) _____ at an output rate great enough to satisfy the entire market (at a price that is _____). Under such circumstances, the firm obviously has an incentive to _____ to the point where it produces all the market will buy of the good, because its costs (decrease, increase) _____ as it continues to expand. Competition cannot be maintained in such a case.

10. A company's assets can be valued by _____ cost or _____ cost, i.e., at what the company paid for them or at what it would cost to replace them. If the _____ does not change much, these two approaches are interchangeable. But if prices are rising, _____ cost will be greater than _____ cost.

11. If a monopolist's demand curve is of unitary elasticity, marginal revenue equals _____. In such a case it would be (possible, impossible) _____ for the monopolist to set marginal cost equal to marginal revenue. The monopolist would try to make its output as _____ as possible, since _____ in output reduce its total cost but not its total revenue.

12. If a monopolist's demand curve is price elastic, its marginal revenue is (positive, negative, zero) _____. If a monopolist's demand curve is price inelastic, its marginal revenue is (positive, negative, zero) _____. A monopolist will not operate at a point on its demand curve where demand is price (elastic, inelastic) _____.

True-False

_____ 1. A profit-maximizing monopolist that does not shut down will always set average revenue greater than marginal cost, if the demand curve for its product slopes downward to the right.

_____ 2. A profit-maximizing monopolist will always set average revenue greater than average total cost in the short run.

_____ 3. If a monopolist is not maximizing its profit per unit of output, it is not setting marginal cost equal to marginal revenue.

_____ 4. Cost-plus-fixed-fee contracts provide less incentive for efficiency than fixed-price contracts, but where the risk to the contractor is very great, they may be the only type of contract that is feasible.

_____ 5. The monopolist's demand curve must always be horizontal.

_____ 6. A monopolist will discontinue production if its losses have to exceed its fixed costs.

_____ 7. Because price levels have been rising in the past 40 years, most regulatory commissions use replacement cost to value a firm's assets.

_____ 8. A monopolist seeks to maximize its profit per unit of output.

_____ 9. Monopoly, like perfect competition, seldom corresponds more than approximately to conditions in real industries, but it is a very useful model.

_____ 10. A monopolist has to take into account the possibility that new firms might arise to challenge its monopoly if it attempted to extract conspicuously high profits. Thus, even the monopolist is subject to some restraint imposed by competitive forces.

_____ 11. Many firms with monopoly power achieved it in considerable part through patents.

_____ 12. When an industry is a natural monopoly, the public often insists that its behavior be regulated by the government.

_____ 13. For both the monopolist and the perfectly competitive firm, profits are maximized by setting the output rate at the point where price equals marginal cost.

_____ 14. Regulatory lag results in rewards for efficiency because, if a regulated firm is efficient, the lag automatically is reduced and profits increase.

Multiple Choice

1. If a firm's marginal cost curve always lies below its average total cost curve, it is likely to be:

   a. a perfectly competitive firm.   d. any of the above.
   b. a monopolistically competitive firm.   e. none of the above.
   c. a monopoly.

2. An industry that formerly was perfectly competitive is monopolized. The monopoly's demand curve is:

   a. the same as the demand curve for an individual firm when the industry was competitive.
   b. the same as the demand curve for the industry's product when the industry was competitive.
   c. more price elastic than either of the above demand curves.
   d. less price elastic than either of the above demand curves.
   e. none of the above.

3. To maximize profit a monopoly should:

   a. set marginal cost equal to price.
   b. set marginal cost equal to input costs.
   c. set marginal revenue equal to marginal cost.
   d. set marginal revenue equal to input costs.
   e. set average cost equal to price.

4. Economists often regard the socially optimal output of any industry as being the output:

   a. where marginal cost equals price.
   b. that a perfectly competitive industry would produce.
   c. where the social value of an extra unit of the good is equal to the social cost of an extra unit of the good.
   d. all of the above.
   e. none of the above.

5. If the marginal cost to society of producing an extra unit of good X is $5, and if the extra value to society of an extra unit of good X is $15 when less than 10 units are produced and $4 when more than 10 units are produced, the socially optimal output of good X is:

   a. less than 10 units.   d. unobtainable from the information
   b. 10 units.   given.
   c. more than 10 units.   e. none of the above.

6. Under monopoly, marginal cost ordinarily is less than price because:

   a. price is less than marginal revenue.
   b. price is greater than marginal revenue.
   c. marginal cost is less than average cost.
   d. marginal cost is greater than average cost.
   e. none of the above.

7. A country's economy consists of two industries, one perfectly competitive and one monopolized. To improve the allocation of resources, it is likely that:

    a. the output of the competitive industry should be reduced.
    b. the output of the monopolistic industry should be increased.
    c. both a and b.
    d. neither a nor b.
    e. a tax should be imposed on the output of the monopolistic industry.

8. A monopolist's total cost equals $100 + 3Q$, where Q is the number of units of output it produces per month. Its demand curve is $P = 200 - Q$, where P is the price of the product. If it produces 20 units of output per month, its total revenue equals:

    a. $4,000.
    b. $3,600.
    c. $400.

    d. $180.
    e. none of the above.

9. In the previous question the marginal revenue from the twentieth unit of output per month equals:

    a. $3,600.
    b. $3,439.
    c. $180.

    d. $400.
    e. none of the above.

10. In question 8 if the monopolist is producing 19 units of output per month:

    a. its profit will increase by $158 if it increases output by 1 unit per month.
    b. its profit will increase by $3 if it increases output by 1 unit per month.
    c. its profit will decrease by $3 if it increases output by 1 unit per month.
    d. its profit will decrease by $158 if it increases output by 1 unit per month.
    e. none of the above.

Discussion and Extension Questions

1. "Monopoly prices do not reflect true opportunity costs to society." Explain.

2. "Even if a monopolist earns no economic profits whatsoever, he or she may harm society." Do you agree? If so, how does the harm come about? Be specific.

3. Is the trucking industry a natural monopoly? Why has the trucking industry been regulated by the Interstate Commerce Commission? What advantages have accrued from deregulation of the trucking industry? Why have some trucking companies been opposed to such deregulation?

4. "Whether or not one considers a firm a monopolist all depends on how the relevant market is defined. If the market is very narrow, many firms would be classified as monopolists; using a very broad definition, there may be no such thing as a monopolist." Explain.

5. Define what is meant by monopoly. Is a monopolist free of all indirect and potential forms of rivalry? What are the most important reasons for monopoly?

6. Prove that a monopolist, to maximize profit, should choose an output rate such that marginal revenue equals marginal cost.

7. How do the price and output set by a monopolist compare with those that would prevail if the industry were perfectly competitive? Why do many economists argue that the allocation of resources under perfect competition is likely to be more socially desirable than under monopoly? Use diagrams to illustrate your arguments.

8. What are some of the criticisms directed at the regulatory commissions and the principles they use? Why has Congress said that the Food and Drug Administration has to be shown that a new drug is effective as well as safe?

Problems

1. The Uneek Corporation is the only producer of battery-powered soup ladles. Suppose that the demand curve facing the firm is as follows:

Quantity of soup ladles produced per day	Price (dollars per soup ladle)
1	30
2	20
3	10
4	6
5	1

a. Using these data fill in the following table for the Uneek Corporation:

Quantity	Total revenue (dollars)	Marginal revenue (dollars)
1	_____	
2	_____	_____
3	_____	_____
4	_____	_____
5	_____	_____

b. Suppose that the Uneek Corporation has a horizontal cost curve, its marginal cost being $9 per soup ladle (see following graph). Its fixed costs are zero. If the Uneek Corporation's costs are as described above, and if it is producing 1 unit of output, how much will a second unit of output (that is, a second ladle) add to its costs? How much will it add to its revenue? Is it profitable to produce a second unit?

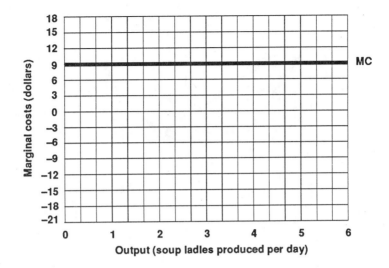

c. Based on the data given above what price should the Uneek Corporation charge?
d. What output should it choose?
e. What is the Uneek Corporation's profit if it produces at the optimal output rate?
f. Suppose that its fixed costs are $10, rather than zero. Will this affect the optimal output rate? Will this affect the firm's profit? If so, how?

2. In a particular industry the minimum value of average cost is reached when a firm produces 1,000 units of output per month. At this output rate, average cost is $1 per unit of output. The demand curve for this product is as follows:

Price (dollars per unit of output)	Quantity (produced per month)
3.00	1,000
2.00	8,000
1.00	12,000
0.50	20,000

a. Is this industry a natural monopoly? Why or why not?
b. If the price is $2, how many firms, each of which is producing an output such that average cost is a minimum, can the market support?

3. The graph below pertains to a monopolist. One of the curves is its demand curve, one is its marginal revenue curve, and one is its marginal cost curve.

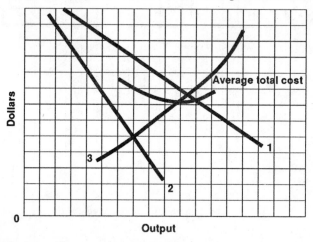

a. What is curve 1?
b. What is curve 2?
c. What is curve 3?
d. Show the output rate that the monopolist will choose and the price it will set.
e. Does the monopolist choose the output rate at which average total cost is a minimum? Do perfectly competitive firms choose such an output rate in the long run?
f. In the graph above show the total profit earned by the monopolist.
g. If the monopolist set price equal to marginal cost, what would be its output rate?

4. Suppose that a hypothetical monopoly has the following demand curve and total costs:

Output sold (per month)	Price	Total revenue	Total cost (per month)	Average total cost	Marginal cost	Marginal revenue	Profit
			(dollars)				
0	50	___	40	___			___
1	45	___	50	___	___	___	___
2	40	___	70	___	___	___	___
3	35	___	95	___	___	___	___
4	30	___	125	___	___	___	___
5	25	___	165	___	___	___	___
6	20	___	225	___	___	___	___

   a. Fill in the blanks of the preceding table.
   b. What output (or outputs) will maximize the monopolist's profits?
   c. What price will the monopolist choose?

5. Suppose that a monopolist has 5 units of output on hand. It can sell this output in one of two markets. The demand curve for the product in each market is shown below:

Market A		Market B	
Price (dollars)	Quantity demanded	Price (dollars)	Quantity demanded
70	1	50	1
65	2	45	2
60	3	40	3
50	4	30	4
40	5	20	5

There is no way that a unit of the good sold in one market can be resold in the other market.

   a. Suppose that the monopolist is selling 4 units in market A and none in market B. Should it sell the fifth unit in market A or market B? Why?
   b. Suppose that the monopolist is selling 4 units in market B and none in market A. Should it sell the fifth unit in market A or market B? Why?
   c. Prove that the monopolist should allocate the goods between markets so that the marginal revenues in the two markets are equal.

6. A monopolist's demand curve is as follows:

Price (dollars)	Quantity demanded
20	0
15	1
10	2
5	3

The monopolist's total cost (in dollars) equals $3 + 20Q$, where Q is its output rate. What output rate will maximize the monopolist's profit?

7. In industry X, a firm's long-run average cost (in dollars) equals $5 + 3/Q$, where Q is the firm's output per year.

   a. Is this industry a natural monopoly? Why or why not?
   b. If this industry is monopolized, and if the monopoly maximizes profit, what is the value of marginal revenue in the long run?
   c. In the long run under the circumstances described in part b, we can be sure that price exceeds a certain amount. What is this amount, and why must price exceed it?

8. A labor union can be viewed as a monopoly for supplying labor services. Use diagrammatic analysis together with the concept of price elasticity of demand to apply what you have learned about monopoly to the way in which a union sets the wage. Your analysis should respond to two specific questions: a. How do the union-set wage and the wage which would be set by competition differ? b. Even though

wages for each working union member might rise when the union sets the wage, show that it is possible that total wages to all members taken together might, in fact, fall when wages are raised to the union level.

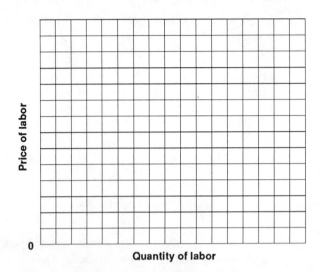

9. Suppose a firm is producing Quarks, and that it has a complete monopoly over Quarks. The following information is given:

Marginal revenue = $1,000 - 20(Q)$
Total revenue = $1,000(Q) - 10(Q^2)$
Marginal cost = $100 + 10(Q)$
where Q = Output of Quarks and P = Price of a Quark

How many Quarks would be sold and at what price if:

a. The firm sets price as a monopoly?
b. The industry (firm) behaves perfectly competitively?

Answers

Matching Questions
1. D   2. C   3. A   4. B   5. F   6. E

Completion Questions
1. $9, $5, $4.50   2. +$1, –$1   3. elastic, inelastic   4. greater, lower   5. average total cost   6. marginal revenue   7. monopoly, supplier, competition   8. market franchise, public facility, service, regulate   9. minimum, profitable, expand, decrease 10. historical, reproduction, price level, replacement, historical   11. zero, impossible, small, decreases   12. positive, negative, inelastic

True-False
1. True   2. False   3. False   4. True   5. False   6. True   7. False   8. False
9. True   10. True   11. True   12. True   13. False   14. False

Multiple Choice

1. c   2. b   3. c   4. d   5. b   6. b   7. c   8. b   9. e   10. a

Problems

1. a.

Total revenue (dollars)	Marginal revenue (dollars)
30	
	10
40	
	−10
30	
	−6
24	
	−19
5	

   b. The second ladle will add $9 to its costs and $10 to its revenue. Yes.
   c. $20.
   d. 2 soup ladles per day.
   e. $22.
   f. No. Yes. It will decrease its profit by $10.
2. a. No. If price is $1, twelve firms of optimal size can exist in the market.
   b. Eight.
3. a. Demand curve.
   b. Marginal revenue.
   c. Marginal cost curve.
   d. It will choose a price of *OP* and an output of *OQ*.

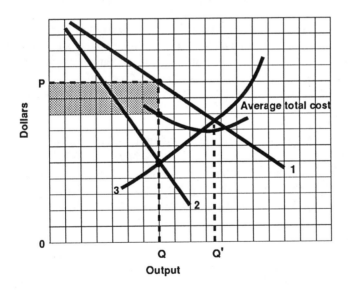

   e. No. Yes.

    f. The shaded area in the graph in the answer to part d equals this profit.

    g. OQ^1 in the graph in the answer to part d.

4. a.

Total Revenue	Average total cost	(dollars)	Marginal cost	Marginal revenue	Profit
0	–				−40
			10	45	
45	50				−5
			20	35	
80	35				10
			25	25	
105	$31^2/_3$				10
			30	15	
120	$31^1/_4$				−5
			40	5	
125	33				−40
			60	−5	
120	$37^1/_2$				−105

    b. 2 or 3 units per month.

    c. $40 or $35.

5. a. The marginal revenue from the fifth unit in market A is zero. The marginal revenue from the first unit in market B is $50. Thus, it should be sold in market B.

    b. The marginal revenue from the fifth unit in market B is −$20. The marginal revenue from the first unit in market A is $70. Thus, it should be sold in market A.

    c. If the marginal revenue in one market is less than in the other, it will pay the monopolist to allocate one more unit to the latter market and one less to the former market. Thus, the monopolist will be maximizing profit only when the marginal revenue in each market is equal.

6. Marginal cost equals $20. The marginal revenue from the first unit of output is $15, from the second unit $5, and from the third unit −$5. Thus, the monopolist should produce nothing.

7. a. Yes, because long-run average cost falls continually as output increases.

    b. The firm's long-run total cost equals $Q(5 + 3/Q) = 3 + 5Q$. Thus, its long-run marginal cost equals $5. Since marginal revenue equals marginal cost if the monopolist maximizes profit, long-run marginal revenue equals $5.

    c. Price exceeds $5, because price exceeds marginal revenue so long as the product's demand curve is downward-sloping to the right.

8. a. The demand and supply curves of labor are shown below. The marginal revenue curve corresponding to the demand curve is also given.

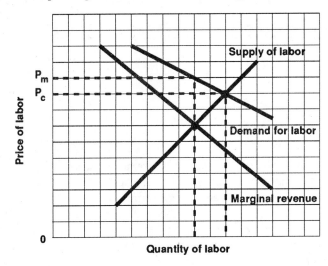

If the union behaves as a monopolist, it will set a wage of P_M. Under competition, the wage would be P_C.

b. If the demand curve for labor is price elastic, an increase in the wage will reduce the total wages. That is, it will reduce the quantity of labor demanded times the wage.

9. a. Since marginal revenue = marginal cost,

$$1,000 - 20Q = 100 + 10Q,$$

which means that $900 = 30Q$, or $Q = 30$.

Since $PQ = 1,000Q - 10Q^2$, the demand curve must be

$$P = 1,000 - 10Q.$$

And if $Q = 30$, P must equal 700.

b. Since the industry's supply curve would be the same as the monopolist's marginal cost curve, the supply curve would be

$$P = 100 + 10Q.$$

As pointed out in part a, the demand curve is

$$P = 1,000 - 10Q.$$

Thus, in a competitive market,

$$100 + 10Q = 1,000 - 10Q$$
$$20Q = 900$$
$$Q = 45.$$

And $P = 1,000 - 10(45) = 550$.

Oligopoly, Game Theory, and Monopolistic Competition

Chapter Profile

Monopolistic competition occurs where there are many sellers whose products are not the same. Thus, the demand curve facing each firm slopes downward to the right. The conditions for long-run equilibrium are that each firm is maximizing profits and that economic profits are zero. According to the theory of monopolistic competition, firms under this form of market organization will tend to operate with excess capacity.

The firm under monopolistic competition is likely to produce less and charge a higher price than a firm under perfect competition. Relative to pure monopoly, monopolistically competitive firms are likely to have lower profits, greater output, and lower prices. Firms under monopolistic competition will, of course, offer a wider variety of styles, brands, and qualities than will firms under perfect competition.

Oligopoly is characterized by a small number of firms and a great deal of interdependence, actual and perceived, among them. Oligopoly is a common market structure in the United States. Conditions in oligopolistic industries tend to promote collusion. A cartel is an open, formal, collusive arrangement. A profit-maximizing cartel will act like a monopolist with a number of plants or divisions, each of which is a member firm. However, in practice, output is unlikely to be allocated among the member firms to minimize total costs, since the allocation process is basically a matter of bargaining. Collusive arrangements often occur, although there are important barriers to effective collusion.

Price leadership is quite common in oligopolistic industries, one or a few firms apparently setting the price and the rest following their lead. Two types of price leadership are the dominant-firm and the barometric-firm model. An example of the former kind of price leadership is the steel industry until a decade or so ago.

A contestable market is a market into which entry is absolutely free, and exit is absolutely costless. In a contestable market, profits are zero, the average cost of production is as low as possible, and price equals marginal cost.

A game is described in terms of its players, rules, payoffs, and information conditions. The relevant features of a two-person game can be shown by the payoff matrix. A dominant strategy is a strategy that is the player's best choice regardless of what the other player does. The prisoners' dilemma is a type of game that is often encountered in oligopoly.

Relative to perfect competition, it seems likely that price and profits will be higher under oligopoly. Moreover, oligopolistic industries will tend to spend more on advertising, product differentiation, and style changes than perfectly competitive industries.

Behavioral Objectives

A. You should be able to define and explain the following key concepts in this chapter:

Monopolistic competition	Tit for tat	Price leader
Oligopoly	Horizontal merger	Contestable market
Pure oligopoly	Vertical merger	Dominant strategy
Differentiated oligopoly	Conglomerate merger	Dominant firm
Product differentiation	Collusion	Barometric firm
Product group	Cartel	Payoff matrix

B. Make sure that you can do each of the following:

1. State how monopolistic competition differs from perfect competition.

2. Explain how price and output are determined under monopolistic competition, both in the short and long run.

3. Compare the price, profits, output, efficiency, and variety of product under monopolistic competition with those under perfect competition.

4. State how oligopoly differs from monopoly.

5. Describe the factors that are responsible for oligopoly.

6. Distinguish between the dominant-firm model and the barometric-firm model of price leadership.

7. Explain how a cartel will determine price and output, and contrast this situation with a case of price leadership.

8. Compare the price, profits, output, efficiency, and variety of product under oligopoly with those under perfect competition.

9. Define a player, a game, a strategy, and a payoff, and describe the essential features of game theory.

10. Describe the theory of contestable markets.

Getting Down to Cases: The Ohio Valley Electric Corporation Case

One of the biggest legal battles in antitrust history occurred in 1965, when the Ohio Valley Electric Corporation sued Westinghouse and General Electric for damages. According to the Ohio Valley Electric Corporation, it had been overcharged for electrical equipment it purchased during the period when the electrical equipment producers conspired to raise prices. In the subsequent trial, it built its case in considerable part on the following graph, which shows the relationship between average order prices and book prices during 1948 to 1963.*

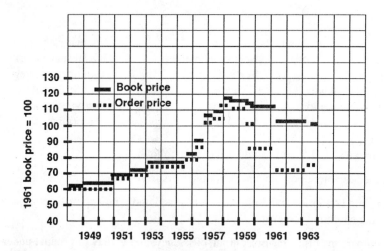

a. The book price was the published price issued by General Electric and other electrical equipment producers. The average order price was the average price actually negotiated for such equipment. Does it appear that this equipment was frequently sold below its book price? Does this show that there was considerable competition among the equipment producers?

b. There was evidence that the electrical equipment producers had held meetings to control prices before 1959. Is the relationship between average order price and book price different in the post-1959 period than in the earlier years? Is this difference what you would expect if the conspiracy ended in 1959?

c. According to the Ohio Valley Electric Corporation, in the absence of a conspiracy, the actual order price would have borne the same relationship to the book price in the early 1950s as in the early 1960s. Specifically, it would have been about 75 percent of the book price. Do you agree? Why or why not?

d. Based on the reasoning in part c, the Ohio Valley Electric Corporation argued that they incurred damages of $8.2 million. But the electrical equipment producers argued that actual prices had moved up and down due to shifts in demand and supply. How would you determine the extent to which each side was correct?

e. Judge Wilfred Feinberg ruled that the damages equaled $5.6 million. How would you determine whether this was a reasonable ruling?

---

* Source: R. Sultan, *Pricing in the Electrical Oligopoly*, Boston: Harvard University, 1974.

Matching Questions

_____ 1. Monopolistic competition

_____ 2. Oligopoly

_____ 3. Player

_____ 4. Strategy

_____ 5. Dominant strategy

_____ 6. Advantage of being first

A. Wal-mart

B. Best regardless of what other player does

C. Steel

D. Retailing

E. A decision-making unit, whether a person or organization

F. What a player will do under each contingency

Completion Questions

1. The demand and cost curves of a monopolistically competitive firm are given below. If the firm charges a price of $4, its profits will equal about _____. If the firm charges a price of $6, its profits will equal about _____. If it charges a price of $8, its profits will equal about _____. In the long run, (entry, exit) _____ will occur in this industry.

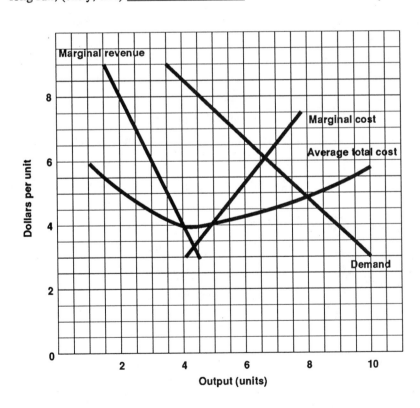

2. A monopolistically competitive firm is in long-run equilibrium. Its marginal revenue equals $5. If its marginal revenue plus its economic profit equal one-half of its price, its price equals $_____ , and its marginal cost equals $_____. In game theory, a strategy is a _____ _____ of what a player will do under each contingency.

3. All firms in an industry have marginal cost curves that are horizontal lines at $5 per unit of output. If they combine to form a cartel, the cartel's marginal cost (will, will not) _____ be $5 per unit of output. If the cartel maximizes profit, its marginal revenue will be (greater than, smaller than, equal to) _____ $5 per unit of output, and its price will be (greater than, smaller than, equal to) _____ $5 per unit of output.

4. Under monopolistic competition, the firm is likely to produce (less, more) _____ and charge a (higher, lower) _____ price than under perfect competition.

5. Relative to pure monopoly, monopolistically competitive firms are likely to have (greater, lower) _____ profits, (greater, lower) _____ output, and (higher, lower) _____ prices.

6. If the _____ dilemma is repeated, a good strategy may be _____ .

7. If the demand curve is the same under oligopoly as under perfect competition, then under oligopoly price will tend to be _____ and output _____ than under perfect competition.

8. Oligopoly occurs in markets where there are (few, many) _____ sellers and it has two forms: one in which all sellers produce an identical product and the other in which the sellers produce somewhat different products. Examples of _____ are the markets for steel, cement, tin cans, and petroleum. Examples of _____ are the markets for automobiles and machinery.

9. Under monopolistic competition, the demand curve slopes (downward, upward) _____ to the right. Consequently, marginal revenue must be (less, more) _____ than price. Thus, under monopolistic competition, marginal cost must also be (less, more) _____ than price, since

marginal revenue must (equal, exceed) _____ marginal cost at the firms' profit-maximizing output rate. But if marginal cost is (less, more) _____ than price, the firm's output rate must be (less, more) _____ and the price (higher, lower) _____—than if marginal cost equals price, which is the case under perfect competition.

10. A(n) _____ is an open, formal, collusive arrangement among firms. In many countries in Europe, _____ are common and legally acceptable. In the United States, most _____ arrangements, whether secret or open, were declared illegal by the Sherman Act, which was passed in _____.

11. There is always a temptation for oligopolists to _____ on any collusive agreement. So long as the other firms stick to the agreement, any firm that _____ its price below that agreed to under the collusive arrangement can take a lot of business away from the other firms and (decrease, increase) _____ its profits substantially, at least in the short run.

12. In order to coordinate their behavior without outright collusion, some industries contain a(n) _____. It is quite common in oligopolistic industries for one or a few firms to _____ the price and for the rest to follow their lead. Two types of _____ leadership are the _____ model and the _____ model.

True-False

_____ 1. Under perfect competition, firms will offer a greater variety of styles, brands, and qualities than under monopolistic competition.

_____ 2. In an oligopoly, any change in one firm's price or output generally influences the sales and profits of its rivals.

_____ 3. Prices in oligopolistic markets tend to fluctuate a good deal more than prices under perfect competition.

_____ 4. In game theory, given the payoff matrix, each firm will always have two equally optimal choices.

_____ 5. Under monopolistic competition there must be a large number of firms in the product group.

_____ 6. The number of firms in the product group must be large enough under monopolistic competition so that each firm expects its actions to go unheeded by its rivals and is unimpeded by possible retaliatory moves on their part.

_____ 7. A firm under monopolistic competition may be somewhat inefficient because it tends to operate with excess capacity.

_____ 8. A cartel may act like a monopolist with a number of plants or divisions, each of which is a member firm.

_____ 9. In practice, it appears that cartels often divide markets geographically or in accord with a firm's level of sales in the past.

_____ 10. During the 1950s there was widespread collusion among about 30 firms selling turbine generators, switchgears, transformers, and related products with total sales of about $1.5 billion per year.

_____ 11. Collusion is often difficult to achieve and maintain because an oligopoly contains an unwieldy number of firms, or the product is quite hetero-geneous or the cost structures of the firms differ considerably.

_____ 12. Oligopolists tend to compete less aggressively through advertising and product differentiation than through direct price reductions.

_____ 13. Oligopolistic industries tend to spend more on advertising, product differentiation, and style changes than perfectly-competitive industries.

_____ 14. A monopolistically competitive firm's short-run demand and cost curves are as follows:

Price (dollars)	Quantity demanded	Total cost (dollars)	Output
8	1	5	1
7	2	7	2
6	3	9	3
4	4	11	4
3	5	20	5

This firm, if it maximizes profit, will choose an output rate of 4.

_____ 15. In the previous question, the number of firms in this industry will tend to increase, if all firms in the industry are like this one.

_____ 16. In question 14, if the firm's fixed cost rises by $5, the firm's short-run output rate will be unaffected.

_____ 17. In question 14, if the firm's costs rise by $10, the number of firms in this industry will tend to decrease (because of exit), if all firms in the industry are like this one.

Multiple Choice

1. The graph pertains to a monopolistically competitive firm:

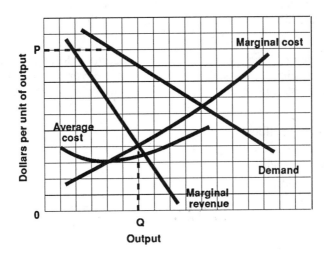

This firm would be foolish to set a price of *OP* because:

   a. marginal revenue exceeds marginal cost at this price.
   b. it exceeds the profit-maximizing price.
   c. it results in an output that is lower than the profit-maximizing output.
   d. all of the above.
   e. only b and c are true.

2. In the previous question, if the firm chooses an output rate of *OQ*:

   a. other firms will tend to enter the industry, since entry is easy.
   b. the firm will make an economic profit.
   c. the firm will set a price of *OP*.
   d. all of the above.
   e. only a and b are true.

3. One major assumption of Chamberlin's theory of monopolistic competition is that:

   a. demand curves will be the same for each firm but cost curves will be different.
   b. each firm's product is a fairly close substitute for the others in the group.
   c. there are just a few firms in each group.
   d. each firm expects its actions to influence those of its rivals.
   e. all of the above.

4. In game theory, a game is basically described in terms of:

   a. players.   d. information conditions that exist.
   b. rules.   e. all of the above.
   c. payoffs.

5. There is general agreement that which of the following models is an adequate general representation of oligopoly behavior?

   a. contestable markets
   b. price leadership
   c. cartel model
   d. cost-plus pricing
   e. none of the above

6. In 1991 industry A was a perfectly competitive industry in long-run equilibrium. In 1992 it was cartelized, the result being that its economic profit was $10 million higher than in 1991. In 1992 its economic profits were:

   a. zero.
   b. less than $10 million.
   c. $10 million.
   d. more than $10 million.
   e. indeterminate on the basis of the available data.

Discussion and Extension Questions

1. Suppose your economics professor states publicly that he grades on a curve (i.e., the top 10 percent of the students get an A, the next 20 percent a B, the next 40 percent a C, the next 20 percent a D, and the lowest 10 percent fail). The whole class could save itself a lot of work then by agreeing privately not to study at all (assuming the love of knowledge is negligible) for the final exam and just let the rankings thus far determine the final grades. Why might such an agreement be difficult to maintain and enforce?

2. At times there has been considerable debate in Congress and elsewhere concerning the desirability of breaking up the major oil firms. Do you believe such a step would be socially desirable? Why or why not?

3. "A cartel merely redistributes income. It takes from the cartel's customers and gives to the cartel members. So long as the latter are as worthy as the former, there are no adverse social consequences." Comment and evaluate.

4. Under monopolistic competition, will the firm produce less than the minimum-cost output in the long run? Why or why not? How will the level of price under monopolistic competition compare with that under perfect competition? Under monopoly?

5. Is game theory a practical tool that can be used to predict oligopolistic behavior? Explain.

6. What is a cartel? How does a profit-maximizing cartel set its price? What is meant by price leadership? Does it occur frequently?

Problems

1. The India Company and the China Company are duopolists. Each firm has two possible strategies. The payoff matrix is as follows:

Possible strategies for the China Company	Possible strategies for the India Company: Strategy A	Strategy B
Strategy 1	China's profit: $7 million India's profit: $5 million	China's profit: $8 million India's profit: $6 million
Strategy 2	China's profit: $6 million India's profit: $5 million	China's profit: $7 million India's profit: $6 million

   a. Does the China Company have a dominant strategy?
   b. Does the India Company have a dominant strategy?
   c. What strategy will the China Company choose?
   d. What strategy will the the India Company choose?

2. The cost curves and demand curve of the Jones Manufacturing Company, a monopolistically competitive firm, are shown below:

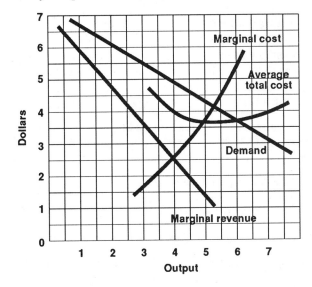

   a. What output rate will this firm choose?
   b. What price will it charge?
   c. How great will be its profits?
   d. Is this a long-run equilibrium situation?

3. Suppose that an industry is composed of 20 firms, each with a horizontal marginal cost curve. In particular, each firm can produce at a marginal cost of $2 per unit of output. Variation in industry output does not affect the cost curve of the individual firms.

   a. If the industry is cartelized, what will the marginal cost curve of the cartel look like?

b. The marginal revenue for the cartel is $3 when it produces 100 units of output, $2 when it produces 200 units of output, and $1 when it produces 300 units of output per month. Will it produce more or less than 100 units of output per month?

c. Will it produce more or less than 300 units per month?

d. Can you tell what output level it will choose? If so, what is it?

4. An oligopolistic industry selling a homogeneous product is composed of two firms. The two firms set the same price and share the total market equally. The demand curve confronting each firm (assuming that the other firm sets the same price as this firm) is shown by the table below. Also each firm's total cost function is shown below:

Price (dollars)	Quantity demanded	Output	Total cost (dollars)
10	5	5	45
9	6	6	47
8	7	7	50
7	8	8	55
6	9	9	65

a. Assuming that each firm is right in believing that the other firm will charge the same price that it does, what is the price that each should charge?

b. Under the assumptions in part a, what output rate should each firm set?

c. Is there bound to be entry into this industry in the long run?

d. Is there any incentive for each firm to cut its price to somewhat below its rival's price? If so, what is it?

5. Suppose that if industry A sets its price above $5 per unit, a swarm of new firms will enter the industry and take a very large proportion of the sales away from the established firms.

a. What effect does this have on the shape of the demand curve confronting the established firms in the industry?

b. What effect do you think that this will have on the industry's pricing practices?

6. Suppose that the payoff matrix for a two-person game is as follows:

Player B's possible strategies	Player A's possible strategies	
	1	2
I	$4,000	$3,000
II	$2,000	$1,500

The two players are A and B. Each has two possible strategies (A's being 1 and 2, B's being I and II). The values in the matrix are gains for B (= losses for A).

a. What is A's optimal strategy?

b. What is B's optimal strategy?

c. Is there an equilibrium solution to this game? What is it?

d. How much will player A lose under the equilibrium solution?

e. How much will player B gain under the equilibrium solution?

Answers

Matching Questions
1. D   2. C   3. E   4. F   5. B   6. A

Completion Questions
1. –$12, $10, $18, entry   2. 10, 5, complete specification   3. will, equal to, greater than   4. less, higher   5. lower, greater, lower   6. prisoners', tit for tat   7. higher, lower   8. few, the former, the latter   9. downward, less, less, equal, less, less, higher   10. cartel, cartels, collusive, 1890   11. cheat, cuts, increase   12. price leader, set, price, dominant-firm, barometric-firm

True-False
1. False   2. True   3. False   4. False   5. True   6. True   7. True   8. True   9. True   10. True   11. True   12. False   13. True   14. False   15. True   16. True   17. True

Multiple Choice
1. d   2. e   3. b   4. e   5. e   6. c

Problems
1. a. Yes.
   b. Yes.
   c. Strategy 1.
   d. Strategy B.
2. a. 4 units of output.
   b. $5.
   c. $4.
   d. No.
3. a. A horizontal line at $2 = MC$.
   b. More.
   c. Less.
   d. Yes. 200 units of output, if it maximizes profit.
4. a. $9.
   b. 6.
   c. Not necessarily; it depends on the extent of the barriers to entry.
   d. Yes, because its demand curve is likely to be very elastic, if the other firm does not match its price cut.
5. a. The demand curve may have a kink at the price of $5; it may be much more price elastic above this price than below it.
   b. The established firms may avoid raising the price above $5, since this would encourage entry.
6. a. Strategy 2.
   b. Strategy I.
   c. Player A adopts strategy 2, player B adopts strategy I.
   d. $3,000.
   e. $3,000.

CHAPTER 12

Industrial Organization and Antitrust Policy

Chapter Profile

The most important reason why economists oppose monopoly is that it imposes a burden on society by misallocating resources. In defense of monopoly power, some economists have asserted that the rate of technological change is likely to be greater in an imperfectly competitive industry than under perfect competition. It does seem unlikely that a perfectly competitive industry would be able—and have the incentive—to carry out the research and development required to promote a rapid rate of technological change in many sectors of the economy. This is an area of continuing controversy. The arguments against monopoly power are by no means open-and-shut.

Economic power in the United States is distributed very unevenly; 100 corporations control over half of the total manufacturing assets of the economy. Moreover, many individual industries are dominated by a few firms. This concentration of power is viewed with concern by many economists and lawyers.

In 1890, the Sherman Act was passed; it outlawed any contract, combination, or conspiracy in restraint of trade and made it illegal to monopolize or attempt to mono-polize. In 1914, Congress passed the Clayton Act, and the Federal Trade Commission was created. A more recent antitrust development was the Celler-Kefauver Anti-Merger Act of 1950.

The real impact of the antitrust laws depends on the interpretation placed on these laws by the courts. In its early cases, the Supreme Court put forth and used the famous rule of reason—that only unreasonable combinations in restraint of trade, not all trusts required conviction under the Sherman Act. The situation changed greatly in the 1940s when the Court decided that Alcoa, because it controlled practically all of the nation's aluminum output, was in violation of the antitrust laws.

The impact of the antitrust laws is also determined by the vigor with which the Antitrust Division of the Justice Department prosecutes cases. This too has varied from period to period.

There are at least two fairly distinct approaches to antitrust policy. One looks primarily and directly at market performance; the other emphasizes market structure. Although there are respected economists in favor of each of these approaches, the second is probably preferred by most experts in this field.

Not all our laws are designed to promote competition and restrict monopoly. On the contrary, some laws are designed to do just the opposite. For example, the patent system confers a temporary monopoly on inventors. And the Robinson-Patman Act and many other laws are designed to restrict competition.

Behavioral Objectives

A. You should be able to define and explain the following key concepts in this chapter:

Market concentration ratio	Tying contract	Market structure
Antitrust laws	Rule of reason	Patent system
Price discrimination	Market performance	Resale price maintenance

B. Make sure that you can do each of the following:

1. State the economic arguments against monopoly, oligopoly, and monopolistic competition on the grounds of resource misallocation.

2. State the arguments for monopoly power put forth by Joseph Schumpeter and John Kenneth Galbraith, and describe the extent to which the available evidence seems to support these arguments.

3. Explain how industrial concentration is measured, and describe the extent of industrial concentration in various sectors of the American economy.

4. Describe the Sherman Act, the Clayton Act, and the Federal Trade Commission Act.

5. Explain the rule of reason, and the changes that have occurred over the past 60 years in the Supreme Court's interpretation of the antitrust laws.

6. Contrast the market performance approach to antitrust policy with the market structure approach.

7. Describe the purpose and nature of the patent system.

8. Describe the Robinson-Patman Act, the Miller-Tydings Act, and other laws aimed at limiting competition in the United States.

9. Indicate the noneconomic arguments against monopoly power and giant firms.

Getting Down to Cases: United States v. E. I. Du Pont de Nemours

In one of the most famous antitrust suits of this century, the government charged Du Pont, the large chemical firm, with "monopolizing, attempting to monopolize and conspiracy to monopolize interstate commerce in cellophane . . . in violation of Section 2 of the Sherman Act." Du Pont produced 75% of the cellophane sold in the United States.

a. Why didn't the government prosecute Du Pont under Section 1 of the Sherman Act?

b. Based on Du Pont's share of the cellophane market, was it clear that Du Pont was in violation of Section 2 of the Sherman Act?

c. The Supreme Court pointed out that, "despite cellophane's advantage, it has to meet competition from other materials in every one of its uses. . . . The overall result is that cellophane accounts for 17.9% of flexible wrapping materials . . ."

How can one tell whether cellophane had to meet competition from other materials, and how stiff this competition was?

d. The Supreme Court also denied that "Du Pont's profits, while liberal . . . demonstrate the existence of a monopoly. . . ." According to the government Du Pont's net profit after taxes was 15.9 percent during the relevant period. How did the Supreme Court come to this conclusion?

e. The Supreme Court decided that Du Pont was not in violation of the Sherman Act. In reaching this decision it pointed to the high cross elasticity of demand existing between cellophane and other flexible packaging materials like pliofilm. Why is this of relevance?

Matching Questions

_____ 1. Automobile industry	A. Outlawed tying contract
_____ 2. Rule of reason	B. Market concentration ratio exceeding 90 percent
_____ 3. Printing industry	C. Used in U.S. Steel case
_____ 4. Market structure criterion	D. Market concentration ratio of less than 10 percent
_____ 5. Miller-Tydings Act	E. Used in Alcoa case
_____ 6. Clayton Act	F. Resale price maintenance

Completion Questions

1. The government (can, cannot) _____ convict firms of violation of the antitrust laws merely by showing that they fixed prices or attempted to do so. The government (does, does not) _____ have to show how much prices were raised. The government (does, does not) _____ have to show what the effects were.

2. The Standard Oil Case, decided in 1911, resulted in _____ _____. The American Tobacco case, decided in 1911, resulted in _____. The U.S. Steel case, decided in 1920, resulted in _____. All of these cases were tried under Section _____ of the _____.

3. The IBM case alleged that IBM has had monopoly power in the market for _____. This case was tried under Section _____ of the _____.

4. While many economists favor the market _____ approach to anti-trust policy, the majority favor the market _____ approach to evaluating undesirable monopolistic characteristics.

5. Many conflicts between the patent system and antitrust policy have been resolved in favor of _____.

6. The market _____ shows the percentage of total sales or production accounted for by the biggest four firms.

7. The _____ outlawed any contract, combination, or conspiracy in restraint of trade and made it illegal to monopolize or attempt to monopolize.

8. If an industry produces up to the point where the social value of an extra unit of the good is more than the cost to society of producing an extra unit, this (is, is not) _____ the socially optimal output rate because a 1-unit (decrease, increase) _____ in the output rate will increase the social value of output by more than the social cost of production.

9. A monopolistic industry produces at a point where the social value of an extra unit of the good (which equals price) is (greater, less) _____ than the cost to society of producing the extra unit (which equals _____ cost).

10. Some economists, like Joseph Schumpeter and John Kenneth Galbraith of Harvard University, have asserted that the rate of technological change is likely to be higher in a(n) _____ competitive industry (i.e., monopoly, oligopoly, etc.) than in a(n) _____ competitive industry.

11. (Contrary to, In accord with) _____ the allegations of Galbraith and others, there is (little, much) _____ evidence that industrial giants are needed in most industries to insure rapid _____ and rapid utilization of new techniques.

True-False

_____ 1. A firm with a 60 percent market share frequently is permitted to go untouched by the antitrust laws, while at the same time 2 firms with 10 percent of a market sometimes are forbidden to merge.

_____ 2. Whether or not price-fixing is illegal depends on the price fixers' share of the market; if their share is small enough, it is not illegal under U.S. law.

_____ 3. If firm A acquires the stock or assets of a competing corporation, this may be illegal based on Section 7 of the Clayton Act, as amended by the Celler-Kefauver Act.

_____ 4. The most important reason why economists oppose monopoly is that monopolists get rich.

_____ 5. Industrial giants are needed in all industries to insure rapid technological change and rapid utilization of new techniques.

_____ 6. In recent years, mergers have often been disallowed by the courts, but not because of the antitrust laws.

_____ 7. The antitrust laws have as yet had no significant effect on business behavior and markets.

_____ 8. The U.S. patent laws grant the inventor exclusive control over the use of his or her invention for 30 years.

_____ 9. The patent system and the antitrust laws tend to push in opposite directions.

_____ 10. If entry is free and rapid, firms in a perfectly competitive industry may have little motivation to innovate.

_____ 11. The profit rate tends to be higher in industries where the concentration ratio is higher.

_____ 12. Monopoly imposes a burden on society by misallocating resources.

_____ 13. Monopoly redistributes income in favor of the monopolists.

_____ 14. Since monopolists do not have to face direct competition, they are likely to be more diligent in controlling costs and in using resources efficiently.

_____ 15. A certain amount of monopoly power is inevitable in practically all real-life situations, since perfect competition is a model that can only be approximated in real life.

_____ 16. Even if General Motors had little power over prices, it would still have considerable economic—and political—power because of its sheer size.

_____ 17. A firm's size is not necessarily a good indicator of the extent of its monopoly power.

_____ 18. It is more difficult to attack existing concentration in an industry than to stop further concentration firms attempt to bring about through merger.

_____ 19. The Robinson-Patman Act says that sellers must not discriminate in price among purchasers of similar grade and quality where the effect might be to drive competitors out of business.

Multiple Choice

1. It is illegal in the United States for rival firms:
   a. to agree to fix prices.
   b. to restrict or pool output.
   c. to share markets on a predetermined basis.
   d. all of the above.
   e. only a and b.

2. It is illegal in the United States for a firm:

    a. to set its price equal to that of one of its competitors.
    b. to merge with a larger firm.
    c. to charge one customer a different price than another under any circumstances.
    d. to license its patents.
    e. none of the above.

3. The most important reason why economists oppose monopoly is that, as compared with perfect competition, monopolists:

    a. reap higher profits.
    b. charge higher prices.
    c. create a misallocation of resources.
    d. are unlikely to be philanthropic.
    e. none of the above.

4. Price tends to exceed marginal cost under:

    a. monopolistic competition.   d. all of the above.
    b. monopoly.   e. none of the above.
    c. oligopoly.

5. Empirical studies indicate that in most industries:

    a. total research and development expenditures would decrease if the largest firms were replaced by somewhat smaller ones.
    b. research and development expenditures carried out by the largest firms are more productive than those carried out by the somewhat smaller ones.
    c. greater concentration of an industry results in a faster diffusion of innovations.
    d. substituting a large number of smaller firms for a few large ones may lead to slower commercial introduction of some innovations.
    e. all of the above.

6. If firms enter into exclusive and tying contracts which substantially lessen competition, this is illegal according to:

    a. Sherman Act, Section 1.   d. Federal Trade Commission Act.
    b. Sherman Act, Section 2.   e. Celler-Kefauver Act.
    c. Clayton Act.

7. If a firm enters into a contract in restraint of trade, this is illegal based on:

    a. Sherman Act, Section 1.   d. Federal Trade Commission Act.
    b. Sherman Act, Section 2.   e. Celler-Kefauver Act.
    c. Clayton Act.

8. The Antitrust Division once sued Bethlehem Steel and Youngstown Sheet and Tube to stop a proposed merger between them. This case was brought under:

    a. Sherman Act, Section 1.
    b. Sherman Act, Section 2.
    c. Robinson-Patman Act.
    d. Federal Trade Commission Act.
    e. Celler-Kefauver Amendment to the Clayton Act.

Discussion and Extension Questions

1. President Reagan's Council of Economic Advisers said that, "There has been a dramatic shift in antitrust policy under this Administration. Enforcement will focus on . . . mergers among dominant firms in an industry, and price-fixing agreements among competing firms." How does this differ from the past? Do you agree with this shift? Why or why not?

2. "It's not fair for the government to have tried to penalize IBM for its success and farsightedness. Why should the government try to break up IBM merely because it is big and prosperous? It seems foolish to dismember one of the most efficient firms in the country." Discuss and evaluate.

3. "In supply and demand analysis, at the equilibrium price the quantity demanded just equals the quantity supplied. Another way of looking at this is that at the equilibrium quantity the value consumers place on the last unit of output just equals the cost to suppliers of providing it. The real case against monopoly is that a monopolist produces at an output where the value to the consumers exceeds the monopolist's cost of production." Do you agree? Why or why not?

4. A few years ago a national magazine ran an article on the increased competition American automobile firms were facing from imported models. The next week a letter to the editor stated that it would be interesting to see if General Motors talked to its engineers or Michigan senators about the problem. What did the reader mean?

5. How would free world trade that allowed the unfettered sales of commodities among nations affect our use of concentration ratios as a measure of market power?

6. According to F. M. Scherer, "The United States, unlike nearly all other industrialized Western nations, has adopted an antitrust policy which holds explicit price-fixing and output-restricting agreements per se illegal, without regard to their reasonableness." Does this policy seem warranted? Why or why not?

7. How does monopoly interfere with the proper functioning of the price system? What are other indictments against monopoly? On what grounds have Schumpeter and Galbraith defended substantial market power by big firms?

8. Does the available evidence indicate that giant firms are required to promote a rapid rate of technological change?

9. Has the United States consistently adopted a policy of promoting competition and controlling monopoly? Explain.

10. Explain the meaning and importance of the rule of reason. Indicate the importance of the Alcoa case. Describe two fairly distinct approaches to antitrust policy.

11. Cite some national policies designed to limit competition and promote monopoly. What are the arguments for the patent system? What are the arguments against the patent system?

Problems

1. When the Aluminum Company of America wanted to acquire the Rome Cable Corporation, this merger was challenged by the government. Each firm's market shares, based on alternative market definitions, are given below:

Definition	Alcoa	Rome
	(percent)	
Bare aluminum conductor wire and cable	32.5	0.3
Insulated aluminum conductor wire and cable	11.6	4.7
Combined aluminum conductor wire and cable	27.8	1.3
All bare conductor wire and cable (aluminum and copper)	10.3	2.0
All insulated conductor wire and cable	0.3	1.3
Combined insulated and bare wire and cable (all metals)	1.8	1.4

   a. Should this merger have been prevented? Why or why not?
   b. In fact, did the Supreme Court prevent the merger?
   c. In fact, did the Supreme Court agree with the district court?

2. Continental Can Company once wanted to merge with the Hazel-Atlas Glass Company. Continental, the second-largest producer of tin cans in the United States, sold about $1/3$ of all tin cans; Hazel-Atlas, the third-largest bottle maker, sold about 1/10 of all glass bottles.

   a. What was the relevant line of commerce?
   b. Should this merger have been prevented? Why or why not?
   c. In fact, did the Supreme Court prevent the merger?

3. a. Continental Can and Hazel-Atlas together accounted for about $1/4$ of the combined glass and metal container market. Bethlehem and Youngstown, two major steel producers, accounted for about 21 percent of the national steel market when they proposed to merge. As noted in an earlier question, this merger was challenged by the Justice Department. Should the two steel companies have been allowed to merge? Why or why not?
   b. According to the companies, Bethlehem sold most of its output in the East, whereas Youngstown sold most of its output in the Midwest. Was this fact of relevance? Why or why not?
   c. In fact, did the district court allow Bethlehem and Youngstown to merge? What reasons did it give for its decision?

4. There are several firms that produce left-handed monkey wrenches. Suppose their sales in 1992 are as follows:

Firm	Sales (millions of dollars)
A	100
B	50
C	40
D	30
E	20
F	5
G	5

a. What is the concentration ratio in the left-handed monkey wrench industry?
b. Would you regard this industry as oligopolistic? Why or why not?
c. Suppose that firm A merges with firm G. What now will be the concentration ratio in this industry?
d. Suppose that, after they merge, firms A and G go out of business. What now will be the concentration ratio in this industry?

5. Firm X, which sells engines, has a uniform price of $500 which it charges all its customers. But after its competitors began to cut their prices in the California market to $400, firm X reduces its price to $400.

a. Does this tend to violate the Clayton Act?
b. If firm X had cut its price to $300, might this tend to violate the Clayton Act?
c. Suppose that firm X decides to purchase enough of the stock of competing firms so that it can exercise control over them to see to it that the price-cutting in the California market stops. Is this legal? If not, what law does it violate?

6. A manufacturer of table salt does not establish the same price for all buyers. Instead, the price varies inversely and substantially with the size of the customer's order. The differences in price are not due to cost differences. The buyers are retail stores, and the large buyers can resell the salt at a lower price than can the small buyers. Is the salt manufacturer's pricing illegal? If so, what law does it violate?

7. We list below a number of U.S. laws, after which we list a number of antitrust provisions. In the blank space before each provision, put the letter corresponding to the U.S. law containing this provision.

A. Sherman Act, Section 1
B. Sherman Act, Section 2
C. Clayton Act
D. Federal Trade Commission Act
E. Celler-Kefauver Act
F. Robinson-Patman Act

_____ a. It is illegal to enter into a contract, combination, or conspiracy in restraint of trade.

_____ b. It is illegal to discriminate among purchasers to an extent that cannot be justified by a difference in cost.

_____ c. It is illegal to use unfair methods of competition.

_____ d. It is illegal to attempt to monopolize trade.

_____ e. It is illegal to enter into exclusive and tying contracts.

_____ f. It is illegal to discriminate among purchases, where the effect might be to drive competitors out of business.

_____ g. It is illegal to employ unfair or deceptive acts or practices.

_____ h. It is illegal to acquire the stock of competing corporations.

Answers

Matching Questions
1. B   2. C   3. D   4. E   5. F   6. A

Completion Questions
1. can, does not, does not   2. the dissolution of Standard Oil, the dissolution of American Tobacco, acquittal, 2, Sherman Act   3. electronic computers, 2, Sherman Act   4. performance, structure   5. the latter   6. concentration ratio   7. Sherman Act   8. is not, increase   9. greater, marginal   10. imperfectly, perfectly   11. Contrary to, little, technological change

True-False
1. True   2. False   3. True   4. False   5. False   6. False   7. False   8. False   9. True   10. True   11. True   12. True   13. True   14. False   15. True   16. True   17. True   18. True   19. True

Multiple Choice
1. d   2. e   3. c   4. d   5. d   6. c   7. a   8. e

Problems
1. The Supreme Court ruled against the merger, whereas the district court permitted it.
2. The district court said cans and bottles were separate lines of commerce, but the Supreme Court emphasized the competition between cans and bottles. The Supreme Court ruled against the merger.
3. a. The district court ruled against the merger.
   b. The court held that transportation costs were small enough so that competition on a national basis was practical.
   c. No. It said the merger would make "even more remote than at present the possibility of any real competition from the smaller members of the industry who follow the leadership of United States Steel (now USX)."
4. a. $220/250 = 88$ percent.
   b. Yes, because the concentration ratio is so high.
   c. 90 percent.
   d. $140/145 = 97$ percent.
5. a. No.
   b. It might be charged that firm X was discriminating to a greater degree than was justified to meet competition.
   c. No. The Celler-Kefauver Act.
6. Yes. The Robinson-Patman Act.
7. a. A
   b. C
   c. D
   d. B
   e. C
   f. F
   g. D
   h. E

Determinants of Wages

Chapter Profile

Under perfect competition, a firm will employ each type of labor in an amount such that its marginal product times the product's price equals its wage. In other words, the firm will employ enough labor so that the value of the marginal product of labor equals labor's price.

The firm's demand curve for labor—which shows, for each price of labor, the amount of labor the firm will use—is the firm's value-of-marginal-product curve (if labor is the only variable input). The market demand curve for labor shows the relationship between its price and the total amount of labor demanded in the market.

Labor's price depends on its market supply curve as well as on its market demand curve. Labor's market supply curve is the relationship between the price of labor and the total amount of labor supplied in the market. Labor's market supply curve may be backward bending.

An input's price is determined under perfect competition in essentially the same way that a product's price is determined: by supply and demand. The price of labor will tend in equilibrium to the level at which the quantity of labor demanded equals the quantity of labor supplied. By the same token, the equilibrium amount of labor utilized is also given by the intersection of the market supply and demand curves.

If there are qualitative differences among workers, the differential in their wages will correspond to the differential in their marginal products. Some of the differences in the wage rates workers receive are due to differences in ability. However, even if all workers were of equal ability, there would still be differences in wage rates to offset differences in the characteristics of various occupations, such as the cost of training and stability of earnings, and in geographical areas, such as variations in the cost of living.

Workers may invest in their own education to signal employers that they are able. A worker may pursue his or her interests and neglect the goals of the employer. To help induce workers to promote the aims of the firm, bonus payment systems are often instituted by employers.

The biggest unions in the United States are the National Education Association, the Teamsters, and the Food and Commercial Workers. Each national union is composed of local unions, which operate within the context of the constitution of the national union.

The AFL-CIO is a federation of national unions created by the merger in 1955 of the American Federation of Labor and the Congress of Industrial Organizations. The AFL-CIO is a very important spokesman for the American labor movement, but because the national unions in the AFL-CIO have given up relatively little of their power to the federation, its authority is limited.

There are several ways that unions can increase wages—by shifting the supply curve of labor to the left, by shifting the demand curve for labor to the right, and by influencing the wage directly.

Collective bargaining is the process of negotiation between union and management over wages and working conditions. An agreement generally specifies the extent and kind of recognition that management gives the union—such as the closed shop, union shop, or open shop. In addition, it specifies the level of wage rates for particular jobs, the length of the workweek, the rate of overtime pay, the extent to which seniority will determine which workers will be first to be laid off, the nature and extent of management's prerogatives, and how grievances between workers and the employer will be handled. The union's power is based to a considerable extent on its right to strike.

Behavioral Objectives

A. You should be able to define and explain the following key concepts in this chapter:

Firm's demand curve for labor	Backward-bending supply curve	Congress of Industrial Organizations
Value of the marginal product of labor	Noncompeting groups	Featherbedding
Market demand curve for labor	Monopsony	Collective bargaining
Derived demand	National union	Closed shop
Market supply curve for labor	Local union	Union shop
	American Federation of Labor	Open shop
	Industrial union	Strike

B. Make sure that you can do each of the following:

1. Explain what economists mean by the labor force and the price of labor.

2. Indicate how, under perfect competition, the firm's demand curve for labor can be derived, given the firm's production function and the price of the product.

3. Cite the principal factors determining the shape of the supply curve for labor.

4. Indicate how the equilibrium price and quantity of labor can be determined, given the market demand and supply curves for labor.

5. Explain why wage differentials occur among workers of various kinds, among occupations, and among areas.

6. Indicate how, under monopsony, the equilibrium price and quantity of labor can be determined.

7. Describe how education is used by workers as a signaling device.

8. Indicate the nature of principal-agent problems in the labor market, and how bonus payments can be used to help induce workers to further the aims of the firm.

9. Use supply and demand curves to indicate three ways that unions can increase wages.

Getting Down to Cases: Salaries on the Diamond

In the early days of baseball, every player was free to sign with any team at the end of the season. Owners of baseball teams found themselves bidding up the price of players, and watched stars switch teams. At a secret meeting in 1879, they agreed that each team could protect five of its players from being hired away.

   a. Before 1879, what factors governed the wage of a baseball player?

   b. After 1879, what factors governed the wage of the five players that a team could protect?

   c. What was the effect of the 1879 agreement on the wage of baseball players?

By 1890, the owners had extended their agreement to include all baseball players. Every player on every team had to work for the team they signed their first contracts with—or leave baseball. The team could trade a player to another team, but the player could not switch teams. Then, in 1975, two pitchers, Dave McNally of the Montreal Expos and Andy Messersmith of the Los Angeles Dodgers, challenged this arrangement. A legal battle ensued.

   d. What arguments do you think that the owners made in support of the existing arrangements?

   e. What arguments do you think that the players made against these arrangements?

   f. Eventually, the rules governing the hiring of baseball players were changed. Players were allowed to declare themselves free agents, and other teams were allowed to bid for their services. Using the concepts described in this chapter, show the likely effect of this change on the wage of a baseball player.

   g. From the mid-1970s to the early 1980s, the average player's salary more than tripled. Is this in accord with your prediction in part f?

Matching Questions

_____ 1. Noncompeting groups   A. Bonus payments

_____ 2. Education   B. Outlawed closed shop

_____ 3. Principal-agent problem   C. Lawyers and surgeons

_____ 4. AFL-CIO   D. Lane Kirkland

_____ 5. Taft-Hartley Act   E. Neglect of employer's interests

_____ 6. Incentive system   F. Signal

Completion Questions

1. In competitive firm X, the marginal product of the first unit of labor is 3 units of output, the marginal product of the second unit of labor is 2 units of output, and the marginal product of the third unit of labor is 1 unit of output. If the price of a unit

of output is $15, the firm will demand _____ unit(s) of labor when the price of a unit of labor is $40, _____ unit(s) of labor when the price of a unit of labor is $25, and _____ unit(s) of labor when the price of a unit of labor is $20.

2. A perfectly competitive firm's demand curve for labor slopes downward and to the right because of the law of _____. This is because the firm's demand curve for labor is the same as its _____ curve, and the _____ is equal to the price of the product times the marginal product of labor.

3. To a monopsonist, the cost of hiring an additional laborer (decreases, increases) _____ as it hires more and more labor. The cost of hiring an additional laborer (exceeds, equals, is less than)_____ the wage that must be paid this worker. For example, if the monopsonist can hire 10 workers at a daily wage of $35 and 11 workers at a daily wage of $40, the cost of hiring the eleventh worker is _____ , as compared with the wage of the eleventh worker, which is _____.

4. The profit-maximizing competitive firm uses each input in an amount such that the input's _____ multiplied by the _____ equals the input's _____.

5. Since inputs are demanded to produce other things, the demand for labor and other inputs is called a(n) _____ demand.

6. Labor's _____ is the relationship between the price of labor and the total amount of labor supplied in the market.

7. _____ is a market structure where there is a single buyer.

8. The supreme governing body of the national union is the _____.

9. As Michael Spence and others have pointed out, education is often used as a _____ by job applicants and employers.

10. A _____ problem may exist because workers pursue their own goals, not those of their employer.

11. Trying to restrict output per worker in order to increase the amount of labor required to do a certain job is called _____.

12. If profit is maximized, the monopsonistic firm will hire labor up to the point at which the extra cost of adding a(n) _____ laborer equals the extra revenue from adding the _____ laborer. The wage rate, as well as the quantity hired, is (higher, lower) _____ under monopsony than under perfect competition.

13. In a(n) _____ shop a worker must be a union member before he or she can be hired. This gives the union more power than a(n) _____ shop, in which the employer can hire nonunion workers who must then become union members in a certain length of time after being hired. In a(n) _____ shop, the employer can hire both union and nonunion workers, and the latter need not join a union once employed.

True-False

_____ 1. If a technological change occurs which increases the marginal productivity of labor, and if at the same time the supply curve of labor shifts to the right, the price of labor must fall.

_____ 2. If a union shifts the supply curve of labor to the left, and if the price elasticity of demand for labor is infinite, the price of labor will rise.

_____ 3. All unions are organizations of workers in a particular trade or occupation.

_____ 4. If the value of the marginal product is greater than the input's price, the perfectly competitive firm can increase its profit by decreasing its utilization of the input.

_____ 5. An example of a backward-bending supply curve might be that for labor.

_____ 6. The differential in wages between skilled and unskilled laborers of the same type will be due, at least in part, to the differential in their marginal products.

_____ 7. The amount of money needed for an all-volunteer army was determined solely on the basis of the market demand curve.

_____ 8. In the United States about $2/3$ of the people employed are white-collar workers (such as salespeople, doctors, secretaries, or managers) and service workers (such as waiters, bartenders, or cooks), while only about $1/3$ are blue-collar workers (such as carpenters, mine workers, or foremen) and farm workers.

_____ 9. A firm's demand curve for an input shows the relationship between the input's price and the amount of the input utilized by the firm. That is, it shows, for each price, the amount of the input that the firm will use.

_____ 10. Beyond some point, increases in wages may result in smaller amounts of labor being supplied.

_____ 11. The reason for a backward-bending supply curve for labor is that, as the price of labor increases, the individual supplying the labor becomes richer and wants to increase his or her amount of leisure time.

_____ 12. The wage for surgeons is higher than for unskilled labor because the demand curve for surgeons is farther to the right and the supply curve for surgeons is farther to the left than the corresponding curves for unskilled labor.

_____ 13. Wage differentials cannot be expected to persist among noncompeting groups because people can move from the low-paid to the high-paid jobs.

_____ 14. Holding the unemployment rate constant, the proportion of the male population that enlists is directly related to the level of military pay (as a percent of civilian pay).

_____ 15. Under perfect competition, the supply curve of labor to an individual firm is a horizontal line.

_____ 16. If the marginal product of an 18-year-old with job experience is twice that of an 18-year-old without job experience, and if the wage for 18-year-olds with experience is 40 percent above the minimum wage, 18-year-olds without experience will not find work.

Multiple Choice

1. Suppose that the production function of a hypothetical competitive firm is as follows:

Number of workers employed per day	Output per day
1	0
2	5
3	20
4	35
5	38

   If the value of the marginal product of a worker is $150 when between 2 and 3 workers are employed per day, the price of a unit of output must be:

   a. $1,000.
   b. $100.
   c. $20.
   d. $10.
   e. none of the above.

2. The price elasticity of demand for a particular input will be greater:

   a. the more easily other inputs can be substituted for it.
   b. the smaller the price elasticity of demand for the product the input helps to produce.
   c. in the short run than in the long run.
   d. all of the above.
   e. none of the above.

3. If the supply curve is backward bending, increases in price (beyond some point) may result in _____ of the input being supplied.

   a. amounts increasing quickly to zero
   b. an imaginary quantity
   c. smaller amounts
   d. a negative amount
   e. none of the above

4. In a national union, the authority to set policy for the union is held by the:

   a. federal government.
   b. local union's officers.
   c. delegates to the convention.
   d. federation.
   e. all of the above.

5. The share of the income going to labor in the United States has been

   a. declining markedly.
   b. failing to decline
   c. subject to great variation, going from 10 to 90 percent.
   d. precisely constant.
   e. none of the above.

6. It makes perfectly good sense for a labor union to want to:

   a. maximize the wage rate.
   b. maximize its marginal revenue.
   c. keep its members fully employed.
   d. all of the above.
   e. none of the above.

Discussion and Extension Questions

1. According to *Business Week,* quarterbacks in the National Football League earn about twice as much as offensive linemen (when players are at the sixth-year level). Why does this wage differential exist? Pro football salaries are about half of those in pro baseball and basketball. What factors help to account for this difference?

2. One study suggests that union workers have over the last several decades earned wages that are 10 to 20 percent higher than the wages paid to nonunion labor. Does that imply that wages in the United States would, on average, be lower if there were no unions?

3. How might a consumer boycott of grapes or lettuce work to the detriment of Mexican-American farm laborers in California?

4. "Keynes regarded wages as fixed; Milton Friedman regards them as flexible. Neither is really correct, and it is important that unions, with their immense power, be willing to settle for limited wage increases to prevent ruinous inflation. Unfortunately, there is no evidence they will do so." Discuss and evaluate.

5. "Unions of state and local workers have far too much power. They can shut down entire regions." Comment and evaluate.

6. "Labor unions are no longer of any consequence. They were beaten by the conservative governments of the 1980s and early 1990s." Comment and evaluate.

7. Describe three ways that unions can increase wages. Give examples where each has occurred.

8. If you were an employer, would you prefer a closed shop, an open shop, or a union shop? Why? Which would you prefer if you were president of the union? Why?

Problems

1. Suppose that the demand curve for lawyers is as follows:

Annual wage (thousands of dollars)	Quantity of labor demanded (thousands of person-years)
30	200
45	180
60	160
75	140
90	120
105	100
120	80

a. Draw the demand curve for lawyers.

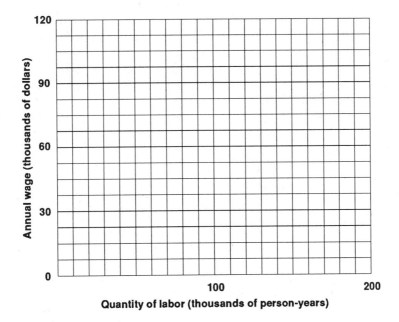

b. Suppose that the supply curve for lawyers is as follows:

Annual wage (thousands of dollars)	Quantity of labor supplied (thousands of person-years)
30	80
45	100
60	120
75	140
90	160
105	180
120	200

Draw the supply curve for lawyers on the graph for part a.

c. What is the equilibrium wage for lawyers if the market is perfectly competitive?
d. Suppose that lawyers form a union, and that the union forces the wage up to $105,000 a year. How many person-years of labor will be supplied but will be unable to find work?

2. Suppose that the relationship between the number of laborers employed per day in a car wash and the number of cars washed per day is as follows:

Number of laborers	Cars washed
1	15
2	40
3	50
4	55

a. Suppose that the owner of the car wash receives $2 for each car wash, and that the price of labor is $20 per day. How many laborers will the owner hire per day?
b. What is the value of the marginal product of labor when between 1 and 2 laborers per day are used? When between 2 and 3 laborers per day are used? When between 3 and 4 laborers per day are used?
c. If the owner of the car wash hires 3 laborers per day, does the value of the marginal product of labor equal the wage?

3. Suppose that the Ace Manufacturing Company is a member of a perfectly competitive industry. Suppose that the relationship between various amounts of labor input and output is as shown below.

Product price (dollars)	Units of labor	Units of output	Marginal product of labor	Value of marginal product (dollars)
10	0	0		
10	1	$2\frac{1}{2}$	_____	_____
10	2	5	_____	_____
10	3	7	_____	_____
10	4	8	_____	_____

a. Fill in the blanks.
b. If you are told that the Ace Manufacturing Company is hiring 3 units of labor, you can establish a range for the value of the wage rate prevailing in the labor market (assuming that the firm maximizes profit). What is this range? Specifically, what is the maximum value that the wage (for a unit of labor) may be? What is the minimum value? Why?
c. Suppose that the Ace Manufacturing Company must pay $20 for a unit of labor. How many units of labor will it hire? Why?

d. In the graph below, draw the Ace Manufacturing Company's demand curve for labor.

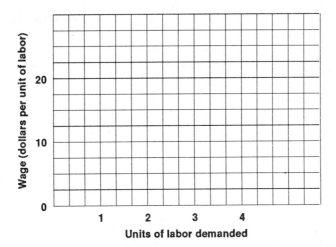

e. Suppose that the Ace Manufacturing Company were a monopsonist rather than a perfectly competitive firm. Do you think it would pay a higher, a lower, or the same wage? Why?

4. The demand and supply curves for musicians in a particular area in 1991 are as shown below.

a. If a union makes the users of musicians demand 50 percent more hours per week of musicians' time than in 1991 at each wage rate, draw the new demand curve in the graph.

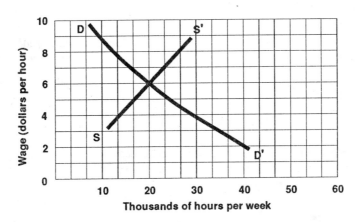

b. After the union shifts the demand curve, perhaps due to featherbedding, what will be the new equilibrium wage? What will be the new equilibrium quantity employed?

5. A perfectly competitive firm has the following value-of-marginal-product curve:

Number of units of labor per day	Value of marginal product (dollars)
1	52
2	47
3	42
4	37
5	32
6	

a. If there are 1,000 firms, all of which have the same value-of-marginal-product curve, the market demand curve for labor is as follows:

Price of labor per day (dollars)	Number of units of labor demanded per day
50	_____
45	_____
40	_____
35	_____

Fill in the blanks above. (Assume that only integer numbers of units of labor can be used.)

b. The supply curve for labor is as follows:

Price of labor per day (dollars)	Number of units of labor supplied per day
35	3,000
40	4,000
45	5,000
50	6,000

What is the equilibrium price of a unit of labor per day?

c. What will be the total amount of labor demanded in the market? What will be the amount demanded by each firm?

d. What will be the extra cost that a firm would incur if it added an extra unit of labor per day?

e. What will be the value of the marginal product of labor for this firm?
f. If a minimum wage of $45 per day were established, what would be the total amount of labor demanded in the market?

6. Firm R, a monopsonist, confronts the supply curve for labor shown below:

Wage rate per hour (dollars)	Number of units of labor supplied per hour	Cost of adding an additional unit of labor per hour (dollars)
3	1	
4	2	_____
5	3	_____
6	4	_____
7	5	_____
8	6	_____

a. Fill in the blanks. (Assume that only integer numbers of units of labor can be used.)
b. Firm R's demand curve for labor is a horizontal line at a wage rate of $8 per hour. What quantity of labor will firm R demand?
c. What will be the equilibrium wage rate?
d. If this were a perfectly competitive labor market, what would be the equilibrium quantity of labor demanded? What would be the equilibrium price?

7. Firm Z, a monopsonist, confronts the supply curve for labor shown below; its demand curve for labor is as shown below:

Supply curve of labor		Demand curve for labor	
Wage rate per hour (dollars)	Number of units of labor supplied per hour	Wage rate per hour (dollars)	Number of units of labor demanded per hour
5	1	9	1
6	2	8	2
7	3	7	3
8	4	6	4
9	5	5	5

a. Firm Z is organized by a union, which demands a wage rate of $9 per hour. Firm Z agrees because it cannot afford a strike. What amount of labor will firm Z demand? What will be the equilibrium wage rate?
b. In the absence of the union, what amount of labor would firm Z demand? What would be the equilibrium wage rate?

Answers

Matching Questions

1. C   2. F   3. E   4. D   5. B   6. A

Completion Questions

1. 1, 2, 2   2. diminishing marginal returns, value-of-marginal-product, value of the marginal product   3. increases, exceeds, $90, $40   4. marginal product, product's price, price   5. derived   6. market supply curve   7. Monopsony   8. convention   9. signal   10. principal-agent   11. featherbedding   12. additional, additional, lower   13. closed, union, open

True-False

1. False   2. False   3. False   4. False   5. True   6. True   7. False
8. True   9. True   10. True   11. True   12. True   13. False
14. True   15. True   16. True

Multiple Choice

1. d   2. a   3. c   4. c   5. b   6. c

Problems

1. a.

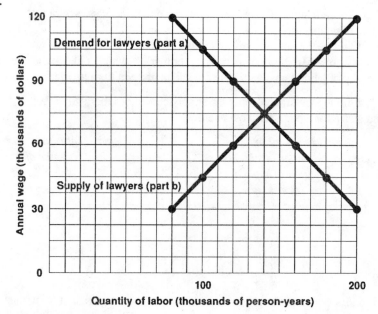

b.   See answer on the graph for part a.
c. $75,000.
d.   80,000.
2. a.   2 or 3.
b. $50, $20, $10.
c.   Yes.

3. a.

Marginal product of labor	Value of marginal product (dollars)
$2\frac{1}{2}$	25
$2\frac{1}{2}$	25
2	20
1	10

   b. The wage must be between $10 and $20, because if it were more than $20, the firm would hire only 2 units of labor, and because if it were less than $10, the firm would hire 4 units of labor.

   c. 3 units of labor or 2 units of labor. Because this will maximize its profit.

   d.

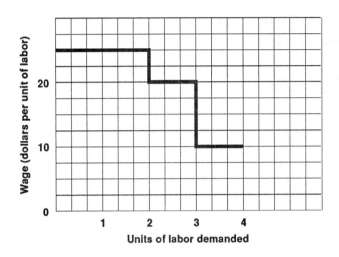

   e. A lower wage, for reasons given in the section of the text on "Monopsony."

4. a.

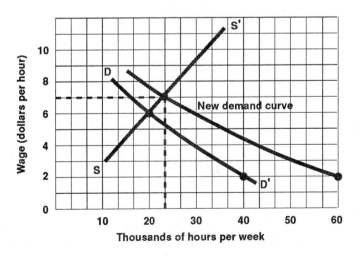

   b. About $7. About 23,000 hours per week.

5. a.

*Number of units of labor
demanded per day*

2,000
3,000
4,000
5,000

b. $40.
c. 4,000 units, 4 units.
d. $40.
e. $42.
f. 3,000 units.

6. a.

*Cost of adding an additional
unit of labor per hour (dollars)*

5
7
9
11
13

b. 3 units per hour.
c. $5.
d. 6 units per hour, $8.

7. a. 1 unit of labor per hour, $9.
b. 2 units of labor per hour, $6.

CHAPTER 14

Interest, Rent, and Profits

Chapter Profile

Interest is a payment for the use of money. Interest rates vary a great deal, depending on the nature of the borrower and the type and riskiness of the loan.

The pure interest rate—the interest rate on riskless loans—is, like any competitive price, determined by the interaction of supply and demand. However, because of the influence of the government on both the demand and supply sides of the market, it is clear that the pure interest rate is to a considerable extent a matter of public policy. One very important function of interest rates is to allocate the supply of loanable funds.

Capital is composed of inputs produced by the economic system itself. Our economy uses very roundabout methods of production and devotes a considerable amount of its productive capacity to the production of capital. If more and more capital is produced during a particular period, consumers must cut further and further into their consumption during that period.

In a capitalist system, each capital good has a market value that can be determined by capitalizing its earnings. Any piece of capital has a rate of return, which indicates its net productivity. An asset's rate of return is the interest rate earned on the investment in the asset. Holding constant an asset's annual return, the asset's worth is higher, the lower the rate of return available on other investments. If firms maximize profits, they must carry out all projects where the rate of return exceeds the interest rate at which they can borrow.

Rent is the return derived by inputs that are fixed in supply. Since the supply of the input is fixed, its price can be lowered without influencing the amount supplied. It is important to know whether a certain payment is a rent, because a reduction of the payment will not influence the availability and use of the input if the payment is a rent. If it is not a rent, however, a reduction of the payment is likely to change the allocation of resources. Thus, if the government imposes taxes on rents, there will be no effect on the supply of resources to the economy.

Another important type of property income is profits. Available statistics on profits are based on the accountant's concept, not the economist's, with the result that they include the opportunity costs of the labor, capital, and land contributed by the owners of the firm.

Two of the important factors responsible for the existence of profits are innovation and uncertainty: profits are the rewards earned by innovators and a payment for risk-bearing. Still another reason for the existence of profits is monopoly power; due to contrived scarcity, profits are made by firms in imperfectly competitive markets.

Behavioral Objectives

A. You should be able to define and explain the following key concepts in this chapter:

Rate of interest	Supply curve for loanable	Capitalization
Pure rate of interest	funds	Land
Demand curve for loanable	Capital budgeting	Rent
funds	Primary inputs	Innovator
Rate of return	Capital	Risk
	Saving	

B. Make sure that you can do each of the following:

1. Describe the demand for loanable funds, the supply of loanable funds, and the determination of the equilibrium rate of interest.

2. Describe the government's influence on the supply curve for loanable funds, and how this influences the interest rate.

3. Indicate how the equilibrium rate of interest is determined, given the demand curve and supply curve for loanable funds.

4. Explain the social functions of the interest rate, and why, even in Communist economies, something like an interest rate must be used.

5. Define an asset's rate of return and explain the principles of capital budgeting.

6. Explain how capitalization can be used to calculate an asset's worth, and how one can compute the present value of a future dollar.

7. Define rent, and explain and evaluate Henry George's argument that rents should be taxed away by the government.

8. Define economic profits, and state the major reasons why they exist.

9. Explain the social function of profit in a capitalist economy.

Getting Down to Cases: Shopping for a Machine Tool

The Martin Tool and Die Company is deciding whether to buy a numerically controlled machine tool or a conventional machine tool. The price of the numerically controlled machine tool is $100,000, while the price of the conventional machine tool is $40,000. Each machine tool is estimated to have a life of five years, after which the scrap value is zero. Each machine tool produces the same quantity (and quality) of output, but the numerically controlled machine tool requires $15,000 less labor per year. In all other respects, the cost of the two machines are the same.

    a. If the Martin Tool and Die Company buys the numerically controlled machine tool (rather than the conventional machine tool), how much more or less will its cash inflow be now, one year from now, and so on? Fill in the blanks below.

Number of years hence	Difference in cash inflow
0	_____
1	_____
2	_____
3	_____
4	_____
5	_____

b. If the interest rate is 10 percent, which machine tool should the Martin Tool and Die Company purchase? Why?

c. If the interest rate is 8 percent, which machine tool should the Martin Tool and Die Company purchase? Why?

d. Based on the above information, can we be sure that the Martin Tool and Die Company should purchase either machine tool? Why or why not?

e. The vice president of manufacturing of the Martin Tool and Die Company says that, if the conventional machine tool is purchased, the rate of return on the investment will be 35 percent. But he is against the purchase of either new machine because the old machine that would be replaced still has several years of useful life. Do you agree? Why or why not?

Matching Questions

_____ 1. Land

_____ 2. Capital budgeting

_____ 3. Capitalization

_____ 4. Frank Knight

_____ 5. Henry George

_____ 6. Rent

A. Intrafirm allocation of investment funds

B. Payment above minimum required to attract amount of input

C. Single tax

D. Computing an asset's worth

E. Fixed in supply

F. Uncertainty as explanation of profit

Completion Questions

1. Mr. Smith buys a bond for $1,000. If the bond pays interest of $50 per year indefinitely, the interest is _____ percent. If the price of the bond increases to $1,500, the interest rate is _____ percent. If the price of the bond falls to $500, the interest rate is _____ percent.

2. If the interest rate is 10 percent, a dollar received a year from now is currently worth _____ , and a dollar received 2 years from now is currently worth

_____ . Thus, a business venture that will pay you both a dollar a year from now and a dollar 2 years from now is currently worth _____ .

3. If the present value of a dollar received 2 years from now is 85.7 cents, the interest rate must be _____ percent. If the present value of $2 received 3 years from now is $1.78, the interest rate must be _____ percent. If the interest rate is more than _____ percent, one dollar received 20 years from now is worth less than 15 cents now.

4. Interest rates vary as a function of the loan's _____ , its _____ , and the cost of _____ .

5. The equilibrium pure interest rate is given by the intersection of the _____ and _____ curves for loanable funds.

6. Holding an asset's annual returns constant, the asset's worth is higher, the (lower, higher) _____ the rate of return available on other investments.

7. _____ is a process of computing an asset's worth.

8. The _____ for loanable funds is the relationship between the quantity of loanable funds supplied and the pure interest rate.

9. Increases in the interest rate tend to (increase, reduce) _____ aggregate investment, thereby (increasing, reducing) _____ gross national product.

10. The price of an input which has a fixed supply is _____ . A(n) _____ is a payment above the minimum necessary to attract this amount of the input.

11. Were the government to impose a tax on rents, there would be (some, no) _____ effect on the supply of resources to the economy. Because he felt rent was _____ and the supply of land (would, would not) _____ be affected by such a tax, Henry George felt that it was justifiable to _____ rent.

12. Critics of George's position argued that land can be improved; thus the supply (is, is not) _____ completely price-inelastic. They further argued that if land rents are _____ , many other kinds of income are likewise.

13. In the accountant's definition, the money the owner of a firm has left after paying wages, interest, and rent, and after providing proper allowance for the depreciation of buildings and equipment, is _____ . The economist's definition differs in that he or she would also deduct the _____ costs of the labor, capital, and land contributed by the owner.

True-False

_____ 1. If Pennsylvania has a usury law that puts a limit of 10 percent on interest rates, and if a bond yielding $100 per year indefinitely is selling for $800 on Wall Street, the quantity of loanable funds supplied is likely to be less than the quantity of loanable funds demanded in Pennsylvania.

_____ 2. If the Federal Reserve pursues a policy of easy money, and at the same time profitable new investment opportunities open up, the equilibrium quantity of loanable funds will increase.

_____ 3. The pure rate of interest is the rate on a riskless loan.

_____ 4. If the firm maximizes profit, it will accept investments where the interest rate exceeds the rate of return.

_____ 5. Interest rates serve to allocate the supply of loanable funds.

_____ 6. If a firm borrows money to buy equipment at an interest cost that is less than the rate of return from the equipment, it will lose money.

_____ 7. Capital budgeting refers to decisions concerning a firm's choice of investment projects.

_____ 8. One reason for the existence of profits is "contrived scarcity" due to monopoly power.

_____ 9. Before taxes, corporation profits average about 50 percent of gross national income.

_____ 10. A very large demand for loanable funds stems from firms which want to borrow money to invest in capital goods like machine tools, buildings, and so forth.

_____ 11. An asset's rate of return is the interest rate earned on the investment in the asset.

_____ 12. The lower the interest rate, the smaller the amount firms will be willing to borrow.

_____ 13. The government is an important factor on the demand side of the market for loanable funds, because it is a big borrower.

_____ 14. In the Middle Ages church law outlawed usury, even though interest continued to be charged.

_____ 15. Although interest is sometimes represented as a product of greedy capitalists, even socialist and Communist economies must use something like an interest rate to help allocate funds.

_____ 16. Labor and land are often called the primary inputs because they are produced outside the economic system.

_____ 17. The process by which people give up a claim on present consumption goods in order to receive consumption goods in the future is called saving.

_____ 18. According to Karl Marx, "surplus value," which includes what we would call profit, is a measure of, and consequence of, exploitation of labor by owners of firms.

_____ 19. Clearly, monopoly profits are socially justified.

Multiple Choice

1. Mrs. X can either pay $50 now (for the coming year) and $50 a year from now (for the next year) for a service that protects against termites. Alternatively, she can pay $100 now (for the coming two years) for this service. Mrs. X should be indifferent between these two alternatives if the rate of interest is:

   a. zero.
   b. 2 percent.
   c. 5 percent.
   d. 10 percent.
   e. none of the above.

2. In the previous question, if the rate of interest is 10 percent, the cost of the second alternative exceeds that of the first alternative by:

   a. zero.
   b. $4.55.
   c. −$5.00.
   d. $5.00.
   e. none of the above.

3. In question 1, if the rate of interest is 8 percent, Mrs. X should be indifferent between the first alternative and paying _____ now (for the coming two years) for this service.

   a. $96.00
   b. $96.30
   c. $100.00
   d. $104.00
   e. none of the above

4. The proportion of national income going to proprietors has:

   a. decreased slightly.
   b. decreased markedly.
   c. increased slightly.
   d. increased markedly.
   e. stayed the same.

5. The largest of the following five income categories in the United States is:

   a. proprietor's income.
   b. corporate profits.
   c. interest.
   d. wages and salaries.
   e. rent.

6. The so-called primary inputs are:

   a. labor and land.
   b. labor and capital.
   c. land and capital.
   d. all of the above.
   e. none of the above.

7. Suppose that the rate of return on alternative investments is 6 percent, and that a particular asset will yield $1,500 per year indefinitely. The asset is worth:

   a. $9,000.
   b. $25,000.
   c. $90,000.
   d. $250,000.
   e. $100,000.

8. If a firm maximizes profit, the rate of return of the least productive project that is accepted by the firm must be _____ the interest rate at which the firm can borrow.

   a. less than
   b. ¹/₂
   c. greater than or equal to
   d. twice
   e. less than or equal to

9. Profits are:

   a. a reward for efficiency.
   b. an incentive for innovation.
   c. an indicator of where resources are needed.
   d. all of the above.
   e. none of the above.

Discussion and Extension Questions

1. "Interest rates are set largely by New York financiers and Washington politicians, not by the market. To a considerable extent, they are set to maximize the profits of the big banks, who control much of the American economy." Discuss and evaluate.

2. "Money really doesn't produce anything. You can stick a dollar bill in the earth, and it won't grow. You can't wear it or eat it. Why should it receive any return? Interest is merely a trick to obtain unearned income for the moneyed classes." Discuss and evaluate.

3. Suppose your paternalistic (and rich) uncle promises you a gift of $10,000 when you "grow up," which he defines as ten years from right now. If the interest rate is currently 6 percent, and it is expected to remain at that level, how much could he give you now instead of $10,000 ten years from now, so that the two gifts would have equal value?

4. What is the relationship between the concept of rent and the concept of opportunity cost?

5. Define what is meant by the rate of interest. What difference, if any, is there between interest and usury?

6. What is the relationship between the riskiness of a loan and the rate of interest?

7. What are the social functions of the interest rate?

8. If the government imposes a tax on economic rent, will this affect the supply of resources to the economy? Why or why not?

9. Describe Joseph Schumpeter's concept of profit. How is it related to his view of the process of economic growth? Describe Frank Knight's concept of profit. How does it differ from Schumpeter's?

Problems

1. Suppose that the demand curve for loanable funds in the United States is as follows:

Interest rate (percent)	Quantity of loanable funds (billions of dollars)
4	60
6	50
8	40
10	30
12	20

   a. Draw the demand curve:

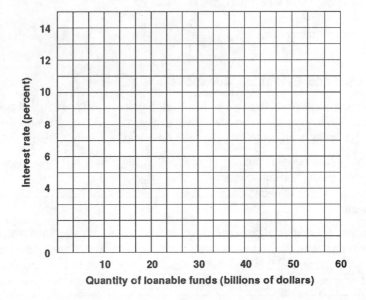

   b. Suppose that the existing supply of loanable funds in the United States is $40 billion. What is the equilibrium interest rate, given the data presented above?
   c. If the interest rate is the one indicated in part b, what is the worth of an asset that yields $1,000 a year permanently?
   d. If the interest rate is the one indicated in part b, and if you are considering investing your money in an investment with a rate of return of 7 percent, should you accept the investment? Why or why not?

2. Using the table in the text (p. 281), determine what the monthly mortgage payment will be if:

   a. The interest rate is 10 percent, the mortgage is $50,000, and it extends for 30 years.

b. The interest rate is 8 percent, the mortgage is $20,000, and it extends for 20 years.

c. The interest rate is 7 percent, the mortgage is $30,000, and it extends for 25 years.

3. Suppose that the supply curve for a particular type of mineral is as shown below:

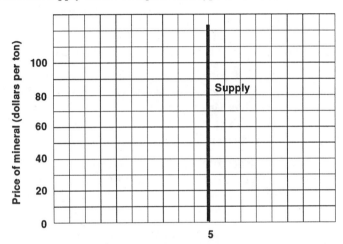

a. Is the price of this mineral a rent?

b. Suppose that a tax of $2 per ton is imposed on the producers of this mineral. What effect will this have on the quantity supplied? Does the answer depend on the demand curve for the mineral?

4. Suppose that the Jones Construction Company can borrow money at 15 percent per year and that it is willing to accept only those (riskless) investments that yield 20 percent per year or more. Is this firm maximizing profit?

5. Suppose that the Jones Construction Company has the following investment opportunities:

Rate of return (percent)	Amount of money the firm can invest at the given rate of return (millions of dollars)
35	5
30	10
25	8
20	9
17	4

a. If it has to pay 15 percent interest, which investment opportunities should it accept?

b. How much less should it invest in these projects if it has to pay 18 percent interest?

6. Mr. Smith buys a very long-term bond that pays annual interest of $50 per year. It is a 5 percent bond that has a face value of $1,000. Mr. Smith bought it in 1955

when the prevailing interest rate was 5 percent, and he paid $1,000 for it. In 1982, the prevailing interest rate was about 10 percent. Approximately how much was the bond worth then?

7. a. Suppose that you will receive $10,000 in three years. How much is it worth now? (Assume that the interest rate is 6 percent.)
   b. How much is it worth to you to get the $10,000 one year earlier—that is, in two years, not three?

8. Mr. Q owns 100 acres of farm land which he rents at $100 per acre.

   a. If the interest rate is 10 percent, how much is Mr. Q's land worth?
   b. Because of a fall in the price of wheat, Mr. Q can rent his land for only $75 per acre. Now how much is Mr. Q's land worth?
   c. Oil is found on Mr. Q's property, the result being that he can rent his land for $400 an acre. Now how much is Mr. Q's land worth?

9. Ms. Q, if she does not undergo any further training, can expect to earn $25,000 per year for the indefinite future. If she takes this year off and goes to school rather than works, she can expect to earn $26,000 a year for the indefinite future. The school is free, but she will not be able to work at all while going to school.

   a. If Ms. Q expects to live and work forever, what rate of return will she earn from this investment in her own education?
   b. Suppose that Ms. Q can obtain 10 percent on alternative investment opportunities. Is this investment worthwhile?
   c. To make this investment worthwhile, how much must she be able to earn per year after the year in school?

10. Firm X must choose between investing in machine A and machine B. The machines do exactly the same work but their purchase prices and maintenance costs differ. The purchase price of machine A is $10,000, while the purchase price of machine B is $5,000. The maintenance cost each year with machine A is $1,000, while the maintenance cost each year with machine B is $1,600. Both machines last so long that it is reasonable to assume (for simplicity) that they last forever.

    a. If the interest rate is 5 percent, which machine should firm X buy? Why?
    b. If the interest rate is 10 percent, which machine should firm X buy? Why?
    c. If the interest rate is 15 percent, which machine should firm X buy? Why?
    d. At what interest rate would firm X be indifferent between the two machines? Why?

Answers

Matching Questions
1. E 2. A 3. D 4. F 5. C 6. B

Completion Questions
1. 5, $3^{1}/_{3}$, 10 2. 90.9 cents, 82.6 cents, 173.5 cents 3. 8, 4, 10 4. riskiness, term, bookkeeping and collection 5. demand, supply 6. lower 7. Capitalization

8. supply curve   9. reduce, reducing   10. rent, rent   11. no, unearned income, would not, tax away   12. is not, "unearned"   13. profit, opportunity

True-False

1. True   2. True   3. True   4. False   5. True   6. False   7. True   8. True
9. False   10. True   11. True   12. False   13. True   14. True   15. True
16. True   17. True   18. True   19. False

Multiple Choice

1. a   2. b   3. b   4. b   5. d   6. a   7. b   8. c   9. d

Problems

1. a.

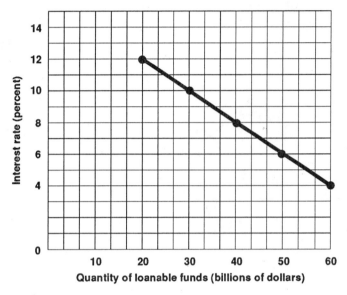

   b.   8 percent.
   c. $12,500.
   d.   No. Because you can get 8 percent if you lend your money elsewhere.
2. a. $8.78 \times 50 = \$439$ per month.
   b. $8.37 \times 20 = \$167.40$ per month.
   c. $7.07 \times 30 = \$212.10$ per month.
3. a.   Yes.
   b.   None. No.
4. No.
5. a.   All shown in the table.
   b. $4 million less.
6. About $500.
7. a.   Using Table 14.2 in the text, we see that it is worth $.839 \times \$10,000$, or $8,390.
   b.   Using Table 14.2, we see that it is worth $.89 \times \$10,000$, or $8,900 to get it in two years. Thus, it is worth $510 more than if you got the money in three years.

8. a. $100,000.
   b. $75,000.
   c. $400,000.
9. a. $1,000 ÷ 25,000 = 4 percent.
   b. No.
   c. $27,500.
10. a. If firm X buys machine A rather than machine B, it is investing an additional $5,000 now in order to reduce annual maintenance costs by $600. Thus, the rate of return on the extra $5,000 investment is $600/$5,000, or 12 percent. Since the interest rate is 5 percent, firm X should make this extra investment; it should buy machine A.
    b. Machine A. See part a.
    c. Machine B. See part a.
    d. 12 percent. See part a.

CHAPTER 15

Income Inequality and Poverty

Chapter Profile

Lorenz curves are used to measure the extent of income inequality. They make it clear that there was a considerable reduction in income inequality in the United States between the late 1920s and the end of World War II.

Many factors are responsible for existing income differentials. Some people are abler, better educated, or luckier than others. Some people have much more property, or more monopoly power than others.

Critics of income inequality argue that it lessens total consumer satisfaction because an extra dollar given to a poor man provides him with more extra satisfaction than the loss of a dollar takes away from a rich man. Also, they argue that income inequality leads to social and political inequality.

Defenders of income inequality points out that it is scientifically impossible to make interpersonal comparisons of utility, and they argue that income inequality is needed to provide incentives for people to work and create, and that it permits greater capital formation.

There is no well-defined income level that can be used in all times and all places to determine poverty. Perhaps the most widely accepted definition of poverty in the United States today is the one developed by the Social Security Administration. It began by multiplying the cost of a minimal nutritionally sound food plan by 3 to get an income level that is used as a poverty line. According to this definition, about 13 percent of the population in the United States fell below this poverty line in 1990.

Nonwhite families, families headed by a female, and very large families are more likely than others to be poor. To a considerable extent, the reasons for their poverty lie beyond the control of the poor themselves. About 1/3 of poor adults have suffered a disability of some sort, or the premature death of the family breadwinner, or family dissolution. Discrimination is also an obvious factor. Most heads of poor families do not have jobs.

Because private charity is deemed inadequate, the United States has authorized its government to carry out various public programs to aid the poor. There are programs to provide the poor with goods and services—for example, food stamp programs. Other programs, like aid to families with dependent children, give them cash.

There is widespread dissatisfaction with existing antipoverty—or "welfare"—programs. They are judged to be inefficient; their costs have increased at an alarming rate; and they provide little incentive for people to get off welfare. One suggestion to remedy these problems is a negative income tax.

Behavioral Objectives

A. You should be able to define and explain the following key concepts in this chapter:

Income inequality	Social Security	Food programs
Lorenz curve	Old-age insurance	Welfare
Progressive tax	Medicare	Aid to families with
Regressive tax	Unemployment	dependent children
Medicaid	insurance	Negative income tax
Tax incidence	Supplemental Security	Break-even income
Poverty	Income Program	

B. Make sure that you can do each of the following:

1. Explain how the Lorenz curve can be used to measure the degree of income inequality.

2. Describe the trends in income inequality in the United States during the past 50 years.

3. Indicate the effects of the tax structure on income inequality in the United States.

4. State the major arguments against income inequality.

5. State the major arguments in favor of income inequality.

6. Describe the Social Security Administration's definition of poverty, and the characteristics of the poor in the United States.

7. Explain the nature of our Social Security programs and the controversies that have occurred concerning these programs in recent years.

8. Describe the characteristics and size of various antipoverty programs in the United States, particularly aid to families with dependent children and the food stamp programs.

9. Explain how a negative income tax would work, and describe the arguments for and against such a program.

Getting Down to Cases: The Economic Effects of Discrimination

According to one definition, discrimination means that equals are treated unequally or that unequals are treated equally. Discrimination in the market place results from two principal sources: the power to discriminate, and the desire to discriminate. Thus, a monopsonistic employer is likely to have the power to discriminate, and if he or she acts as if nonmoney costs are connected with hiring women, blacks, Native Americans, Hispanics, or other groups, the result is likely to be discrimination in the relevant labor market.

a. With discrimination of this sort, are resources allocated solely on the basis of marginal productivity? Are the incomes of minority groups reduced?

b. Suppose that the production possibilities curve for this society is as shown below:

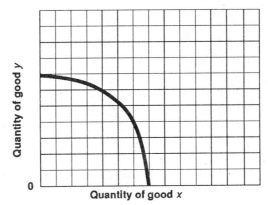

Does discrimination of this sort push this curve outward? Inward? Does it result in society's being at a point inside the production possibilities curve?

c. According to one study, a New York City store quoted three different prices for the same television set—$125 to a white law student, $139 to a Puerto Rican housewife, and $200 to a black housewife. Is this evidence of discrimination? (Or is it due to other factors such as the perceived differences in the probability of payment?) Should such price differences be tolerated in a democratic society?

d. School districts use revenues from the local property tax and grants-in-aid (mostly from the state) to pay for education. Is there a direct or inverse relationship between a district's per capita income and its education expenditures per pupil? Does this relationship reflect discrimination? (How should discrimination be defined?)

e. According to Lester Thurow, "The institutions of government are an important link in implementing discrimination. Either directly through legal restrictions or indirectly through harassment and expenditure decisions, the coercive power of the white community flows through local, state, and federal government institutions." Do you agree with this statement? Is it true in all parts of the country? How would you test its validity?

Matching Questions

_____	1. Progressive tax	A. Designed to reduce pay differentials between sexes for the same work
_____	2. Equal Pay Act of 1963	B. *A Theory of Justice*
_____	3. Regressive tax	C. Estate tax
_____	4. Aid to families with dependent children	D. Hospitalization insurance
_____	5. John Rawls	E. Sales tax
_____	6. Medicare	F. Cash payments to poor

Completion Questions

1. Suppose that families earning $4,000 or less per year pay no taxes and receive a welfare payment equal to the difference between their earned income and $4,000. If such a family earns $3,000, its total income is _____. If such a family earns $4,000, its total income is _____ . There is (considerable, little, no) _____ incentive to earn more income up to $4,000.

2. In country A, the lowest-income 40 percent of the families receive 10 percent of the income, and the highest-income 10 percent of the families receive 30 percent of the income. One point on country A's Lorenz curve is found by plotting _____ percent on the horizontal axis against _____ percent on the vertical axis. Another point on country A's Lorenz curve is found by plotting _____ percent on the horizontal axis against _____ percent on the vertical axis.

3. The most important single program to aid the poor gives aid to _____.

4. The proposal calling for poor families to receive a payment, while families with incomes above a certain minimum would pay a graduated tax, is called a(n) _____.

5. A commonly used diagram for measuring income inequality is the _____.

6. The federal income tax is (progressive, regressive) _____ , whereas the sales tax is (progressive, regressive) _____.

7. Were incomes equal for all families, the Lorenz curve would be a _____ line connecting the _____ of the diagram with its _____ righthand corner.

8. The _____ Act, passed in 1935, established a government-sponsored _____ system providing compulsory old-age insurance for both workers and self-employed people, as well as _____ insurance.

9. Assume that a negative income tax exists whereby the government pays each family (of four people) an amount equal to $3,000 – I/3, where I is the family's earned income. Families earning less than _____ per year will receive some payment from the government. The maximum amount that any family can receive from the government is _____ per year. If the poverty line is $5,000, a family must earn _____ to reach this line.

10. The amount that a family pays for a given tax is shown below, at each of a number of income levels of the family. This tax is progressive when a family's income is less than _____ , proportional when a family's income is between _____ and _____ , and regressive when a family's income exceeds _____ .

Income (dollars)	Tax (dollars)
$1,000	$10
$5,000	$100
$10,000	$300
$20,000	$600
$30,000	$900
$50,000	$1,200
$100,000	$2,000

True-False

_____ 1. The demand curve for unskilled labor is $P = 5 - 2Q$, and the supply curve for unskilled labor is $P = 3Q$, where P is the wage rate (in dollars per hour) and Q is the quantity of labor (in millions of hours). If a minimum wage of $5 an hour is established, all unskilled labor will be unemployed.

_____ 2. In the previous question, if a minimum wage of $4.50 an hour is established, the quantity supplied of unskilled labor will exceed the quantity demanded by 1.5 million hours.

_____ 3. There has been a great reduction in income inequality in the United States in the past 25 years.

_____ 4. Every industrialized country has greater income inequality than every less developed country.

_____ 5. The Lorenz curve plots the percentage of people, going from the poorest up, on the horizontal axis, and the percentage of total goods and services consumed on the vertical axis.

_____ 6. In the United States, inequality of after-tax income is more than inequality of before-tax income.

_____ 7. To finance old-age insurance, payroll taxes must be paid by each worker and his or her employer.

_____ 8. If the government gives all families of four persons $4,000 per year and imposes a tax of 25 percent on earned income, a family's disposable income would be greater than its earned income if its earned income is less than $16,000 per year.

Multiple Choice

1. If a negative income tax is established whereby the government pays each family (of four people) an amount equal to $3,000 - .6I$, where I is earned income (in dollars), and families who receive no such payment must pay taxes, the break-even income is:

   a. $9,000.
   b. $6,000.
   c. $5,000

   d. $3,000.
   e. none of the above

2. If the negative income tax in the previous question were adopted, a family below the break-even income that increased its earned income by $1 would net:

   a. nothing.
   b. 40 cents.
   c. 60 cents.

   d. $1.
   e. none of the above.

3. The Social Security system is:

   a. an ordinary insurance system.
   b. mandatory, not voluntary.
   c. financed by a regressive tax on earnings.
   d. all of the above.
   e. only b and c are true.

4. In 1990 it was estimated by the federal government that a family of four (including two children) to be just above the poverty line needed an annual income of:

   a. less than $2,000.
   b. between $2,000 and $3,000.
   c. between $6,000 and $8,500.

   d. between $4,500 and $6,000.
   e. between $13,000 and $14,000.

5. Blacks as compared to whites:

   a. have just about the same average income.
   b. are just as likely to complete high school.
   c. are just as likely to have a job.
   d. are more likely to be excluded from certain occupations.
   e. all of the above.

6. Which of the following kinds of families is most likely to be poor?

    a. white family with 6 members
    b. black family with 2 members
    c. black family with 6 members
    d. white family with 2 members
    e. all of the above are equally likely to be poor

7. Which of the following is not a progressive tax?

    a. inheritance tax
    b. federal income tax
    c. estate tax
    d. payroll tax
    e. all of the above

8. Suppose that each family must pay each year either $500 or 5 percent of its income (whichever is greater) to support local schools. This tax is:

    a. regressive for families with incomes under $10,000.
    b. proportional to income for families with incomes over $10,000.
    c. both a and b.
    d. more progressive than the federal income tax.
    e. none of the above.

9. Suppose that each family in nation A receives $1,000 in benefits from federal highways, and that each family pays $500 plus 10 percent of its income in taxes to pay for the maintenance of these highways.

    a. This government program provides more benefits to families with incomes under $4,000 than they pay for.
    b. Families with incomes over $6,000 pay more for this program than the benefits are worth to them.
    c. Families with incomes under $555 have negative disposable incomes.
    d. both a and b.
    e. all of the above.

Discussion and Extension Questions

1. In finding solutions for poverty would you like to distinguish between individuals who are temporarily (or voluntarily) poor—like students—and those who are more likely to remain poor over a longer period of time?

2. Suppose that over the next generation or so, we have more older people and fewer younger people. How will this alter the Social Security programs, both from the cost and benefit sides?

3. Should the prize money at professional tennis tournaments be distributed equally between men and women players? Why might the men be paid more? When should the women be paid more?

4. Generation-skipping trusts are one device the wealthy have used to avoid estate taxes. As put by one expert, "You provide income to your child for life, then to your grandchildren who are living today, with principal to their children at age 21." What

are the gains and costs to society of allowing the use of such trusts? Are you for or against permitting their use?

5. "Since one cannot make interpersonal comparisons of utility (or satisfaction), there is no way to tell whether progressive taxes are really to be preferred over regressive ones." Comment and evaluate.

6. What would the Lorenz curve look like if incomes were the same for all families? In the United States, are incomes more equally distributed than 50 years ago? Explain.

7. Is a sales tax progressive or regressive? Why? Is the personal income tax progressive or regressive? Why?

8. Suppose that the amount paid for a particular tax is related to the income of the taxpayer in the following way:

Income (dollars)	Tax (dollars)
1,000	50
10,000	600
100,000	7,000

Is this tax progressive or regressive?

9. What are some of the salient characteristics of poor families in the United States? What is meant by a negative income tax? Do you favor or oppose such a scheme?

Problems

1. a. If the Lorenz curves for the income distributions of countries A and B are as shown below, which country has more income inequality?

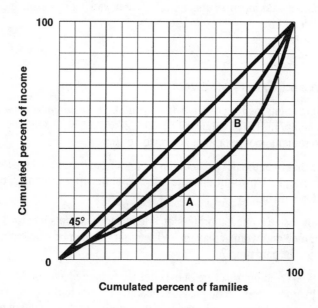

b. In country A, what percentage of the total income is received by the top 7 percent of the families? By the top 20 percent of the families? By the top 50 percent of the families?

c. In country B, what percentage of the total income is received by the top 7 percent of the families? By the top 20 percent of the families? By the top 50 percent of the families?

2. Suppose that the income distribution in the nation of Canam is as follows:

Money income (dollars)	Percent of families	Percent of total income received
Under 4,000	1	0.1
4,000-7,999	9	2.9
8,000-11,999	30	12.0
12,000-15,999	30	25.0
16,000-19,999	20	30.0
20,000 and over	10	30.0

a. Plot the Lorenz curve:

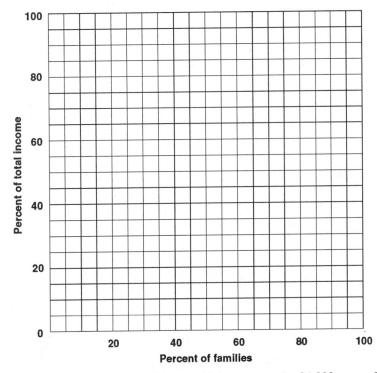

b. Suppose that the families in Canam with incomes under $4,000 are enabled to earn $10,000, and the incomes of all other families remain fixed. What percent of families are in each income class?

c. Suppose that the extra income to the Canam poor (described in part b) leads to the following results:

Money income (dollars)	Percent of total income received
Under 4,000	0
4,000-7,999	2.8
8,000-11,999	12.5
12,0000-15,999	24.9
16,000-19,999	29.9
20,000 and over	29.9

Plot the new Lorenz curve:

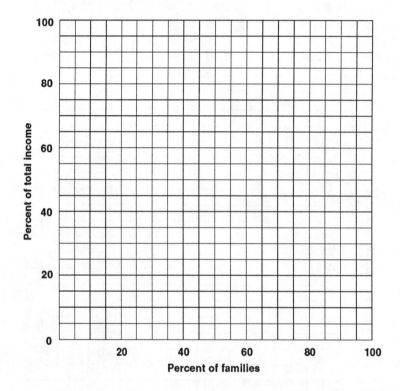

3. Suppose that the break-even income under a negative income tax is $4,000. This is the income at which a family of four neither pays nor receives taxes. Suppose that such a family receives 50 percent of the difference between its income and the break-even income, if its income is below the break-even income, and that it pays 25 percent of the difference between its income and the break-even income, if its income exceeds the break-even income.

a. In the table below, indicate how much a family at each income level would receive or pay in taxes.

Family income (dollars)	Payment received (dollars)	Taxes paid (dollars)
2,000	_____	_____
3,000	_____	_____
4,000	_____	_____
5,000	_____	_____
6,000	_____	_____
7,000	_____	_____
8,000	_____	_____
10,000	_____	_____
20,000	_____	_____

b. What incentive is there for an unemployed person heading a family with an income of $2,000 to get a job?

4. Suppose that the demand and supply curves for unskilled labor in a perfectly competitive labor market in the land of Canam are as shown below:

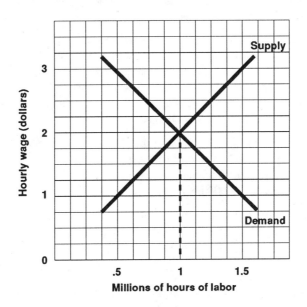

a. If a minimum wage of $2.50 per hour is established, what will be the effect on the total employment of unskilled labor?
b. What will be the effect on the total income received by unskilled workers?
c. Will the minimum wage solve the poverty problem in Canam?

5. a. Suppose that the amount of tax paid by a person with income equal to X is given by the formula

$$T = \frac{X}{3}$$

where T is the amount of the tax. Is this tax progressive or regressive? Why?

   b. Suppose that the formula is

$$T = \frac{X}{5} + \frac{X^2}{9}$$

Is the tax now progressive or regressive? Why?

6. Nation X's tax system exempts the first $5,000 of a person's income and taxes away 50 percent of the rest.

   a. Suppose that Mr. Poor's before-tax income is $10,000 and Mr. Rich's before-tax income is $50,000. Mr. Rich's before-tax income is five times Mr. Poor's. What is the ratio of Mr. Rich's after-tax income to Mr. Poor's?

   b. Is it true that, if any person has 5 times as much before-tax income as another person, the former person's after-tax income will be less than 5 times as much as the latter person's? Why or why not?

   c. Does nation X's tax system tend to reduce the inequality of income? Is the tax system progressive or regressive? Why?

7. Nation Y is considering three alternative tax systems. The first would exempt the first $5,000 of a person's income and tax away 50 percent of the rest. The second would exempt the first $8,000 of a person's income and tax away 70 percent of the rest. The third would exempt the first $10,000 of a person's income and tax away the rest. Nation Y's government assumes that the nation's total output will be the same regardless of which tax system is adopted. Do you agree? Why or why not?

8. Nation Z changes its tax system. After the change, the first $5,000 of a person's income is exempted and 50 percent of the rest is taxed away. Before the change, the first $2,500 of a person's income was exempted, and 1/3 of the rest was taxed away. John Jameson worked 2,000 hours at a wage rate of $5 per hour before the change.

   a. If he continues to work as much as before the tax change, will his after-tax income change?

   b. Assuming that he could vary the number of hours he worked, was an extra hour of leisure worth more or less than $3.33 to him before the change in the tax system? Why or why not?

   c. Was an extra hour of leisure worth more than $2.50 to him after the change in the tax system? Why or why not?

9. The table below shows how much, according to the Family Assistance Plan proposed by President Nixon in 1969, a family would receive in welfare payments, given that its earned income was a particular amount.

Earned income (dollars)	Welfare payment (dollars)
500	1,600
1,000	1,460
2,000	960
3,000	460

a. Assuming no taxes have to be paid on earned income under $3,000, what percentage of an extra dollar of earned income would a person keep if his or her income were $600?

b. What percentage of an extra dollar of earned income would a person keep if his or her income were $1,500?

c. What percentage of an extra dollar of earned income would a person keep if his or her income were $2,500?

d. In evaluating the Family Assistance Plan, why would the answers to previous parts of this question be relevant?

Answers

Matching Questions
1. C   2. A   3. E   4. F   5. B   6. D

Completion Questions
1. $4,000, $4,000, no   2. 40, 10, 90, 70   3. families with dependent children
4. negative income tax   5. Lorenz curve   6. progressive, regressive   7. straight, origin, upper   8. Social Security, social insurance, unemployment   9. $9,000, $3,000, $3,000   10. $10,000, $10,000, $30,000, $30,000

True-False
1. True   2. False   3. False   4. False   5. False   6. False   7. True   8. True

Multiple Choice
1. c   2. b   3. e   4. e   5. d   6. c   7. d   8. c   9. e

Problems

1. a. Country A
   b. About 20 percent, about 47 percent, about 70 percent.
   c. About 13 percent, about 33 percent, about 63 percent.

2. a.

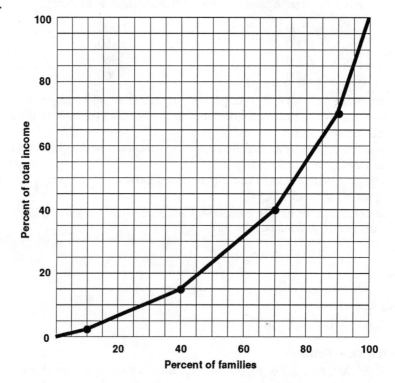

b.

Money income (dollars)	Percent of families
Under 4,000	0
4,000–7,999	9
8,000–11,999	31
12,000–15,999	30
16,000–19,999	20
20,000 and over	10

c.

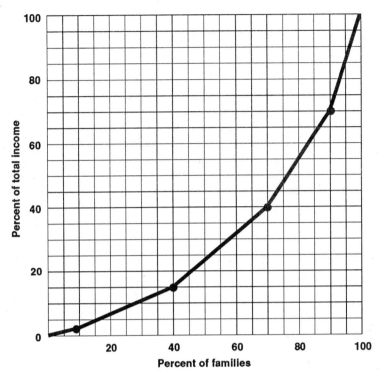

3. a.

Payment received (dollars)	Taxes paid (dollars)
1,000	–
500	–
0	–
–	250
–	500
–	750
–	1,000
–	1,500
–	4,000

b. He will keep 50 cents of every dollar he earns, since the payments he receives decline by 50 cents for every dollar he earns.

4. a. Employment will decline from 1 million hours of labor to .75 million hours of labor.

b. Income will decline from $2 million to $1.875 million.

c. No.

5. a. It is neither regressive nor progressive, since the amount of the tax is proportional to income.

   b. Progressive, because $\dfrac{T}{X} = \dfrac{1}{5} + \dfrac{X}{9}$, which means that $\dfrac{T}{X}$ increases as X increases.

6. a. 3.67 to 1.

   b. No. If one person has a before-tax income of $5,000, and another has a before-tax income of $1,000, the former person's after-tax income will not be less than 5 times as much as the latter person's.

   c. Yes. Progressive because the proportion of income going for taxes rises with income.

7. No. In the third tax system, there would be no incentive to earn more than $10,000. In the second tax system, the incentive to earn more than $8,000 would not be very strong.

8. a. No.

   b. More, because if this were not the case, he would work an extra hour before the change in the tax system. After taxes, he would receive $3.33 for each extra hour he worked.

   c. More, because if this were not the case, he would work an extra hour after the change in the tax system. After taxes, he would receive $2.50 for each extra hour he worked.

9. a. 72 percent.

   b. 50 percent.

   c. 50 percent.

   d. Because it is generally believed that a welfare program should contain incentives for welfare recipients to increase their earned income and get off welfare.

The Economic Role
of the Government

Chapter Profile

The price system suffers from some important limitations: (1) the distribution of income generated by the price system may be neither the best nor the fairest that might be obtained; (2) the price system cannot handle public goods adequately; (3) external economies or diseconomies cause too little or too much of certain goods to be produced.

To a considerable extent, the government's role in the economy has developed in response to these limitations of the price system. But there are wide differences of opinion on the proper role of government in economic affairs. Conservatives tend to be suspicious of "big government," while liberals are inclined to believe that the government should do more.

In the past 50 years, government spending has increased considerably, both in absolute terms and as a percent of total output. (It is now about $1/3$ of our total output.) To a large extent, this increase has been due to our greater military responsibilities, as well as to the fact that, as their incomes have risen, our citizens have demanded more schools, highways, and other goods and services provided by government.

One example of the role of government in the American economy is the farm program. Because people and resources have not moved out of agriculture as rapidly as the price system dictated, farm incomes have tended to be relatively low.

In response to political pressures from the farm blocs, the government set in motion a series of programs to aid farmers. A cornerstone of these programs was the concept of parity, which said that the price farmers receive should increase at the same rate as the prices of the goods and services farmers buy.

The government instituted price supports to keep farm prices above their equilibrium level. But since the support prices exceeded the equilibrium prices, there was a surplus of the commodities that the government had to purchase and store. To help reduce these surpluses, the government tried to restrict the output of farm products and expand the demand for them.

CHAPTER SIXTEEN

Behavioral Objectives

A. You should be able to define and explain the following key concepts in this chapter:

Public goods	Transfer payments	Income tax
External economy	Price supports	Property tax
External diseconomy	Depression	Sales tax
Antitrust laws	Private sector	Parity
Welfare payments	Public sector	

B. Make sure that you can do each of the following:

1. Explain the major limitations of the price system, and be sure to include the concepts of external economies and diseconomies, as well as public goods.

2. Describe the conservative and liberal positions concerning the proper economic role of government, and the differences between them.

3. Explain the principal ways in which the U.S. government tries to insure a proper legal, social, and competitive framework for the price system.

4. Indicate the principal ways in which the U.S. government tries to redistribute income and stabilize the economy.

5. Use supply and demand curves to show the effects of external economies and diseconomies on the optimal output of a competitive industry.

6. Describe the growth over time in the size of government expenditures (federal, state, and local), and the reasons for this growth.

7. Describe what the government (federal, state, and local) spends its money on, and the kinds of taxes that bring in the bulk of its tax revenues.

8. Indicate the nature of our farm problems, and the factors causing them.

9. Explain both the pre-1973 price-support programs and our current farm programs, using supply and demand curves.

10. Describe the leading criticisms of our government farm programs, as well as the arguments for them.

Getting Down to Cases: Majority Rule and Social Choice

Decisions concerning government expenditures and taxes are political decisions. In democracies, such decisions are made by majority rule. Kenneth Arrow, Stanford's Nobel laureate, has carried out some fundamental studies of majority rule and social choice. To illustrate simply the sorts of results obtained by Arrow and other economists, suppose that a society consists of three members, John Blue, William Gray, and James Green. Suppose too that each member of society must vote on three possible levels of the government budget in this simple society: high, medium, and low. Each person's vote has equal weight in determining the outcome. Further, suppose that the preferences of the three people with respect to budget levels are as indicated below:

222

	Blue	Gray	Green
First preference	High	Low	Medium
Second preference	Medium	High	Low
Third preference	Low	Medium	High

a. Suppose that the choice is between a high budget and a low one. Which will be chosen?

b. Suppose that the choice is between a low budget and a medium one. Which will be chosen?

c. Given the results of a and b, what seems to be the level of the government budget that will win, based on majority rule?

d. What if we alter the sequence in which the choices are made. Suppose that the choice first is between a medium and a low budget, and that the winner is then compared with a high budget. What seems to be the level of the government budget that will win, based on majority rule? Is your answer the same as in c?

e. Suppose that William Gray prefers a low budget to a medium budget to a high budget (and Blue's and Green's preferences remain as shown above). Does the voting sequence still matter? Or is the winner (based on majority rule) the same, regardless of the sequence in which the choices are made?

Matching Question

_____ 1. External diseconomy   A. National defense

_____ 2. External economy   B. Given in return for no product or service

_____ 3. Property tax   C. Uncompensated help

_____ 4. Parity   D. Farm programs

_____ 5. Public good   E. Uncompensated harm

_____ 6. Transfer payment   F. Important to local governments

Completion Questions

1. The _____ make it illegal for firms to collude or to attempt to monopolize the sale of a product.

2. The government often tries by establishing _____ to control the activities of firms in markets where competition cannot be expected to prevail.

3. Public goods are generally paid for by _____.

4. The _____ states that a farmer should be able to exchange a given quantity of his or her output for as much of nonfarm goods and services as he or she could at some point in the past.

5. Frequently in the past, the government support programs have set a price that is (above, below) _____ the equilibrium price.

6. At the federal level the biggest money raiser is the _____ tax.

7. Some _____ cannot be provided through the price system because there is no way to _____ a citizen from consuming the good. For example, there is no way to _____ a citizen from benefiting from national expenditures on defense, whether he or she _____ money toward defense or not. Consequently, the _____ cannot be used to provide such goods.

8. A(n) _____ is said to occur when consumption or production by one person or firm results in uncompensated benefits to another person or firm. A good example of a(n) _____ exists where fundamental research carried out by one firm is used by another firm.

9. Where external economies exist, it is generally agreed that the price system will produce too (little, much) _____ of the good in question and that the government should _____ the amount produced by private enterprise. This is the basic rationale for much of the government's huge _____ in basic science.

10. A(n) _____ is said to occur when consumption or production by one person or firm results in incompensated costs to another person or firm. A good example of a(n) _____ occurs when a firm dumps pollutants into a stream and makes the water unfit for use by firms and people downstream.

11. State governments now spend (less, more) _____ than the federal government, although before World War I, they spent (less, more) _____.

12. About _____ of the federal expenditures goes for defense and other items connected with international relations and national security. About _____ goes for Social Security, Medicare, income security, health, and education. The rest goes to support farm, transportation, housing, and other such programs, as well as to run Congress, the courts, and the executive branch of the federal government.

True-False

_____ 1. The research activities of industrial firms often result in external economies.

_____ 2. The government should impose taxes on goods that result in external economies in order to promote an optimal allocation of resources.

_____ 3. Public goods frequently are sold in the private market.

_____ 4. The government relies on the legitimate and systematic use of force.

_____ 5. Prices determined in noncompetitive markets provide incorrect signals regarding what consumers want and how scarce resources and commodities are.

_____ 6. The price system cannot be used to handle the production and distribution of public goods in an optimal manner.

_____ 7. The government should discourage the production of goods and services that entail external economies.

_____ 8. Government expenditures in the United States have grown much more rapidly than total output in this century.

_____ 9. Poor countries (with little industry) spend a higher percentage of output on government services than do the industrialized countries.

_____ 10. When the support price of a farm product exceeded the equilibrium price, a surplus of the product was likely to result.

_____ 11. The government produces most of the goods and services it provides. For example, the federal government supports over half of the research and development carried out in the United States, and practically all of it is carried out in government laboratories.

_____ 12. There has been little movement toward public ownership in the United States, despite occasional cries to the contrary on the hustings and in the press. Perhaps the most important and controversial area where government ownership has been extended appreciably in the last 60 years has been in electric power.

_____ 13. At the federal level the personal income tax brings in almost half of the tax revenue collected by the federal government. The next most important taxes at the federal level are the social security, payroll, and employment taxes, and the corporation income tax.

_____ 14. The market demand curve for food is likely to shift to the right very greatly as per capita income rises, because consumption of food per capita faces natural biological and other limitations.

_____ 15. The quantity of farm products supplied tends to be relatively sensitive to price, because the farmers have only limited control over their output. (Weather, floods, insects, and other such factors are very important.)

_____ 16. The less developed countries were permitted by Public Law 480 to buy our farm products with their own currencies, rather than dollars.

_____ 17. To be equitable, each and every citizen should pay an equal amount to the government in taxes.

Multiple Choice

1. The functions of taxes are:

   a. to reduce the amount of resources at the disposal of firms and individuals.
   b. to increase the amount of resources at the disposal of the government.
   c. to raise money needed to finance government expenditures.
   d. to redistribute income.
   e. all of the above.

2. An economic activity that would be unlikely to be financed or subsidized by the government is:

   a. basic scientific research.
   b. development of new weapons systems.
   c. development of new smog-control devices.
   d. development of improved varieties of corn.
   e. none of the above.

3. Which of the following is *not* a public good?

   a. national defense
   b. the services of the U.S. Army
   c. a smog-free environment
   d. blood donated to the Red Cross
   e. the Apollo space program

4. If government activities could be made more efficient, this would permit:

   a. an increase in the output of public goods.
   b. an increase in the output of private (nonpublic) goods.
   c. an increase in either the output of private goods or the output of public goods or both.
   d. no increase in output since the added efficiency would be offset by higher wages for government workers.
   e. none of the above.

5. The government's farm price support programs can be defended by pointing out that:

   a. they have reduced the surpluses of farm products.
   b. the quantity demanded of farm products is not very sensitive to price.
   c. the quantity supplied of farm products is not very sensitive to price.
   d. the rate of technological change in United States agriculture has been very high.
   e. none of the above.

6. Establishing a legal and social framework to enable the price system to work effectively and making sure that markets remain reasonably competitive are jobs for:

   a. the consumer.
   b. the government.
   c. the price system.
   d. the church.
   e. none of the above.

7. Government expenditures represent about what percentage of total output in the United States?

   a. 10%
   b. 20%
   c. 35%
   d. 50%
   e. 60%

8. The largest source of revenue for states is the:

   a. income tax.
   b. highway user tax.
   c. sales (and excise) taxes.
   d. property tax.
   e. estate tax.

9. Which of the following is a limitation of the price system?

   a. The distribution of income may be "unfair" or quite unequal.
   b. Some goods and services cannot be provided because a consumer cannot be excluded whether he or she pays or not.
   c. Production or consumption of a good by one firm may have adverse effects on another.
   d. all of the above.
   e. none of the above.

10. To help reduce farm surpluses, the government in the past has tried to:

   a. restrict output of farm products.
   b. shift demand curve for farm products to the left.
   c. cut down on exports.
   d. all of the above.
   e. none of the above.

11. If the opportunity cost to society of using certain resources in agriculture is higher than the value of the farm products these resources can produce,

   a. the opportunity cost should be reduced by paying these resources less.
   b. the opportunity cost should be reduced by encouraging a shorter workweek in agriculture.
   c. the value of the farm products these resources can produce should be increased by raising the price of farm products.
   d. these resources should be encouraged to leave farming, if society wants to maximize the value of its total output.
   e. none of the above.

Discussion and Extension Questions

1. Former president Ford has been quoted as saying that, "A government big enough to give you everything you want is a government big enough to take from you everything you have." Do you agree? Why or why not? How relevant do you think this statement is for the determination of public policy?

2. *Business Week* has said: "By prematurely deregulating telecommunications, the Federal Communications Commission may be hindering rather than fostering competition." How can this be?

3. What principle developed in the chapter helps explain the government's program in 1976 to provide the public with free innoculations against the so-called swine influenza?

4. Figure 16.1 (and the related discussion) illustrates how government intervention can improve the allocation of resources when there are external economies or disecono-

mies present. Can you show as well how it is possible for such intervention to fail to improve upon, and maybe even worsen, the allocation of resources?

5. "If we wanted to maintain income levels among farmers, payments to poor farmers by the government would be more direct and effective than the present farm program." Comment and evaluate.

6. What are the principal limitations of the price system? It is generally agreed that government must establish the "rules of the game." What does this mean? It is also agreed that the government must see to it that markets remain reasonably competitive. Why?

7. Describe the rationale for the government's efforts to redistribute income. Do all government programs transfer income from rich to poor? Explain.

8. It is generally agreed that the government should discourage the production of goods and services that entail external diseconomies. What are external diseconomies? Give some examples.

9. Why are government expenditures so much bigger now than forty years ago?

Problems

1. The paper industry has the demand and supply curves shown below:

Price of paper (dollars per ton)	Quantity demanded	Quantity supplied
	(millions of tons)	
2	80	40
3	70	50
4	60	60
5	50	70

a. Suppose that this industry results in substantial external diseconomies. What can be said about its optimal output rate?

b. In the graph below, draw the supply and demand curves for paper. Does the supply curve reflect the true social costs of producing the product? If not, will a supply curve reflecting the true social costs lie above or below the supply curve you have drawn?

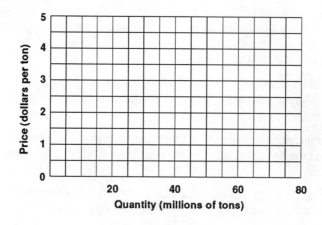

c. What is the equilibrium price of paper? From the point of view of reflecting the true social costs, is this price the correct one, or too low or too high?

2. Suppose that for the past decade the United States has been faced with apple crops far in excess of demand. As Secretary of Agriculture, it is your job to present to Congress a bill to provide price supports for apples. In presenting your case, you assume that the support price for apples will be OP, and that output will be restricted to 1,000 million bushels of apples.

   a If the demand curve for apples is as shown, how much will the government have to purchase?

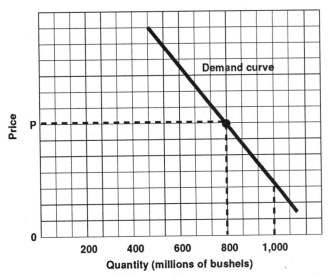

b. If farmers sold the 1,000 million bushels of apples for the best price they could get in the open market, what price would they get?

c. By how much would the demand curve have to shift, and in what direction, in order to eliminate the surplus, if the government supports the price of a bushel of apples at OP?

3. The town of Lucretia is faced with a serious smog problem. The smog can be dispelled if an air treatment plant is installed at an annual cost of $1 million. There is no way to clean up the air for some but not all of the town's population. Each of the town's families acts independently, and no single family can afford to carry out the project by itself. Why doesn't a private firm build the air treatment plant and sell its services to the town's families (acting individually)?

4. Indicate the economic rationale for the government's carrying out the following functions:

   a. regulating the sale and development of drugs.
   b. maintaining an army.
   c. granting aid to families with dependent children.
   d. supporting agricultural experiment stations.
   e. establishing the Antitrust Division of the Department of Justice.
   f. imposing an income tax.
   g. establishing unemployment insurance.

5. In the United States, what processes are used to reallocate resources from the private sector (firms and individuals) to the government?

6. Besides its smog problem, the town of Lucretia has a transportation problem which it hopes can be solved by building a new road through the center of town. There are three types of roads that can be built, their annual costs and benefits to the townspeople being as follows:

Road	Total cost (dollars)	Total benefit (dollars)
No road	0	0
Road 10 miles long	5 million	8 million
Road 20 miles long	12 million	16 million
Road 30 miles long	20 million	20 million

a. What is the extra annual cost of building a 20-mile road rather than a 10-mile road? What is the extra annual cost of building a 30-mile road rather than a 20-mile road?

b. What is the extra annual benefit from building a 20-mile road rather than a 10-mile road? What is the extra annual benefit from building a 30-mile road rather than building a 20-mile road?

c. Should the town build one of these roads? If so, which one?

7. Suppose that the demand and supply curves for good X are as follows:

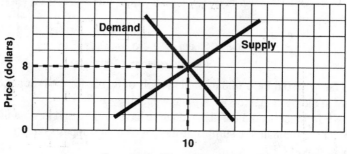

a. If the market for good X is in equilibrium, how much would consumers be willing to pay for an additional unit of good X?

b. The supply curve shows the extra cost of producing an extra unit of good X. If the market for good X is in equilibrium, how much would it cost to produce an extra unit of good X?

c. If the social costs of producing good X *exceed* the private costs, will the social cost of producing an extra unit of good X be equal to the amount consumers would be willing to pay for this extra unit? If not, will the social cost of the extra unit be greater or less than the amount consumers would pay for it? Why?

d. Under the circumstances described in part c, indicate why the socially optimal output of good X is less than 10 million units per year.

e. If the social costs of producing good X were *less* than the private costs, indicate why the optimal output of good X would be more than 10 million units per year.

8. Suppose that the demand curve for soybeans is as follows:

Price (dollars per bushel)	Quantity demanded (billions of bushels per year)
4	2.1
5	2.0
6	1.9
7	1.8
8	1.7

The government supports the price of soybeans at $6 per bushel and restricts soybean output to 2.1 billion bushels per year.

a. How much do farmers receive for their soybean crop under these circumstances?
b. How much would farmers receive for their soybean crop if the government no longer supports the soybean price and if farmers continue to produce 2.1 billion bushels per year?
c. If the farmers producing soybeans were to band together and fix the price, which of the above prices would they choose? Why?

9. In the absence of government output restrictions, the supply curve for soybeans is $P = 2.5Q$, where P is the price (in dollars per bushel) of soybeans and Q is the annual output of soybeans (in billions of bushels.)

a. If the government sets a support price for soybeans of $4 per bushel, will farmers produce their full quota of 2.1 billion bushels per year?
b. If the government abandons its price support for soybeans but maintains the output quota of 2.1 billion bushels per year, will the price and output differ from that under a completely free market? If so how? (Illustrate with a diagram. Assume that the demand curve in the previous problem is valid.)

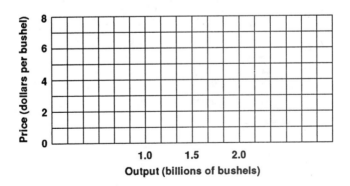

c. If the government wants the quantity of soybeans supplied to be double the quantity that would be supplied in a free market, how high should it support the price of soybeans to elicit this quantity?

Answers

Matching Questions

1. E   2. C   3. F   4. D   5. A   6. B

Completion Questions

1. antitrust laws   2. regulatory commissions   3. taxes   4. concept of parity
5. above   6. personal income   7. goods and services, exclude, prevent, pays, price
system   8. external economy, external economy   9. little, supplement, investment
10. external diseconomy, external diseconomy   11. less, more   12. $1/4$, $1/2$

True-False

1. True   2. False   3. False   4. True   5. True   6. True   7. False   8. True
9. False   10. True   11. False   12. True   13. True   14. False   15. False
16. True   17. False

Multiple Choice

1. e   2. e   3. d   4. c   5. e   6. b   7. c   8. c   9. d   10. a   11. d

Problems

1. a.   It is less than 60 million tons.
   b.   The supply curve does not reflect the true social costs. A supply curve reflecting
        these costs would be above and to the left of the one shown below.

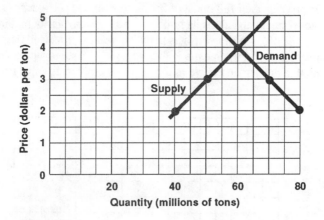

   c. $4. Too low.
2. a.   200 million bushels.
   b.   *OX* in the diagram at the top of the next page:

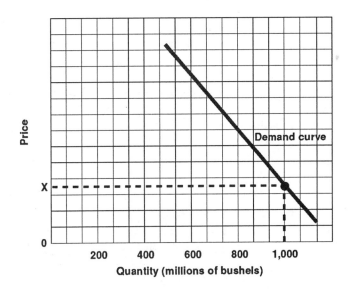

c. The demand curve would have to shift to the right by 200 million bushels.
3. If any family buys smog-free air, it automatically buys it for others too, regardless of whether the latter pay for it or not. And since no family can afford the cost, so long as families act independently, it will be unprofitable for a private firm to carry out this project.
4. a. The government must make sure that goods like drugs are properly labeled and reasonably safe.
   b. National defense is a public good.
   c. Redistribution of income is an accepted concern of government.
   d. There are external economies from such research.
   e. The government must try to maintain reasonably competitive markets.
   f. Redistribution of income is an accepted concern of government.
   g. Redistribution of income and economic stabilization are accepted concerns of government.
5. Taxes and borrowing are used for this purpose.
6. a. $7 million. $8 million.
   b. $8 million. $4 million.
   c. Yes. Road 20 miles long, because the extra benefit from the road 30 miles long is less than the extra cost.
7. a. $8.
   b. $8.
   c. No. It will be greater than the amount that consumers would be willing to pay for it, since consumers would be willing to pay only $8 for it, but its social cost exceeds $8.

    d. The optimal output of good X is less than 10 million units per year because the optimal output is at the intersection of the demand curve with the supply curve reflecting social costs. Because this supply curve lies to the left of the industry's supply curve (in the diagram), the optimal output must be less than 10 million units per year.

    e. If the social costs of producing good X were less than the private costs, the supply curve reflecting social costs would lie to the right of the industry's supply curve. Thus, the intersection of the supply curve reflecting social costs with the demand curve would be at an output exceeding 10 million units per year.

8. a. $6 × 2.1 billion, or $12.6 billion.

    b. $4 × 2.1 billion, or $8.4 billion.

    c. $8, because the amount they receive ($8 × 1.7 billion, or $13.6 billion) is greater than at any lower price, and their costs at this price must be no greater than at lower prices since they are producing less. Thus, their profit must be highest at a price of $8.

9. a If the price is P, $Q = 0.4P$ in the absence of government output restrictions. Thus, if $P = 4$, $Q = 1.6$. Consequently, farmers will not produce their full quota of 2.1 billion bushels.

    b. The demand and supply curves are shown below:

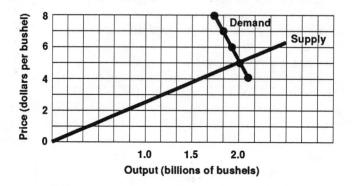

Price will be $5, and output will be 2.0 billion bushels. Since this is less than the output quota, the free-market outcome will prevail.

    c. To elicit 4.0 billion bushels, the price must be set at 2.5 × 4.0 dollars, or $10 per bushel.

Government and the Environment

Chapter Profile

As a result of human activities, great quantities of chemicals, industrial wastes, pesticides, fertilizers, animal wastes, and human wastes are being dumped into the atmosphere and into the rivers, lakes, and oceans.

Waste disposal and other pollution-causing activities result in external diseconomies. The firms and individuals that pollute the water and air (and other parts of the environment) pay less than the true social costs of disposing of their wastes, with part of the true social cost being borne by other firms and individuals who must pay to clean up the water or air, or who must live with the consequences.

The divergence of private from social costs prevents the market system from leading to an optimal allocation of resources. Because the polluters do not pay the full cost of waste disposal, their products are artificially cheap, with the result that too much is produced of them.

The government can help to remedy the breakdown of the market system in several ways: (1) by issuing regulations for waste disposal and other activities influencing the environment; (2) by establishing effluent fees–charges a polluter must pay to the government for discharging wastes; (3) by issuing transferable emissions permits; (4) by granting tax credits to firms that introduce pollution-control equipment. In addition, the federal government can, and does, help local governments meet the costs of waste treatment. Two important advantages of effluent fees or transferable emissions permits are that they are more likely to result in the use of the minimum-cost way to achieve a given reduction in pollution and that they require far less information in the hands of the relevant government agencies than direct regulation.

It is extremely difficult to determine how clean the environment should be. The sensible goal for society is to permit the level of pollution that minimizes the sum of the costs of pollution and the costs of controlling pollution; but no one has a very clear idea of what these costs are, and to a large extent the choices must be made through the political process.

Behavioral Objectives

A. You should be able to define and explain the following key concepts in this chapter:

External diseconomy	Transferable emissions	Direct regulation
Private costs	permits	Effluent fees
Social costs	Air pollution	Tax credits
Water pollution		

B. Make sure that you can do each of the following:

1. Describe the nature and extent of environmental pollution in the United States.

2. Explain why because external diseconomies exist, the private costs of using air and water are less than the social costs, with the result that there is excessive pollution.

3. Indicate the reasons why pollution does not necessarily have to increase with economic growth, population growth, or technological change.

4. Explain why economists tend to prefer transferable emissions permits or effluent fees over other kinds of public policies designed to reduce pollution.

5. Describe recent public policies toward environmental pollution in the United States.

6. Indicate how the optimal level of pollution depends upon both the cost of pollution and the cost of pollution control.

Getting Down to Cases: Pollution Rights in Los Angeles

Suppose that the city of Los Angeles decides to auction off pollution rights. Alternative prices of a certificate allowing the purchaser to put a ton of pollution in the atmosphere are shown below. The total amount of such certificates that would be purchased at each price is also shown below:

Price per ton (dollars)	Number of certificates demanded (each certificate being for 1 ton)
10,000	0
8,000	600
6,000	1,200
4,000	1,800
2,000	2,400
0	3,000

a. The city government decides that the optimal quantity of pollution is 1,800 tons. What will be the price of a certificate?

b. How much money will the city collect from the sale of certificates?

c. If the city does not set a fee on pollution, how many tons of pollution will be put in the air?

d. Is the major purpose of such an auction to collect money for the city? Why or why not?

e. Suppose that firm A can cut back its pollution relatively cheaply but firm B cannot. Will this fee result in firm A's cutting back on its pollution more than firm B will? Why or why not?

f. From the point of view of society, should firm A cut back on its pollution to a greater extent than firm B? Why or why not?

Matching Questions

_____ 1. Zero economic growth	A. No increase in per capita output
_____ 2. Combustion of fossil fuels	B. Water pollution
_____ 3. Zero pollution	C. Not a sensible goal
_____ 4. Detergents	D. Air pollution
_____ 5. EPA	E. Government agency
_____ 6. Effluent fee	F. Charge for polluting

Completion Questions

1. When important external diseconomies are present, government can try to reduce pollution through _____ , _____ and/or _____.

2. _____ are charges that a polluter must pay to the government for discharging waste. Faced with an effluent fee, a polluter will find it profitable to reduce waste discharge to the point where the cost of reducing an additional unit of waste is _____ the effluent fee.

3. An agency which establishes standards for air and water quality is the _____.

4. Environmentalists (opposed, supported) _____ the trans-Alaskan pipeline.

5. The sensible goal for our society is to minimize the sum of the costs of pollution and the _____.

6. A major contributor to air pollution is the combustion of _____ fuels, particularly _____ and _____ products.

7. If a paper mill uses water and then treats it to restore its quality, there is no divergence between _____ and _____ cost. In other words, there are no _____.

8. Electric power companies (have, have not) _____ paid the full cost of disposing of wastes in the atmosphere. Thus they have charged an artificially (high, low) _____ price, and the public has been induced to use (less, more) _____ electric power than is socially desirable.

9. Effluent _____ are an integral part of the institutional arrangements governing water quality in the Ruhr. The amount a firm has to pay depends on how much and what kinds of _____ it pumps into the rivers of the Ruhr valley.

True-False

_____ 1. The price system is unlikely to allocate resources efficiently in the presence of significant external diseconomies.

_____ 2. When polluters do not pay the true cost of waste disposal, too little of their products is produced.

_____ 3. As national output goes up, it is most likely that pollution levels will fall considerably.

_____ 4. If polluters are forced to pay the social costs of disposing of their wastes, the prices of many goods we buy must rise.

_____ 5. The price system is based on the supposition that the full cost of using each resource is borne by the person or firm that uses it.

_____ 6. Immediately after cans and no-deposit bottles were introduced, the consumer of beverages no longer had to pay for the cost of disposing of the cans or bottles.

_____ 7. Technological change is a potential hero in the fight against pollution, because the creation of new technology is an important way to reduce the harmful side effects of existing techniques.

_____ 8. The average American is responsible for much less pollution than the average citizen of most other countries.

_____ 9. Economists favor transferable emissions permits or effluent fees because this approach requires far less information in the hands of the relevant government agencies than does direct regulation.

_____ 10. Subsidies to promote the purchase of particular types of pollution-control equipment may result in relatively inefficient and costly reductions in pollution.

_____ 11. The federal government has disbursed funds to promote research and development to prevent and control the pollution of the atmosphere.

_____ 12. In 1969, the Congress established a new agency—the Council on Environmental Quality—to oversee and plan the nation's pollution control programs.

_____ 13. The Environmental Protection Agency has estimated that it would cost about $2 billion to remove all of the water pollutants from industrial and municipal sources.

_____ 14. The sensible goal for our society is to minimize the sum of the costs of pollution and the costs of controlling pollution.

Multiple Choice

1. At the current level of pollution suppose that the social cost of reducing pollution by one unit is less than the social benefit of reducing pollution by one unit. If so:

    a. the current level of pollution is optimal.

    b. there is too little pollution from society's point of view.

    c. there is too much pollution from society's point of view.

    d. all pollution should be eliminated.

    e. existing pollution control measures should be dropped.

2. If a market for pollution rights were established, the government would issue a limited number of certificates to pollute. Then:

    a. a firm could sell some of its certificates to other firms or individuals if it found it worthwhile to do so.

    b. a firm could buy some of its certificates from other firms or individuals if it found it worthwhile to do so.

    c. the price of a certificate would be set by supply and demand.

    d. all of the above.

    e. none of the above.

3. Taylor Bingham and Allen Miedema have estimated that the cost of reducing sulfur emissions to current standards in St. Louis, Missouri, would be about $50 million per year if direct controls were used and about $29 million if effluent fees were used. The lower cost with effluent fees is due to the fact that:

    a. there are large differences in abatement costs among polluters.

    b. effluent fees induce larger reductions in sulfur emissions among steam-electric power plants (where such reductions are cheap) than among oil refineries (where such reductions are expensive).

    c. direct controls do not result in the cost of reducing emission by one unit being the same for all polluters.

    d. all of the above.

    e. none of the above.

4. Bingham and Miedema estimated that an effluent fee of 13 cents per pound of sulfur discharge would induce the required curtailment of emissions in St. Louis, while in Cleveland the effluent fee would have to be 19 cents per pound. Such differences in the effluent fee may be due to:

    a. differences between cities in the amount by which the total emission of sulfur is to be reduced.

    b. differences between cities in industrial composition.

    c. differences between cities in the technology used in each industry.

    d. all of the above.

    e. none of the above.

Discussion and Extension Questions

1. The optimal amount of pollution is not zero; we're quite sure of that. However, how do we know that we currently have too much pollution? Is it possible that we do not have enough pollution yet? Is more, not less, the direction in which we should be moving?

2. Can you utilize your understanding of cost-benefit analysis, opportunity costs, and other economic principles you have absorbed to roughly analyze how one would decide whether or not a particular state should pass legislation to ban throw-away or disposable bottles and cans for soft drinks and beer? Should manufacturers also be forbidden to use throw-away containers for macaroni? Detergents? Baby food? Should consumers have to pay a deposit on egg cartons?

3. Show how too much pollution, from society's point of view, is likely to arise if the private costs of using water and air for waste disposal are less than the social costs. Is it likely that the output rate of heavy polluters is too high, from a social point of view? Why or why not? Show how, once cans and no-deposit bottles were introduced, an external diseconomy arose with regard to disposal of these items. Are there any states that now require a deposit on bottles?

4. Must economic growth necessarily result in increased pollution? Should the rate of technological change be slowed in order to reduce pollution? Explain.

5. Explain how transferable emissions permits can be used to reduce pollution. What are their advantages? Why do many economists prefer them over direct regulation? Over tax credits for pollution-control equipment?

Problems

1. a. Suppose that the cost to society of various levels of pollution is as follows:

Pollution (millions of tons per year)	Cost (billions of dollars per year)
1	3
2	6
3	10
4	15
5	22
6	30
7	40
8	60

Plot this relationship in the graph on the next page:

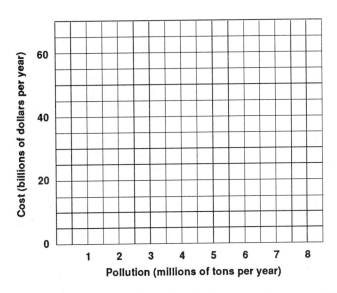

b. Suppose that the cost to society of pollution control varies as follows with the level of pollution:

Pollution (millions of tons per year)	Cost (billions of dollars per year)
1	50
2	40
3	32
4	25
5	19
6	14
7	9
8	5

Plot this relationship on the graph below:

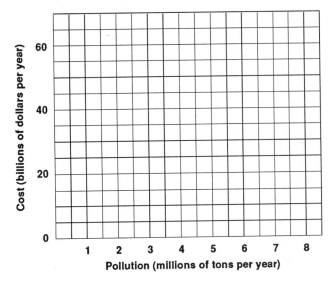

c. Does it make sense to plot the sum of the costs in parts a and b against the level of pollution? If so, plot this relationship on the following graph, and tell what this relationship means.

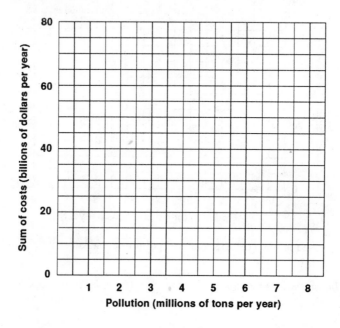

d. Given the data in parts a and b, what is the optimal level of pollution? Why isn't it sensible to aim for zero pollution?

2. States, such as Oregon and Vermont, have passed laws that all carbonated-beverage containers must carry a minimum refundable deposit.

a. According to the director of communications services for American Can Company, "What *is* happening in Oregon is that consumers are paying $10 million more a year for beer and soft drinks than they did before the bottle bill became law. Retail price increases . . . have far exceeded those in neighboring states." Why do you think that this was true?

b. According to this executive of American Can Company, "Oregon (and Vermont) consumers are denied their free choice of container. . . . " Is this true? According to William Baumol and Wallace Oates, this amounts to "a denial of . . . the freedom to pollute unpenalized." Do you agree?

3. According to one study of the Delaware River, the extra social costs involved in going from one level of pollution abatement to another are shown below. Also shown are the extra benefits to society in going from one level of pollution to another. (All figures are in millions of dollars.)

Transition	Extra cost	Extra benefit
From abatement level 1 to 2	35	200
From abatement level 2 to 3	20	20
From abatement level 3 to 4	130	10
From abatement level 4 to 5	245	25

a. If abatement level 1 is currently being achieved, is it socially worthwhile to advance to abatement level 2? Why or why not?
b. Is it socially worthwhile to advance to abatement level 3? Why or why not?
c. Is it socially worthwhile to advance to abatement level 4? Why or why not?
d. Is it socially worthwhile to advance to abatement level 5? Why or why not?

Answers

Matching Questions
1. A   2. D   3. C   4. B   5. E   6. F

Completion Questions
1. direct regulation, effluent fees, transferable emissions permits   2. Effluent fees, equal to   3. Environmental Protection Agency   4. opposed   5. costs of controlling pollution   6. fossil, coal, oil   7. private, social, external diseconomies   8. have not, low, more   9. fees, waste

True-False
1. True   2. False   3. False   4. True   5. True   6. True   7. True   8. False   9. True   10. True   11. True   12. True   13. False   14. True

Multiple Choice
1. c   2. d   3. d   4. d

Problems
1. a.

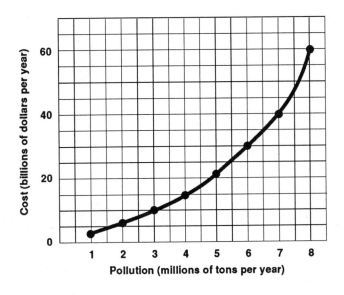

b.

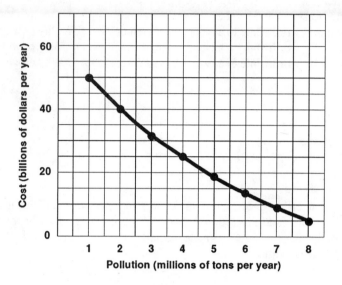

c.

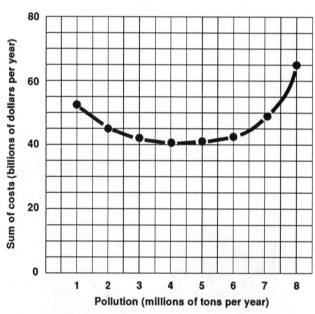

Yes. This relationship shows how the total costs—both pollution costs and pollution control costs—vary with the amount of pollution.

d. 4 million tons. Because it costs more to reduce the pollution (below 4 million tons) than it is worth.

2. a. Because of increased costs of handling, sorting, washing, returning, and refilling bottles, according to this executive.
   b. The issue is too complex to permit a very brief answer, but many economists would agree with Baumol and Oates.
3. a. Yes, because the benefit exceeds the cost.
   b. No, because the benefit does not exceed the cost.
   c. No, because the benefit does not exceed the cost.
   d. No, because the benefit does not exceed the cost.

CHAPTER 18

International Trade

Chapter Profile

International trade permits specialization, and specialization increases output. This is the benefit of trade, both for individuals and for nations. Country A has an absolute advantage over country B in the production of a good when country A can produce a unit of the good with less resources than can country B.

Trade can be mutually beneficial even if one country has an absolute advantage in the production of all goods. Specialization and trade depend on comparative, not absolute advantage. A nation is said to have a comparative advantage in those products where its efficiency relative to other nations is highest.

Trade can be mutually beneficial if a country specializes in the products where it has a comparative advantage and imports the products where it has a comparative disadvantage.

The principle of comparative advantage can be used to predict the pattern of world trade. If markets are relatively free and competitive, producers will automatically be led to produce in accord with comparative advantage. If a country has a comparative advantage in the production of a certain good, it will turn out—after the price of the good in various countries is equalized and total world output of the good equals total world demand—that this country is an exporter of the good under free trade.

Specialization is not the only reason for trade: others are economies of scale, learning, and differences in national tastes. Also some countries develop new products and processes which they export to other countries until the technology becomes widely available.

A tariff is a tax imposed by the government on imports, the purpose being to cut down on imports in order to protect domestic industry and workers from foreign competition. Tariffs benefit the protected industry at the expense of the general public, and, in general, a tariff costs the general public more than the protected industry (and its workers and suppliers) gains.

Quotas are another barrier to free trade. They too reduce trade, raise prices, protect domestic industry from foreign competition, and reduce the standard of living of the nation as a whole.

Tariffs, quotas, and other barriers to free trade are sometimes justified on the basis of national security and other noneconomic considerations. Moreover, tariffs and other forms of protection are sometimes justified to protect infant industries, to prevent a country from being too dependent on only a few industries, and to carry out other such national objectives.

Although only about 10 percent of our gross national product, foreign trade is of very considerable importance to the American economy. Many of our industries rely on foreign countries for raw materials or for markets, and our consumers buy many kinds of imported goods.

In our early years we were a very protectionist country. Our tariffs remained relatively high until the 1930s, when a movement began toward freer trade. Also, during the 1960s, there was a significant reduction in our tariffs. But more recently, as some of our industries (like steel and autos) have been hit hard by imports, there has been a strong push for more protectionist measures.

Behavioral Objectives

A. You should be able to define and explain the following key concepts in this chapter:

Exports	Trading possibilities	Quota
Imports	curve	Export subsidy
Absolute advantage	Terms of trade	European Economic
Comparative advantage	Multinational firm	Community
Production possibilities	Tariff	(Common Market)
curve	Prohibitive tariff	

B. Make sure that you can do each of the following:

1. Describe the size and composition of American exports and imports.

2. State the advantages, both to nations and individuals, of specialization and trade.

3. Show that specialization and trade can increase world output.

4. Use production possibilities curves and trading possibilities curves to show that, if two countries specialize in the production of goods where they have a comparative advantage, both can benefit.

5. Use supply and demand curves to indicate the determinants of the amount of a particular commodity that will be exported by one country to another country.

6. Explain how economies of scale, learning, and technological change result in international trade.

7. Describe the effects of multinational firms and some of the principal reasons for their growth.

8. Indicate the social costs arising from tariffs and quotas.

9. Describe the arguments for tariffs and quotas.

10. Provide a brief history of tariffs in the United States.

Getting Down to Cases: Economic Effects of an Export Ban

On various occasions, the United States government has prohibited the export of particular commodities. For example, in 1980, the government prohibited the export of more than 8 million tons of grain to the (former) Soviet Union. Suppose that the government were to prohibit the export of all wheat grown in the United States. In other words, all wheat would have to be sold to domestic buyers. The demand curve for wheat among such buyers and the supply curve for wheat in the United States are shown below:

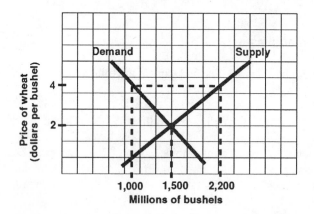

a. If the price of wheat was $4 per bushel before wheat exports were prohibited, how much less wheat will U.S. farmers sell? How much additional wheat will U.S. buyers consume?

b. What is the maximum amount that U.S. buyers would pay for the additional wheat they consume?

c. How much would foreign buyers pay for the extra wheat that U.S. buyers consume? Is this more than the maximum amount that the U.S. buyers would pay for this extra wheat? How much more?

d. Suppose that U.S. producers of wheat forgo profits of $3,700 million because they sell less wheat at a lower price than if exports were allowed. If we add this forgone profit to the amount that foreign buyers would pay for the extra wheat consumed by U.S. buyers, and if we deduct the maximum amount that U.S. buyers would pay for the extra wheat they consume, is the result a reasonable measure of the loss to U.S. producers and consumers due to the prohibition of wheat exports?

e. Do both U.S. producers and U.S. consumers of wheat incur losses because of the prohibition of wheat exports? If not, are the losses of the losers greater or less than the gains of the gainers?

Matching Questions

_____ 1. Multinational firm	A. Limit on imports
_____ 2. Absolute advantage	B. The Treaty of Rome
_____ 3. European Common Market	C. Hoffman-LaRoche
_____ 4. Tariff	D. Stops imports completely
_____ 5. Quota	E. Tax on imports
_____ 6. Prohibitive tariff	F. Country A more efficient than country B

Completion Questions

1. In the absence of trade, suppose that wheat would sell for $3 per bushel in the United States and for £2 in England and that cloth would sell for $3 per yard in the United States and for £0.5 in England. If 1£ = $2.25, the United States will (export, import) _____ wheat because American wheat can be bought for £_____ by the English. England will (export, import) _____ cloth because English cloth can be bought for $_____ by Americans.

2. If the United States exports corn to France, this results in a(n) (increase, decrease) _____ in the price of corn in the United States and a(n) (increase, decrease) _____ in the price of corn in France. If France exports wine to the United States, this results in a(n) (increase, decrease) _____ in the price of wine in the United States and a(n) (increase, decrease) _____ in the price of wine in France.

3. Relative to 100 years ago, the United States exports (fewer, more) _____ manufactured goods and (fewer, more) _____ raw materials.

4. Trade permits specialization, and specialization increases _____.

5. Specialization and trade depend on _____ advantage between countries.

6. The _____ curve shows the maximum amount of one product that can be produced, given various outputs of an alternative product.

7. Assuming for simplicity that only two countries exist, the price of a good tends to settle at the level where the amount of the good that one country exports (equals, is unequal to) _____ the amount that the other country imports.

8. Both a(n) _____ and a(n) _____ generally increase the price of an imported good. Two ways in which governments try to help protect their domestic industries are by _____ and _____.

9. One country has a(n) _____ advantage over another when it can produce one unit of a good with fewer resources than can the other country.

10. During the 1960s about _____ percent of our exports were finished manufactured goods; only about _____ percent were raw materials and foodstuffs.

11. Agricultural commodities like coffee, sugar, bananas, and cocoa make up about _____ of our imports. Petroleum and its products comprise over _____. Over _____ of our imports are manufactured goods like bicycles from England or radios from Japan.

12. Suppose that one country has a comparative advantage in producing one good and another country has a comparative advantage in producing another good. Then if each country specializes in producing the good in which it (has, has not) _____ the comparative advantage, each (can, can not) _____ benefit from trade.

13. _____ will indicate whether a country has a comparative advantage or disadvantage in producing a commodity. If there is a comparative advantage, after the price of a good in various countries is equalized and total world output of the good equals total world demand for it, a country will (export, import) _____ the good under free trade and competition.

14. Specialization can reduce production costs to a lower level than would be possible if each nation tried to be _____.

15. In some cases firms have established overseas branches to control foreign sources of _____. In other cases they have invested overseas in an effort to _____ their competitive position. Very frequently firms have established foreign branches to exploit a(n) _____ lead.

16. A firm with a technological edge over its competitors often prefers to exploit its technology in foreign markets through wholly owned _____ rather than through _____ or other means.

17. Country A can produce a bushel of wheat or a ton of steel with 1 unit of resources. Country B can produce 3 bushels of wheat or $1^1/_2$ tons of steel with 1 unit of resources. Country A (has, does not have) _____ a comparative advantage in the production of wheat, and it (has, does not have) _____ a comparative advantage in the production of steel. Country B (has, does not have)

_____ a comparative advantage in the production of wheat, and it
(has, does not have) _____ a comparative advantage in the
production of steel. Country A has an absolute advantage in the production of
_____. Country B has an absolute advantage in the production of

_____.

True-False

_____ 1. If Brazil could produce each and every good and service with 80 percent as much of each and every input as Argentina, Brazil would have a comparative advantage over Argentina in all goods and services.

_____ 2. If the United States has relatively bountiful supplies of land relative to Japan, and Japan has relatively bountiful supplies of labor relative to the United States, and if the production of electronic goods requires relatively little land and large amounts of labor, while the production of grain requires relatively little labor and large amounts of land, Japan is likely to export electronic goods.

_____ 3. Both the poorer and the richer countries of the world tend to trade largely with the industrialized countries.

_____ 4. Even though one country may be more efficient than another at producing two commodities, both countries may benefit if each specializes and trades.

_____ 5. The United States tends to export products with a high technological component.

_____ 6. The protection of certain industries for the purpose of national defense is the only argument ever given for barriers to free trade.

_____ 7. Under free trade a nation's economic welfare is always lower than under a tariff.

_____ 8. Western Europe and Canada take about $1/2$ of our exports, and Latin America takes over 10 percent.

_____ 9. Quotas can be even more effective than tariffs in keeping foreign goods out of a country.

_____ 10. International differences in resource endowments and in the relative quantity of various types of human and nonhuman resources are important bases for specialization.

_____ 11. One of the most important effects of the multinational firm has been to integrate the economies of the world more closely into a world-wide system.

_____ 12. The purpose of a tariff is to cut down on imports in order to protect domestic industry and workers from foreign competition.

_____ 13. Export subsidies and other such measures frequently lead to counter-measures. For example, to counter foreign export subsidies, the U.S. government imposes duties against such subsidies on goods sold here.

_____ 14. Tariffs or other forms of protection are sometimes justified to foster the growth and development of young industries.

_____ 15. If country A uses 20 percent less of all inputs to produce every good and service than does country B, there may be no advantage in two-way trade between these two countries.

Multiple Choice

1. Country C can produce a ton of food or 4 tons of coal with 1 unit of resources. Country D can produce 2 tons of food or 5 tons of coal with 1 unit of resources.

   a. Country C will export food and import coal.
   b. Country D will export food and import coal.
   c. Country C will neither import nor export food.
   d. Country D will neither import nor export coal.
   e. none of the above.

2. If France exports wine to England and England exports textiles to France, an increase in the price of wine (relative to the price of textiles) means:

   a. an improvement for France in the terms of trade.
   b. a change in the slope of France's trading possibility curve.
   c. a change in the slope of England's trading possibility curve.
   d. all of the above.
   e. only a and b are true.

3. Which of the following is not advanced as a reason for specialization and trade?

   a. economies of scale
   b. learning
   c. difference in national tastes
   d. need for some self-sufficiency
   e. all of the above

4. The purpose of a tariff is to:

   a. reduce imports to protect domestic industry and workers from foreign competition.
   b. produce revenue to pay for shipping costs.
   c. reduce costs.
   d. all of the above.
   e. none of the above.

5. One difference between tariffs and quotas is that only tariffs:

   a. reduce trade.
   b. raise prices.
   c. provide the government with revenue.
   d. reduce the standard of living of the nation as a whole.
   e. none of the above.

6. In addition to national defense, tariffs and other forms of protection are sometimes defended on the grounds that they:

   a. promote growth and development of young industries.
   b. protect domestic jobs and reduce unemployment.
   c. prevent overdependence of a country on only a few industries.
   d. improve a country's terms of trade.
   e. all of the above.

7. Which of the following is not a major impediment to free trade?

   a. tariffs
   b. quotas
   c. export subsidies
   d. all are impediments
   e. none are impediments

8. Oil import quotas:

   a. cost American consumers billions of dollars per year during the late 1960s.
   b. were removed in 1973.
   c. both a and b.
   d. neither a nor b.
   e. never occurred in the U.S.

9. If the United States specializes in wheat and England specializes in Scotch whiskey, and if wheat is on the vertical axis and Scotch whiskey is on the horizontal axis, the U.S. trading possibilities curve is flatter (that is, closer to being a horizontal line) if:

   a. the price of a fifth of Scotch whiskey is low relative to the price of a bushel of wheat.
   b. the price of a bushel of wheat is low relative to the price of a fifth of Scotch whiskey.
   c. the typical U.S. consumer prefers a fifth of Scotch to a bushel of wheat.
   d. the typical English consumer prefers a fifth of Scotch to a bushel of wheat.
   e. none of the above.

Discussion and Extension Questions

1. *Business Week* has written: "The story of U.S. merchandise trade in April has a familiar ring: Imports rose, exports fell, and the trade deficit widened." According to some observers, the U.S. government should impose quotas and tariffs to reduce the flood of imported goods. Do you agree? Why or why not?

2. "It is a foolish and dangerous thing for U.S. firms to export their technology since this will result in foreign firms' imitating our products and beating us in foreign markets." Discuss and evaluate.

3. In an emergency people frequently are called upon to carry out tasks that are far removed from their normal occupations. Suppose that four people escape from a ship wreck and are marooned on a desert island. One member of the group, a college graduate, is given the job of sweeping the floor. He complains that this is a poor use of his talents. Using the theory of comparative advantage, explain why he may be wrong.

4. Why do the less developed countries tend to trade with the industrialized countries, not with one another?

5. What is the basic argument for trade rather than trying to be self-sufficient?

6. Explain how international trade results from gaps in technology.

7. What have been some of the economic effects of the multinational firms on the world economy?

8. Choose an argument which has been used to justify tariffs and then write two statements—one which defends and one which attacks this argument.

9. Do you think that an oil import quota can be justified by considerations of national defense?

10. Is it better to "buy American" because we then have both the goods and the money? Explain.

11. If the free flow of goods will lead to an increase in world output, would we also press for a free flow of people across countries (i.e., no immigration restrictions)?

Problems

1. Suppose that the demand and supply curves for transistor radios in the United States are as follows:

Price (dollars)	Quantity demanded (millions)	Quantity supplied (millions)
5	5	2
10	4	3
15	3	4
20	2	5

Further suppose that the demand and supply curves for transistor radios in Japan are:

Price (expressed in dollar equivalent of Japanese price)	Quantity demanded (millions)	Quantity supplied (millions)
5	2.5	1
10	2.0	3
15	1.5	5
20	1.0	7

a. Suppose that there is free trade in transistor radios. What will be the equilibrium price?
b. Which country will export transistor radios to the other country?
c. How large will be the exports?
d. Suppose that the United States imposes a tariff of $10 per transistor radio. What will happen to exports and imports?

2. Suppose that the United States can produce 3 electronic computers or 3,000 cases of wine with 1 unit of resources, while France can produce 1 electronic computer or 5,000 cases of wine with 1 unit of resources.

a. Will specialization increase world output?
b. Is this an example of absolute or comparative advantage?
c. If the maximum number of computers that can be produced per year in the United States is 1,000, draw the U.S. production possibilities curve on the graph below.

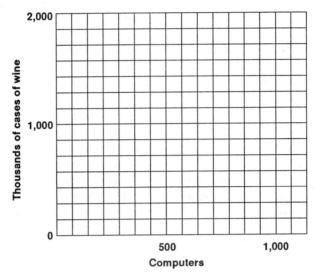

d. In the diagram above draw the trading possibilities curve if the United States produces only computers and trades them for French wine (at a price for each computer that is equivalent to 2,000 cases of French wine). Does this curve lie above the production possibilities curve?
e. If the maximum number of cases of wine that can be produced per year in France is 2 million, draw the French production possibilities curve below.

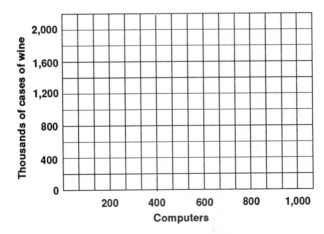

f. In the diagram above draw the trading possibilities curve if France produces only wine and trades it for U.S. computers (at a price for each computer that is equivalent to 2,000 cases of French wine). Does this curve lie above the production possibilities curve?

3. Suppose that labor is the only input and that two countries, Argentina and Brazil, can produce the following amounts of two commodities, bananas and nuts, with a day of labor:

	Bananas (lbs.)	Nuts (lbs.)
Argentina	10	3
Brazil	5	4

a. In order for both countries to gain from trade, between what limits must the ratio of the prices lie?
b. Suppose that there is free trade and the price of bananas increases relative to the price of nuts. Is this change in the terms of trade to the advantage of Argentina or Brazil?

4. Countries A and B are neighbors and produce only food and machines. Both countries' production possibilities curves are straight lines. Country A has 500 units of resources, while country B has 200 units of resources. In country A, a unit of resources can produce 22 units of food or 11 units of machinery. In country B, a unit of resources can produce 15 units of food or 10 units of machinery. Before there was any international trade, output in the two countries was:

	Output	
	Food	Machinery
Country A	836 units	1,320 units
Country B	2,250 units	500 units

a. What is the price of a unit of machinery (in terms of food) in each of the countries when they do not trade with each other? Explain why.
b. Can the two countries benefit from international trade? If so, explain why.
c. Between what limits will the ratio of the price of machinery to the price of food be once international trade begins?

5. In problem 2, suppose that the price of a computer rises from the equivalent of 2,000 cases of wine to the equivalent of 4,000 cases of wine. In other words, one computer now exchanges for 4,000 cases of wine, rather than 2,000 cases of wine.

a. Draw the new trading possibilities curves for the United States and France in the graphs in parts c and e of problem 2.
b. Do the results indicate that the United States can consume less than before? More than before? Explain.
c. Do the results indicate that France can consume less than before? More than before? Explain.

6. Countries D and E have not traded with each other because of political differences. Suddenly, they reconcile their political differences and begin to trade. Cigars are relatively cheap, but beef is relatively expensive in country D. Beef is relatively cheap, but cigars are relatively expensive in country E.

a. When these countries begin to trade, will the demand for cigars produced in country D increase or decrease? Will the price of cigars increase or decrease in country D?

b. Will the demand for cigars produced in country E increase or decrease? Will the price of cigars increase or decrease in country E?
c. Will the demand for beef produced in country D increase or decrease? Will the price of beef increase or decrease in country D?
d. Will the demand for beef produced in country E increase or decrease? Will the price of beef increase or decrease in country E?
e. Will the demand for resources used in country D to produce cigars increase or decrease? Will the demand for resources used in country E to produce beef increase or decrease?
f. Will the demand for resources used in country E to produce cigars increase or decrease? Will the demand for resources used in country D to produce beef increase or decrease?

7. Country G's production possibilities curve is shown below. So is country H's production possibilities curve. The only goods produced in either country are food and clothing.

| | Country G | | | Country H | |
Possibility	Food output	Clothing output	Possibility	Food output	Clothing output
A	0	32	A	0	24
B	5	24	B	4	18
C	10	16	C	8	12
D	15	8	D	12	6
E	20	0	E	16	0

a. In country G what is the cost of clothing in terms of food?
b. In country H what is the cost of clothing in terms of food?
c. If countries G and H engage in trade, which country will export food? Which country will export clothing?
d. If countries G and H engage in trade, between what limits will the terms of trade lie?

Answers

Matching Questions
1. C   2. F   3. B   4. E   5. A   6. D

Completion Questions
1. export, $1^1/_3$, export, $1^1/_8$ 2. increase, decrease, decrease, increase   3. more, fewer
4. output   5. comparative   6. production possibilities   7. equals   8. tariff, quota, tariffs, quotas   9. absolute   10. 60, 20   11. $^1/_{10}$, 10 percent, $^1/_2$ 12. has, can
13. Market forces, export   14. self-sufficient   15. raw materials, defend, technological
16. subsidiaries, licensing   17. does not have, has, has, does not have, neither, both

True-False
1. False   2. True   3. True   4. True   5. True   6. False   7. False   8. True
9. True   10. True   11. True   12. True   13. True   14. True   15. True

Multiple Choice

1. b   2. d   3. d   4. a   5. c   6. e   7. d   8. c   9. a

Problems

1. a. $10.
   b,c. Japan will export 1 million transistor radios to the United States
   d. Exports and imports will drop.
2. a. Yes.
   b. The United States has an absolute advantage in computers; France has the same in wine.
   c.

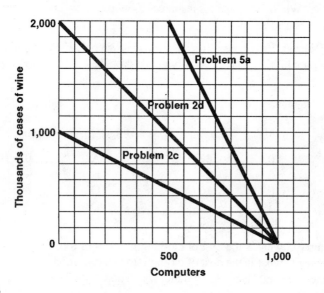

   d. Yes
   e.

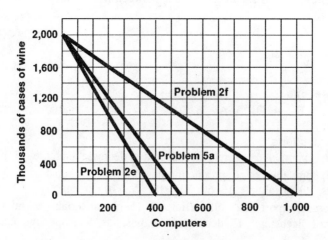

   f. See answer to e. It lies above the production possibilities curve.

3. a. The price of a pound of bananas must be between $^3/_{10}$ and $^8/_{10}$ of the price of a pound of nuts.
   b. Argentina.
4. a. The price of machinery is double that of food in country A and is $1^1/_2$ times that of food in country B, because of the relative costs of machinery and food in each country.
   b. Yes, because country A has a comparative advantage in food and country B has a comparative advantage in machinery.
   c. The ratio will be between 1.5 and 2.0.
5. a. See answers to c and e of Problem 2.
   b. More.
   c. Less.
6. a. Increase. Increase.
   b. Decrease. Decrease.
   c. Decrease. Decrease.
   d. Increase. Increase.
   e. Increase. Increase.
   f. Decrease. Decrease.
7. a. An extra unit of clothing costs $^5/_8$ of a unit of food.
   b. An extra unit of clothing costs $^2/_3$ of a unit of food.
   c. Country H. Country G.
   d. The price of a unit of clothing will lie between $^5/_8$ and $^2/_3$ of the price of a unit of food.

The Communist Countries and Marxism

Chapter Profile

According to Karl Marx the fundamental causes of political and social change are socioeconomic factors. He viewed history as a series of class struggles, the present class struggle being between the capitalists, who own the means of production, and the workers.

In Marx's view the struggle will eventually result in the defeat of capitalism, which will be replaced by socialism, a transitional stage toward communism. To Marx communism was the ultimate, perfect form of economic system.

Marx, who subscribed to a labor theory of value, believed that the workers create a surplus value, the difference between the value of what they produce and the subsistence wage they receive. Capital formation, in Marx's view, comes about as a consequence of this surplus value.

The Soviet Union, the first country to embrace Marxian socialism, was a command economy where power was concentrated in the hands of a relatively few Communist officials who made the big decisions on what was to be produced, how it was to be produced, and who was to receive how much. The government owned the factories, mines, equipment, and other means of production.

The top officials of the Communist Party established the overall goals for the economy. The detailed production plans to realize these broad goals were drawn up by Gosplan, the State Planning Commission. These plans were reviewed by individual industries and plants, and after negotiations and revision, Gosplan issued the final plan.

In the Soviet Union the government, not the market, set prices. Prices facing producers were set in such a way that a firm of average efficiency would make neither a profit nor a loss. Prices facing consumers were set to ration the consumer goods produced and to raise the planned revenue needed for investment. The difference between the price to the consumer and the price to the producer was the turnover tax.

In 1987, Mikhail Gorbachev called for radical changes in the Soviet economy, including the elimination of day-to-day management of the economy by agencies like Gosplan and the end of the controlled and subsidized price system. While these proposals did not have a major impact, there continued to be considerable ferment in the Soviet Union during the late 1980s and early 1990s, and some talk that there might be a transition to free markets. In late 1991, the Soviet Union fell apart, as various republics seemed to become autonomous. Political change seemed to occur so rapidly that all that safely could be said was that the situation was in flux.

A second type of communist system is found in China. China's first five-year plan was an ambitious and ruthless drive toward industrialization that seemed to achieve its objectives, but Mao's Great Leap Forward was a disaster that set back the country's economic development.

Marxian socialism—or communism—is not the only brand of socialism. There are many democratic socialist parties and governments that occupy a middle ground between our more capitalistic system and the communist systems.

In the United States so-called radical economics is based largely on Marxism. The radical economists challenge the methods and assumptions of conventional economics and advocate basic institutional change.

Behavioral Objectives

A. You should be able to define and explain the following key concepts in this chapter:

Communism	Marxism	Quota
Capitalist	Five-year plan	Turnover tax
Proletariat	Gosplan	Piece rates
Socialism	Gosbank	Democratic socialism
Value	Command economy	Radical economics
Surplus value		

B. Make sure that you can do each of the following:

1. Describe Karl Marx's theory of the class struggle.

2. Explain Marx's theory of value.

3. Describe Marx's predictions concerning capitalism and the extent to which they have come true.

4. Indicate the nature of economic planning in the (former) Soviet Union.

5. Describe how prices were set in the Soviet Union, and compare the extent of income inequality there with that in the United States.

6. Evaluate the performance of the (former) Soviet economy from the points of view of growth, efficiency, and equity.

7. Indicate the nature of the Chinese economy.

8. Describe the economic history of China since World War II.

9. Indicate how democratic socialist parties and governments differ from communist parties and governments.

10. Describe radical economics, and explain its relationship to Marxian doctrines.

Getting Down to Cases: The Convergence Hypothesis

According to some observers, the communist and capitalist systems are converging. Believers in this convergence hypothesis say that differences between the policies and institutions of the two systems are getting smaller.

a. Is there any evidence that China is beginning to rely less on central planning and to allow more autonomy for individual plant managers? If so, describe this evidence.

b. Is there any evidence that the United States is relying more on governmental intervention and less on markets? If so, describe this evidence.

c. Is there any evidence that the political tensions between the United States and China declined during the 1980s and early 1990s?

d. Is it likely that the differences between communist and capitalist countries will be negligible in the next decade or two?

e. Is Chinese agriculture becoming more like U.S. agriculture?

f. Is the Chinese economic growth rate becoming closer to that of the United States?

g. Is American industrial management becoming more like that in China?

h. Are Chinese workers becoming more like those in the United States?

i. If the United States and China do tend to converge, will this have an effect on our political system?

Matching Questions

_____ 1. Capitalists	A. Launched in China in 1958
_____ 2. Socialism	B. Own the means of production
_____ 3. Proletariat	C. State planning commission
_____ 4. Great Leap Forward	D. Workers
_____ 5. Mikhail Gorbachev	E. A transitional stage, according to Marx
_____ 6. Gosplan	F. Soviet Union

Completion Questions

1. In the Soviet Union detailed production plans, on the basis of data from various ministries, were drawn up by _____.

2. An economy like that which prevailed in the Soviet Union, where people are told what to do, is called a(n) _____ economy.

3. In the United States prices are set by the market, whereas in the Soviet Union they were set by the _____.

4. In the Soviet Union the difference between the price to the consumer and the price to the producer was called a(n) _____.

5. The Swedish socialist government and Britain's Labor party are both examples of

   _____.

6. According to Marx, every economic system—ancient, feudal, or modern—develops certain defects or internal _____ , which eventually cause it to give way to a(n) (new, old) _____ system.

7. According to Marx the value of any commodity—that is, its price relative to other commodities—is determined by the amount of _____ time used in its manufacture. In other words, if one item requires twice as much _____ time to produce as another, the price of the former is _____ that of the latter.

8. According to Marx wages tend to equal the lowest level consistent with the _____ of the worker, because capitalists are driven by the _____ motive.

9. Combining his theory of value and his theory of wages, Marx concluded that workers produce a(n) _____ value—a value above and beyond the subsistence wage they receive—which is taken by the _____. This surplus value arises because the capitalists make the workers labor for longer hours than are required to produce an amount of output equal to their

   _____.

10. In Marx's view capitalism would eventually reveal certain fundamental weaknesses that would hasten its demise. As more and more capital is accumulated, Marx felt that the _____ would be driven down, that _____ would increase, that business cycles would become more _____ , and that monopoly would _____.

11. Marx did not visualize an immediate progression to communism. Instead he saw _____ as a way-station on the road to communism. _____ would be a "dictatorship of the proletariat." The workers would rule. Specifically, they would control the _____ , which according to Marx is merely a tool of the propertied class under

   _____.

12. After an unspecified length of time, Marx felt that socialism would give way to _____ , his ideal system. _____ would be a

classless society, with all men as brothers, everyone working and no one owning capital or exploiting his fellow man. Under _____ , the state would become obsolete and wither away. The principle of income distribution would be: "From each according to his ability, to each according to his

_____."

13. The top officials of the _____ Party established the overall goals for the Soviet economy. These goals were generally enunciated in a(n) _____ plan.

14. Whereas _____ are the chief means of allocating resources in the United States, _____ has been the chief means in communist economies. Whereas the _____ motive is an important determinant of producer behavior in the United States, _____ has been the chief determinant of producer behavior in communist economies.

15. Whereas _____ are free to select their product, output, and price in the United States, these matters have been determined by _____ in communist economies. Whereas farms are owned by _____ in the United States, there were _____ farms in the Soviet Union.

16. Cyclical unemployment tended to be (higher, lower) _____ in the Soviet Union than in the United States. Income from all sources tended to be (more, less) _____ equally distributed in the Soviet Union than in the United States. Unions tended to be a (more, less) _____ powerful check on management's powers in the Soviet Union than in the United States.

True-False

_____ 1. Marx felt that capitalism would be succeeded directly by communism.

_____ 2. In the Soviet Union prices to producers were set so that a firm of average efficiency would run neither a profit nor a loss.

_____ 3. The extent of income inequality (for all types of income) in the Soviet Union was about the same as that in the United States.

_____ 4. Per capita gross national product in the United States was more than twice that in the Soviet Union.

_____ 5. Gorbachev seemed to encourage manager autonomy.

_____ 6. Radical economics is based largely on Marxism.

_____ 7. In accord with Marx's views most productive resources in the Soviet Union were publicly owned.

_____ 8. When the Soviet plan was published, the Gosbank gave each manager enough money to buy the resources—labor, materials, and so on—allocated to him or her.

_____ 9. The State Control Commission had inspectors who visited plants and went over the records of the Gosbank.

_____ 10. The manager of an industrial plant in the USSR was told that to fulfill the plan he or she had to produce a certain amount, his or her quota.

_____ 11. In the USSR prices of inputs did not reflect the relative scarcity of inputs, as they do in capitalistic economies.

_____ 12. The gap between the price to the consumer and the price to the producer was called the turnaround tax in the USSR.

_____ 13. Having succeeded in pushing the economy ahead in the five-year plan of 1942–47, in 1948 China's leaders launched a more ambitious plan, called the Great Leap Forward.

_____ 14. The bulk of China's population is engaged in agriculture.

_____ 15. In 1978, China's Central Committee approved a new system of incentives for China's peasants.

_____ 16. In the Soviet Union profits and losses were determinants of whether the output of particular goods (like shoes and bread) should be expanded or reduced.

_____ 17. In the Soviet Union all clothing and household furnishings were owned by the state or by collective farms.

_____ 18. Prices in the Soviet Union were determined by the demand and supply of products and resources.

_____ 19. In planning the output and capacity of various industries, the Chinese can make plans for one industry without reference to what is planned for other industries without reducing economic efficiency.

_____ 20. One of the advantages of central planning over a market economy is that the planners require less information than do firms because all that the planners have to decide is what will be produced, not how it will be produced.

Multiple Choice

1. The possible advantages to the United States of increased U.S.-Russian technology transfer are:

   a. improved East-West political relations.
   b. improved access to Russian technology.
   c. increased U.S. exports.
   d. all of the above.
   e. none of the above.

2. Under communism, according to Marx:

    a. the state would be all-powerful.
    b. income would be related to the amount a person produced.
    c. no individual would own capital.
    d. no one would work.
    e. none of the above.

3. Which of the following predictions made by Marx has proved accurate?

    a. The working class would experience greater and greater misery.
    b. The rate of profit would fall.
    c. Greater warfare would occur between capitalists and workers.
    d. None of the above.
    e. All of the above.

4. Which of the following is both a communist country and an LDC?

    a. South Africa
    b. China
    c. Iran
    d. India
    e. Venezuela

5. Workers in the Soviet Union:

    a. were unable to change jobs.
    b. often were paid on a piece-work basis.
    c. were unable to choose how much bread, cheese, and other such items to buy.
    d. all of the above.
    e. none of the above.

6. The Soviet economy was hampered by:

    a. little innovation in the non-defense sector.
    b. slow diffusion of new techniques in the non-defense sector.
    c. the production of goods that were unsalable.
    d. all of the above.
    e. none of the above.

7. Soviet society was handicapped by:

    a. little or no improvements in education in the Soviet Union.
    b. little or no system of social insurance for workers.
    c. little or no transfer of technology from the West.
    d. all of the above.
    e. none of the above.

8. The turnover tax in the Soviet Union:

    a. did not affect the price of a consumer good.
    b. affected the income that the Soviet consumer had to spend.
    c. was turned over to the firms to finance modernization and expansion of plant and equipment.
    d. all of the above.
    e. none of the above.

9. In the Soviet Union prices performed the following function:

    a. prices determined how much of various goods was produced.
    b. prices determined how much of various resources was allocated to particular plants.
    c. prices were used to ration goods among consumers.
    d. all of the above.
    e. none of the above.

Discussion and Extension Questions

1. Obviously, it is difficult to tell which of the many economic systems is the best; it depends on how much weight you give to certain variables, like security, freedom, stability, efficiency, and so forth. It's hard to compute which country has the highest level of citizen welfare or utility. Could you devise a test which might shed some light on the problem of determining which nation was best satisfying its citizens?

2. According to *Business Week*, "Agriculture remains the Achilles' heel of the Russian economy." According to *U.S. News & World Report*, "Many analysts, including some Russians when talking privately, are convinced that inefficient organization, a lack of incentives, and rigid central planning and controls greatly compounded natural troubles [in agriculture]." Discuss the facets of Soviet organization, incentives, and planning that the critics refer to, and why they may have had this effect.

3. Lloyd Reynolds has written that, "There is no reasonable doubt that most Chinese are better off in material terms than they were in 1949. They are also better off than the average Indian, Pakistani, or Indonesian." How did the Chinese increase per capita income? How can one estimate how well off the Chinese are?

4. "The Soviet Union was far more efficient than the West, because it did not tolerate unemployment." Comment and evaluate.

5. "The Soviet Union was in trouble economically, one of the basic reasons being its inability to innovate." Comment and evaluate.

6. Describe briefly Karl Marx's view of the fundamental causes of political changes and the course of history. According to Marx what determines the value of any commodity? According to Marx how would income be distributed under socialism? Under communism?

7. Did the state "wither away" in the Soviet version of communism? Explain. What were some of the problems in Soviet planning?

8. Was Communist China's Great Leap Forward a success? Why or why not?

9. Have China's experiments with a more decentralized economic system paid off?

10. What criticisms do the radical economists direct at conventional economics? What are some of the criticisms of radical economics?

Problems

1. Abram Bergson, in his Wicksell Lectures, presented the following data (for 1960):

Country	Real national income per employed worker (U.S. = 100)	Percent of nonfarm activities in total employment
U.S	100	92
France	58	79
Germany	58	86
U.K.	56	96
Italy	40	68
Japan	27	70
USSR	39	61

a. Use the graph below to determine whether the relationship between real national income per employed worker and the percent of nonfarm activities in total employment was direct or inverse.

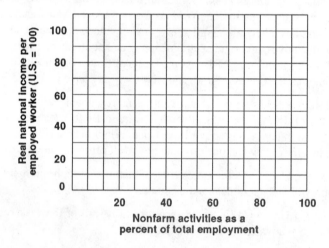

b. What does this relationship mean? Can we be sure that changes in one variable cause changes in the other variable?

c. With regard to output per employed worker, how did the Soviet Union compare with Japan, Italy, and the United States, according to these figures?

2. According to Stanley Cohn the GNP's of the United States and USSR were as follows:

	United States	USSR
	(billions of 1966 U.S. dollars)	
1950	414	140
1955	508	185
1960	565	253
1965	711	326
1969	838	395

a. Did it appear that the percentage gap between the Soviet GNP and the U.S. GNP was declining during the 1950s and 1960s?
b. Did it appear that the Soviet GNP would equal ours in the next decade? Why or why not?

3. Suppose that the market demand curve for shoes in the Soviet Union was as follows:

Price (in rubles)	Quantity demanded (hundreds of million pairs)
150	5.0
120	5.5
90	6.0

a. If the Soviet planners decided to produce 550 million pairs of shoes, what would be the sum of the price to the producer and the turnover tax per pair?
b. If the price to the producer of a pair of shoes was 90 rubles, what would be the turnover tax?
c. If the planners decided to produce 600 million pairs of shoes, what would be the turnover tax if the price to the producer of a pair of shoes was 85 rubles?

Answers

Matching Questions
1. B   2. E   3. D   4. A   5. F   6. C

Completion Questions
1. Gosplan   2. command   3. government   4. turnover tax   5. democratic socialism
6. contradictions, new   7. labor, labor, twice   8. subsistence, profit   9. surplus, capitalists, wage   10. profit rate, unemployment, severe, grow   11. socialism, Socialism, government, capitalism   12. communism, Communism, communism, needs   13. Communist, five-year   14. markets, government planning, profit, the government's plan   15. firms, the government, private individuals or groups, collective   16. lower, more, less

True-False
1. False   2. True   3. False   4. True   5. True   6. True   7. True   8. True
9. True   10. True   11. True   12. False   13. False   14. True   15. True
16. False   17. False   18. False   19. False   20. False

Multiple Choice
1. d   2. c   3. d   4. b   5. b   6. d   7. e   8. e   9. c

Problems

1. a.   The relationship was direct.

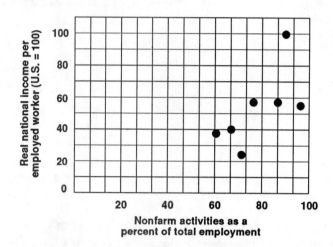

   b.   Apparently real output per employed worker tended to be higher in nations where a relatively large percentage of the labor force was not in agriculture. Obviously, however, this relationship by itself does not establish any sort of line of causation.

   c.   It was almost 50 percent higher than Japan, about the same as Italy, and less than $1/2$ of the United States.

2. a.   Yes.

   b.   No, because the gap was narrowing too slowly.

3. a.   120 rubles.

   b.   30 rubles.

   c.   5 rubles.